**THE
BLACK
PANTHER
PARTY
IN A CITY
NEAR
YOU**

THE BLACK PANTHER PARTY IN A CITY NEAR YOU

EDITED BY Judson L. Jeffries

The University of
Georgia Press
ATHENS

© 2018 by the University of Georgia Press
Athens, Georgia 30602
www.ugapress.org
All rights reserved
Set in by 10/13 Kepler Std Regular by Kaelin Chappell Broaddus

Most University of Georgia Press titles are
available from popular e-book vendors.

Printed digitally

Library of Congress Cataloging-in-Publication Data

Names: Jeffries, J. L. (Judson L.), 1965–, editor, author.
Title: The Black Panther Party in a city near you / Judson L. Jeffries.
Description: Athens, GA : The University of Georgia Press, [2018] | Includes index.
Identifiers: LCCN 2017032685| ISBN 9780820351988 (hardcover : alk. paper) |
    ISBN 9780820351971 (pbk. : alk. paper) | ISBN 9780820351995 (ebook)
Subjects: LCSH: Black Panther Party—History. | African Americans—
    Politics and government—20th century. | African Americans—Civil rights—
    History—20th century. | African Americans—Services for—History—20th century. |
    Poor—Services for—United States—History—20th century. | Civil rights movements—
    United States—History—20th century. | United States—Race relations—History—
    20th century. | United States—History, Local.
Classification: LCC E185.615 .J434 2018 | DDC 322.4/20973—dc23
    LC record available at https://lccn.loc.gov/2017032685

CONTENTS

Introduction:
Painting a More Complete Portrait...
the Third Installment 1
JUDSON L. JEFFRIES AND DUNCAN MACLAURY

Wake up Georgia, the Panthers Are Here!
The Georgia Chapter of
the Black Panther Party
in Atlanta, 1970–1973 12
CHARLES E. JONES

Exceptional Headwinds:
The Black Panthers in D.C. 52
JOHN PREUSSER

The Black Panther Party and
Community Development in Boston 89
DUNCAN MACLAURY, JUDSON L. JEFFRIES,
AND SARAH NICKLAS

From Civil Rights to Black Power in Texas:
Dallas to Denton and Back to Dallas 137
AVA TIYE KINSEY AND JUDSON L. JEFFRIES

Conclusion:
The Black Panther Party in Summation 194
CURTIS AUSTIN

Contributors 201

Index 203

THE BLACK PANTHER PARTY
IN A CITY
NEAR
YOU

Introduction

Painting a More Complete Portrait ...
the Third Installment

JUDSON L. JEFFRIES AND DUNCAN MACLAURY

We can think of no radical organization of the twentieth century that exploded onto the American scene with more flair and chutzpah than the Black Panther Party for Self-Defense (BPP). Although the organization's founding coincided with the mid-sixties color television revolution, it was not until February 1967, when Panthers marched into the San Francisco airport in dramatic fashion and escorted Betty Shabazz to the *Ramparts* office—for an interview with Eldridge Cleaver—that the Bay Area mass media caught wind of them. Several weeks later, the BPP garnered national media attention when a delegation of Panthers descended upon Sacramento, the state's seat of power, on May 2, to protest a bill that was designed (no matter how thinly veiled) to undercut the Panthers' ability to effectively and assertively monitor the actions of Bay Area police officers. Police needed monitoring, especially given the U.S. Supreme Court ruling in *Miranda v. Arizona* the prior year requiring officers to inform suspects of their rights before questioning them. Then in October 1967, just days before Halloween, in the early morning hours, Panther cofounder Huey P. Newton was arrested after an encounter with two police officers that left one dead and the other wounded. With the death penalty a real possibility, Eldridge Cleaver, the Panthers' minister of information, turned Newton's incarceration into a cause célèbre. Taking their lead from the party's national headquarters in Oakland, Panthers sprang into action. As David Hilliard, the party's chief of staff, later wrote, "In less than a week ... we created the Huey Newton Defense Committee and held the first rallies at the courthouse ... we borrowed a psychedelically painted double-deck bus from one of the local white political communes, cruising the streets blaring, '"Free Huey! Free Huey!' Can a Black man get a fair trial in America—even if he was defending his life against a white policeman?"[1]

One year later, as Newton languished in a jail cell and his detractors called for the death penalty, young Bobby Hutton, the party's first recruit, was shot down on the streets of Oakland on April 6, 1968, two days after the assassination of Dr. Martin Luther King Jr., when several Panthers, led by Cleaver, engaged in an ill-advised ambush of police officers as revenge for King's murder. These are the images etched in the minds of many whose perceptions of the Panthers are framed by Hollywood-like storylines that unfolded in the Bay Area press and to some degree in Chicago and Los Angeles, where local police conducted deadly raids on the party. It is these morbid and fatalistic theatrics that many people associate with the Black Panther Party. Between 1967 and 1970, the party, for many, was must-see TV. Had the Panthers' confrontations and standoffs with police been made into a feature film, it would likely have compared favorably to Sergio Leone and Ennio Morricone's hugely popular, gun-slinging spaghetti westerns of that era.

Despite the histrionics that played out on the streets of Chicago, Los Angeles, and Oakland, these were not commonplace in other cities and are not representative of Panther goings-on nationally. This is not to say that raids of Panther offices and gunplay between Panthers and the police never occurred in other places. Clearly they did. One could write a book on the raids that occurred on Panther dwellings in 1969 and 1970 alone. However, the notion that Panther-police gunplay occurred nightly over the course of the organization's existence is off target. This is one of the reasons it is important to chronicle BPP history branch by branch and chapter by chapter, to contextualize the party and to represent it accurately, something the mainstream U.S. media has never done. Addison Gayle Jr. is spot-on in his 1970 book *The Black Situation* when he states matter-of-factly that "most whites are incapable of portraying Blacks with any degree of reality." Whites' "approach to Blacks can only travel the gamut from crude distortion to condescension occasioned by racism either unconscious or overt," Gayle writes.[2] He points to William Styron's portrait of the rebel Nat Turner as a case in point. The southern existential novelist depicts Turner as an outcast, a man at odds with his kind and humane white masters, a man who revolts for reasons of self-interest rather than for the collective whole. Gayle submits that those who criticized Styron for his portrait of Turner, who demanded that Turner be portrayed accurately and truthfully, were wasting their time as whites are neither mentally nor culturally up to the task. Styron, like many whites, views black subjects through the lens of his own white experience and produces not complex, multidimensional people but caricatures and exaggerated stereotypes, bestowing upon them his own values, mores, and ethics. Saddled by homosexual tendencies, Styron's Turner is, in the end, presented as a sad sack of a prisoner who begs Jehovah's forgiveness for the slayings for which he and his band of rebels were responsible.[3] Gayle goes on to suggest that Nat Turner in the hands of Richard Wright, Amiri Baraka, or John Williams would have been wholly different. Styron saw in Turner what he wanted to see, and what he didn't actually see he manufactured. So it was in the U.S. mainstream media as far as the Black Panther Party was concerned.

A review of coverage of the party in major newspapers and magazines and news telecasts in the sixties would undoubtedly reveal a disproportionate number of stories that titillate more than inform. The Panthers' health and dental clinics, free breakfast programs, and clothing and shoe giveaways did rate some coverage, but news media are like the entertainment industry in that they valorize suspense and high drama. There was not much suspense in activists administering sickle-cell anemia tests, running errands for senior citizens, and setting up tuberculosis and lead-poisoning testing stations at supermarkets. If an accurate feature film had been made about the Panthers, its rating would not have been R, as many might imagine, but PG.

The Black Panther Party in a City near You is the latest in a series intended to paint a more complete portrait of the Black Power movement's most widely known organization. *Comrades: A Local History of the Black Panther Party* (Indiana University Press, 2007) looked at the Panthers' organization in Baltimore, Winston-Salem, Cleveland, Indianapolis, Milwaukee, Philadelphia, and Los Angeles. *On the Ground: The Black Panther Party in Communities across America* (University of Mississippi Press, 2010) covered Panther activities in Seattle, Kansas City, New Orleans, Houston, Des Moines, and Detroit. As in these volumes, contributors to *The Black Panther Party in a City near You* excavate, chronicle, and document the Panthers' activity in cities other than those typically associated with the party (e.g., Oakland, Chicago, and New York). Over the years, former BPP leaders have maintained that at one time the organization boasted more than forty branches and chapters around the country. If this is true, it is likely that many African American urbanites were at least somewhat familiar with Panther activities. Even if they lived in cities with no party branch, they probably heard about the Panthers through family and friends who lived where the Panthers were not only visible but a force to be reckoned with.

No matter how many branches, it needs to be made clear that some Panther offices were more embedded in the community than others. Hence the offices enjoyed varying levels of success, and the impact was more compelling in some places than in others. Our research further indicates that not all of these branches and chapters operated simultaneously. Some offices had closed down by the time others were opened, and in a few cases they were offices in name only. For instance, Columbus, Ohio, is reported to have had a branch of the Black Panther Party, according to official records kept at national headquarters in California. However, conversations with one longtime resident of Bronzeville, one of Columbus's historically black neighborhoods, elicited only a faint recollection of "guys walking around town with berets and leather jackets, calling themselves Panthers." When another Columbus native, a nonagenarian reared in a part of town called the Hilltop, was asked about the presence of Black Panthers in central Ohio, he remarked, "If they were here, I don't know anything about it."[4] In a 2007 conversation, the late Nommo X, one of the city's most well-known activists, quipped, "If there were Black Panthers here in town they didn't do much except sell papers every now and then.... There were no breakfast programs or anything like that here.... I don't even remember an office."[5] A deeper investigation found a short-lived office of the National Committee to Combat Fascism (NCCF), but no official branch of the BPP. As noted by Leon Valentine Hobbs, a member of the Seattle chapter for several years before being called to Oakland in the early 1970s, "Not every office that was supposedly a branch of the Black Panther Party was rolling...they may have been an actual branch for all I know, but what were they doing? We were rolling in Seattle...we were moving; Seattle had it going on...no one can say otherwise, that's indisputable.... [but] some of these other branches...I don't know."[6]

This project has deliberately focused only on official Black Panther Party branches and chapters, some of which evolved from offices of the NCCF. Those NCCF offices or other Panther affiliates such as community information centers that were never granted official charter status by the party's central committee are generally outside the scope of the series.[7] Moreover, we focus on branches and chapters that we believe played an important role in the political, social, and economic milieus of their respective cities and communities—as Hobbs put it, "those branches and chapters that were rolling."[8]

Until the publication of *Comrades* and *On the Ground*, only two of the thirteen branches and chapters they covered had been the subject of a scholarly investigation, New Orleans and Des Moines.[9] Well-done case studies of Black Panther Party branches are essential and make real intellectual contributions to our understanding of this multifaceted, complex, and nuanced militant group. We recognized early on that if there is to be systematic research in this area, meaningful data on a bevy of party branches and chapters in different industrial centers and in every region of the country must be collected. The case studies that follow in this book are crisp, easy to follow, and clear in their presentation. Our objective is to cast light on old questions that we hope will in turn prompt new questions—all with the intent of *gaining greater insight into the history of the Black Panther Party*.

By identifying and interrogating the many connecting and moving parts of the Black Panther Party, we help bring greater understanding of the party's history. Studies that continue to privilege Oakland at the expense of other locales represent a missed opportunity to bring much-needed clarity. As case in point, in their ballyhooed 2012 book *Black against Empire: The History of the Black Panther Party*, Joshua Bloom and Waldo Martin provide a finely detailed account of aspects of the BPP that have already been explored.¹⁰ To the neophyte, perhaps, Bloom and Martin's book is priceless, but its focus is not new. On the other hand, Alondra Nelson's *Body and Soul: The Black Panther Party and the Fight against Medical Discrimination* delves into an underexplored dimension of the BPP, looking at its promotion of radical health care.¹¹ We argue that this sort of refocusing, rather than just rehashing Panther history, is imperative in order for Black Panther Party scholarship to evolve. Like Bloom and Martin, Peniel Joseph, a scholar of Black Power, focuses on Oakland problematically. In his 2009 essay on the Black Power movement, Joseph divides BPP history into three periods: 1966 to 1971 (the violent revolution phase), 1971 to 1974 (the electoral campaign of Bobby Seale), and 1974 to 1982 (the decline from powerful Oakland concentration to insignificance).¹² This division, although one with which students of Panther history are familiar, only works as a skeletal outline—and only when it is viewed through the lens of the organization's top leadership. When not viewed through the lens of Oakland, the model breaks down. From 1967 to 1972, local branches of the BPP sprang up around the country, and this rapid growth both encouraged and alarmed the party leaders in Oakland. These branches were fueled and sustained by the raw passion, creative energy, and doggedness of party members throughout the United States. The historiographic attempt to situate and encompass all the local branches and chapters within a phase of the national organization—particularly one defined as "violent"—erases the autonomy of the people involved. This reductionism not only narrows the purview of Panther historiography, it elides facts that may be contrary to official views.

Although the Black Panther Party can be accurately framed as Oakland-centered between October 1966 and the end of 1967, and then again after 1973, in the six intervening years the variety of branches and chapters—and the Panther international office in Algiers—made the party a multifaceted organization. What we have found is that while there are some facets of the BPP that were universal, each branch or chapter had its own unique set of circumstances and therefore applied the party's ten-point program and platform accordingly. Additionally, members of those branches and chapters varied in their socioeconomic makeup, experience with the justice system, political acumen, and level of political consciousness.

While discussion of Oakland is necessary in any account of Panther history, we take care to unearth and bring to light Panther activity in other cities and in other parts of the country. The organization cannot be defined solely by its central headquarters and its top leaders. Furthermore, if, as students of Panther history, we acknowledge that the Panthers were genuinely attempting to foment revolution, then it only makes sense that we build on the history of the party's birthplace by delving into the various unexamined BPP chapters and branches across the country. Had the Panthers been successful in bringing about a revolution, Oakland might have been the flashpoint, but one city does not a revolution make. The Panthers rallied thousands nationwide for the cause of black liberation, self-determination, and freedom while providing essential services to the country's underserved. Understanding the work of Panther regional branches and chapters is essential to understanding the Black Panther Party as a whole.

As was intimated in *Comrades*, the BPP was much more than an organization, it was a cultural and political happening, a movement. The group's iconic attire, an amalgamation of French and Latin American revolutionary garb with a black American style, influenced a generation of college students, community activists, and revolutionaries around the globe. And the BPP was transcendent. No organization of the era elicited its volume of supporters, sympathizers, followers, admirers, allies, imitators, wannabes, and groupies. It could well be argued that the Black Panther Party was a subset of the Black Power movement. This may explain why many within and outside of academia deliberately or unwittingly place the BPP at the center of Black Power movement analysis. The party's substantive and symbolic impact in the United States and abroad was glaring, as groups that resembled the Panthers in organizational structure, objectives, dress, ideology, posture, and community service–oriented approach popped up as far away as Australia, Barbados, Great Britain, and Israel.

The BPP's appeal was in part due to the group's larger than life figures. No black militant organization of the Vietnam War era had more star power than the Black Panther Party. Huey P. Newton, Bobby Seale, Kathleen Cleaver, Elaine Brown, Eldridge Cleaver, and Fred Hampton are to this day household names. As with the previous two volumes in the series, we maintain that the Black Panther Party's success is owed largely to those Panthers whose names are virtually unknown to the wider public. Their stories form the foundation of our work. The writers of these essays have been fortunate in that many former party members have been willing to share their stories. Like West African griots, Talmudic Jews, and Native Americans, we encourage the age-old tradition of storytelling. We have taken special care to document in print stories for the most part previously unknown to those outside of one person's small circle. Making people's stories a part of the public record is important for many reasons, one of which is to "assure that real-life experiences and memories of people cannot be so easily omitted, edited, shredded, or swept away."[13] Moreover, oral history offers "increased understanding and living content to the otherwise one-dimensional information offered by documents alone."[14] When appropriate, we augment these stories with historical anecdotes from other sources, such as personal papers and newspaper accounts of the day.

The Black Panther Party in a City near You examines Panther branches in four cities, from Dallas to Boston. Each chapter foregrounds Panthers who performed the tedious, laborious grunt work that comes with establishing community survival programs, a facet of the BPP that has been given short shrift historically as it was by mainstream media during the party's apex. With personalities highlighted, readers can visualize these American patriots who sacrificed so much so that future generations might enjoy the most basic of "unalienable rights ... Life, Liberty, and the Pursuit of Happiness," in the words of revolutionary Thomas Jefferson.

The Black Panther Party was militant in ideology and sometimes militaristic in disposition, and its survivors are veterans, just as are those who have served in the U.S. armed forces. The Panthers whose stories comprise this volume served on the ground and made sacrifices but receive no retirement pay or pension. Many who stood on the front lines are afflicted with some of the same maladies that plague war veterans. The "walking wounded," as former Panther Raymond "Masai" Hewitt once referred to them: "the ones who survived, veterans from our war with the police and government, as hurt as any who had served in Vietnam."[15] Yet there are no VA hospitals for Panther veterans, no GI Bill, and no special loan programs. Their sole reward is the satisfaction of knowing that their work made a difference and perhaps the hope that those who benefited from their sacrifices may one day come to understand or acknowledge this somehow. Many people wonder as they age whether or not they have made a difference. Former Panthers do not have that problem. Scores of testimonies of men and women who benefited from the Panthers' programs attest to that. The Panthers also set an example of unwavering resistance that is hard to quantify but nonetheless made an indelible impression on some. A Portland, Oregon, native recalls vividly the day that the Portland Panthers showed up at his high school after the Panthers learned that black students were being harassed. This gentleman, now in his sixties, refers to the leader of the Portland branch, Kent Ford, as his Dr. Martin Luther King Jr.[16]

Reginald Major, author of *A Panther Is a Black Cat*, points out that the Panthers were soldiers at war in "the jungle which is America," warriors "moving to bring greatness to the American Experience" by "completing the work begun by the revolution of 1776."[17] Many Panthers were also military veterans who had fought for their country. Maurice "Mojo" Powell in Oakland, Reginald "Malik" Edwards in D.C., Malik Rahim in New Orleans, and Robert Bryan in Los Angeles were all Vietnam War combat veterans. Some older Panthers such as Ellis White in San Francisco were Korean War veterans. A number had served in elite units such as the army's 82nd Airborne Division, 101st Airborne Division, and 173rd Airborne Brigade.[18] Some had earned such medals as the Silver Star, Bronze Star, and Purple Heart. Vietnam veterans Elmer "Geronimo" Pratt and Portland's Tommy Mills were two such highly decorated soldiers, both having served in the U.S. Army.

By fighting against American oppression at home, the Panthers were fighting *for* a country that was as much theirs as it was anyone else's. After all, the United States was in large part built on the backs of their ancestors, for which they had received no remuneration. Contrary to what some have unwittingly accepted, the Panthers did not promote the country's destruction. They did, however, warn of the perils of capitalism long before Manning Marable penned his 1983 book *How Capitalism Underdeveloped Black America*. "America's 'democratic government' and 'free enterprise' system are structured deliberately and specifically to maximize Black oppression," argued Marable. Capitalism prospered not in spite of the marginalization of Blacks but "because of the brutal exploitation of Blacks and workers and consumers."[19] These views reflected those of the Panthers, who had also warned that because of capitalism black workers were becomingly increasingly obsolete. Out of capitalism, an America had developed that was technologically advanced, deeply racist, increasingly overcrowded, unapologetically pragmatic, and openly hostile to blacks.[20] Once an economic asset, blacks had become an economic burden. What the Panthers advocated was a more just and democratic America, and they concurred with Dr. Martin Luther King Jr., who in a speech on April 3, 1968, the day before he was assassinated, beseeched, "All we say to America is, 'Be true to what you said on paper.'"[21] Like the so-called brilliant democracy of Athens, democracy in America was built on and sustained by slavery and by the subjugation of women.

The Panthers knew that the United States would never actualize its full potential if its people did not force it to do so. They understood that dissent is a cornerstone of a healthy and prosperous country and that any attempts to repress dissent needed to be met with uncompromising resistance. To act otherwise would be un-American and treasonous.

As in the two previous volumes in this series, considerable attention is devoted to local community survival programs, as many of them had a far greater impact than is often acknowledged. The testimony of some of those who benefited bears that out. Indeed some of the programs instituted by Panthers across the country are still in operation, albeit under different auspices. The importance of studying the work of rank-and-file Panthers cannot be overstated. For every Huey P. Newton there was a Leroy Haynes in Dallas, and for every Elaine Brown there was a Sandra Ford in Portland and an Audrea Jones in Boston. What were their motives for joining the Black Panther Party? Without knowing who these Panthers were, without understanding how and why they did the things they did, one is ill equipped to contextualize the organization's many successes and failures.

Our case studies approach features the voices of Panther foot soldiers who went door to door educating women about breast cancer, were invited into public schools to test kids for lead poisoning, set up health and dental clinics, walked kids to school, and arranged transportation for people to visit family members in prison. These Panthers were responding to the immediate needs of their communities. As Bobby Seale pointed out in *Seize the Time*, the Panthers wanted to establish "a broad, massive, people's type of political machinery" that served the needs of their respective communities.[22] At the same time, the Panthers maintained that it was important to understand the larger context of their struggle. From the Panthers' standpoint, the liberation of black Americans was inextricably tied to the global struggles for self-determination of all oppressed people, especially people of color.[23]

The opening of local party branches and chapters was predicated upon the social forces and circumstances particular to a city. Therefore, it is important to discuss black people's station (in some cases, their predicament or plight) in each of the cities featured in this book in the decades leading up to the founding of a Panther branch or chapter. One should not expect each essay to cover every event that unfolded during the branch's history, nor should one expect to find the names of every member of a branch or chapter. We do not pretend to offer an exhaustive history of any of these branches. Instead it is our hope that this book will prompt others to build on our work and embark on fuller studies of the branches and chapters examined here and in the two earlier volumes. Since the latter were published in 2007 and 2010, scholarly books have been published on Panther activity in Milwaukee, New Orleans, Philadelphia, Portland, and Chicago.[24] Cities also appear in the foreground of some memoirs and autobiographies by former Panthers, such as Baltimore in Steve McCutchen's *We Were Free for a While: Back to Back in the Black Panther Party* (Baltimore: PublishAmerica, 2008). While valuable, these latter books lack the detachment and impartiality that is expected of scholarly works. Still, they have helped provide a more complete portrait of an organization composed of many parts and many people.

The contributors to this volume have different writing styles, and some of the essays are considerably longer than others, but various factors account for the length. For example, some branches or chapters functioned for a longer time than others. Some branches had more resources than others and thus were able to put in place more community survival programs, and some branches had fewer members. Former Panthers are not equally accessible for interviews, thus presenting the researcher with the unenviable task of relying on other kinds of data, in some cases derived from less reliable sources such as mainstream newspapers. Some branches and chapters were subjected to more ferocious police repression (in quantity and scope) than that experienced by others, hence there may be far more yet to uncover and report.

This book adds to a growing Black Panther Party narrative by focusing on the foot soldiers, without whom there would have been no national organization. For almost half a century they have been content to live in virtual anonymity, but our long-term project has sought to remedy that. The following essays shine light on those Panthers who not only have been omitted from films and documentaries but also whose names haven't even appeared in the credits or notes. Through our work their voices, personalities, and deeds ring loudly, and thus they are afforded the credit and recognition that has eluded them for so long.

NOTES

1. David Hilliard and Lewis Cole, *This Side of Glory* (Boston: Little Brown, 1993), 3.
2. Addison Gayle Jr., *The Black Situation* (New York: Dell, 1970), 38, 184.
3. William Styron, *The Confessions of Nat Turner* (New York: Random House, 1967).
4. John B. Williams, conversation with Judson L. Jeffries, March 12, 2013.
5. Nommo X, conversation with Judson L. Jeffries, April 4, 2007.
6. Leon Valentine Hobbs, conversation with Judson L. Jeffries, April 28, 2008.
7. There is at least one exception. Charles E. Jones, "Arm Yourself or Harm Yourself: People's Party II and the Black Panther Party in Houston, Texas," in *On the Ground: The Black Panther Party in Communities across America*, ed. Judson L. Jeffries (Jackson: University of Mississippi Press, 2010), 3–40, presents a nuanced history of the People's Party II and maintains that this group was eventually given a Panther charter, but others disagree with this claim.
8. In *On the Ground* I referred to these branches and chapters as "substantive," meaning only those branches and chapters that had a physical office out of which business was conducted, were in operation for at least one year, offered a free breakfast program for at least one year, and had a record of hawking the *Black Panther* newspaper. Jeffries, *On the Ground*, xv (note 1). Having a record of selling the newspaper means that there should be, on the part of longtime residents of a particular community, some memory of the newspaper being sold on the street regularly by members of the BPP. Not every Panther branch met this criterion, and those not meeting it would not be considered substantive by my definition. It is unlikely that branches that fell short of meeting these criteria would have had a significant impact on the political affairs of any community.
9. Orissa Arend, *Showdown in Desire: The Black Panthers Take a Stand in New Orleans* (University of Arkansas Press, 2000); Reynaldo Anderson, "Practical Internationalists: The Story of the Des Moines, Iowa, Black Panther Party," in *Groundwork: Local Black Freedom Movements in America*, ed. Jeanne Theoharis and Komozi Woodard (New York: New York University Press, 2005), 282–99.
10. Joshua Bloom and Waldo Martin, *Black against Empire: The History and Politics of the Black Panther Party* (Berkeley: University of California Press, 2012).
11. Alondra Nelson, *Body and Soul: The Black Panther Party and the Fight against Medical Discrimination* (Minneapolis: University of Minnesota Press, 2013).
12. Peniel E. Joseph, "The Black Power Movement: A State of the Field," *Journal of American History* 96, no. 3 (December 2009): 762.
13. Bruce C. Berg, *Qualitative Research Methods for the Social Sciences* (New York: Simon and Schuster, 1995).
14. Jeffries, *On the Ground*, xii.
15. Quoted in David Hilliard and Lewis Cole, *This Side of Glory* (Boston: Little Brown, 1993), 5.

16. Lucas N. N. Burke and Judson L. Jeffries, *The Portland Black Panthers: Empowering Albina and Remaking a City* (Seattle: University of Washington Press, 2016), 229.

17. Reginald Major, *A Panther Is a Black Cat* (New York: William Morrow, 1971), 280–82.

18. Flores A. Forbes, *Will You Die with Me?* (New York: Atria Books, 2006), 124.

19. Manning Marable, *How Capitalism Underdeveloped Black America* (Boston: South End Press, 1983), 2.

20. Samuel F. Yette, *The Choice: The Issue of Black Survival in America* (Silver Spring, Md.: Cottage Books, 1971), 18.

21. Martin Luther King Jr., "I've Been to the Mountaintop," American Rhetoric, http://www.americanrhetoric.com/speeches/mlkivebeentothemountaintop.htm.

22. Bobby Seale, *Seize the Time: The Story of the Black Panther Party and Huey P. Newton* (New York: Random House, 1970), 412.

23. Jeffries, *On the Ground*, xi.

24. Andrew Witt, *The Black Panthers in the Midwest: The Community Programs and Services of the Black Panther Party in Milwaukee, 1966–1977* (New York: Routledge, 2007); Orissa Arend, *Showdown in Desire: The Black Panthers Take a Stand in New Orleans* (Fayetteville: University of Arkansas Press, 2010); Jakobi Williams, *From the Bullet to the Ballot: The Illinois Chapter of the Black Panther Party and Racial Coalition Politics in Chicago* (Chapel Hill: University of North Carolina Press, 2013); Omari L. Dyson, *The Black Panther Party and Transformative Pedagogy: Place-Based Education in Philadelphia* (Lanham, Md.: Lexington Books, 2014); Lucas N. N. Burke and Judson L. Jeffries, *The Portland Black Panthers: Empowering Albina and Remaking a City* (Seattle: University of Washington Press, 2016).

Wake up Georgia, the Panthers Are Here!

The Georgia Chapter of the Black Panther Party in Atlanta, 1970–1973

CHARLES E. JONES

More than three decades after the 1982 demise of the Black Panther Party, it remains a symbol of the turbulent sixties, a watershed decade of the nation's journey toward racial equality and social justice. The party's imagery and praxis still resonate in contemporary popular culture as in academia, as indicated by an explosion of literature on the Panthers in recent years. To date no other Black Power organization or white leftist group of the sixties has received such extensive academic inquiry. By and large, the historiography of the Black Panther Party is skewed toward the Oakland-based headquarters and party affiliates located in major northern and western cities. Four fairly recent publications, Lucas N. N. Burke and Judson L. Jeffries's *The Portland Black Panthers: Empowering Albina and Remaking a City*, Omari L. Dyson's *The Black Panther Party and Transformative Pedagogy*, Jakobi Williams's insightful study *From the Bullet to the Ballot: The Illinois Chapter of the Black Panther Party and Racial Coalition Politics in Chicago*, and Joshua Bloom and Waldo Martin's *Black against Empire: The History and Politics of the Black Panther Party*, a provocative yet primarily Oakland-centric history of the organization, reflect this current big-city preference in the literature on the Panthers.

Scholarly attention to Panther experiences elsewhere in the country, particularly the South, has been uneven. Earlier research documents BPP organizing efforts in Atlanta, Winston-Salem, New Orleans, and Houston.[1] This essay builds upon historian Winston Grady-Willis's synopsis of BPP activities in Atlanta, found in his superb study *Challenging U.S. Apartheid: Atlanta and Black Struggles for Human Rights, 1960–1977*. He examines local Panther dynamics as a part of a larger discussion of Atlanta's "black activist politics," a quest "to realize the full meaning of self-determination in four contexts: grassroots neighborhood activism, radical Black nationalism, progressive Black electoral political activism, and explicitly women-centered activism."[2] Under the auspices of "radical Black nationalism," Grady-Willis provides an informative yet abbreviated treatment of BPP organizing in Atlanta. The following analysis offers an in-depth assessment of the Georgia chapter of the Black Panther Party in Atlanta, adding to the emerging body of literature on BPP southern activism. It also contributes to the important scholarly endeavor spearheaded by Judson L. Jeffries "to paint a more complete portrait" of the Black Panther Party by examining the histories of its various local organizational entities.[3]

The chapter designation of the Atlanta Panther affiliate was but one of several actions of the BPP national leaders underscoring the strategic importance of the Georgia party outpost. For instance, on September 8, 1971, Huey P. Newton announced the relocation of the organization's Oakland headquarters to Atlanta, and later, that fall, he deployed Ron Carter, an Oakland-based party member, to work with the Atlanta affiliate. The BPP central committee's discussions about purchasing the former national office building of the Student Nonviolent Coordinating Committee (SNCC), to serve as the headquarters of the affiliate, further distinguishes the Georgia chapter of the party, making it evidently both valued and privileged by national party leaders.

During its four-year existence (1970–1973), the Atlanta Panther unit experienced limited success. Gene Ferguson, a former rank-and-file member, recalls that the Georgia chapter of the BPP "never got to be a dominant force like in California and other places, but there was a small core group of us who sold the Panther newspaper and did a lot of organizing for the National organization."[4] This essay offers evidence that substantiates Ferguson's candid assessment. It analyzes the Georgia chapter's origins, membership, leadership, survival programs, and gender relations and examines such key external factors as local political culture, alliances and coalitions, media coverage, and political repression. Attention to these important internal and external factors will illuminate the organization's inability to establish a stronger and more sustained Panther presence in Atlanta.

Atlanta affiliate dynamics will also be contextualized within the broader organizational developments, leadership turnover, and policy shifts of the national office in Oakland. I will investigate the interplay between the Oakland headquarters and the Atlanta outpost, with its distinctive organizing style, and analyze the latter as part of broader BPP mobilization in the South, drawing upon the experiences of other southern party affiliates. The essay concludes with a discussion of the critical factors undermining the effectiveness of the Atlanta BPP formation. This work relies on a wide variety of sources, including government documents (federal and local), interviews, archival materials (including BPP organizational records), mainstream newspapers, and the *Black Panther* newspaper and other alternative presses.[5]

The Atlanta Landscape

At the onset of the 1970s, the winds of political change, driven in part by shifting socioeconomic demographics reached Atlanta, the capital of Georgia. The two highest elective offices of the city, mayor and vice mayor, were occupied respectively by Sam Massell, a wealthy, liberal, Jewish realtor, and Maynard Jackson, a lawyer and the grandson of John Wesley Dobbs, a prominent member of the city's black elite. The 1969 municipal elections had propelled five African Americans to Atlanta's city council and three to the school board. The elections were a watershed following a long period of white electoral hegemony in Atlanta. The city's power elite had endorsed neither Massell, who had previously served two consecutive terms as vice mayor, nor Jackson, a political novice who had had the impudence to challenge segregationist Herman Talmadge for his seat in the U.S. Senate during 1968.[6]

Both Massell and Jackson relied on the increasing clout of the black electorate for their victories. Massell defeated Rodney Cook, a Republican state legislator who was endorsed by the downtown business elites, with 44.2 percent of the black vote in the general election, which increased to 92 percent during the runoff contest due to the absence of Horace Tate, the black mayoral candidate of the general election. Maynard Jackson handily defeated Milton Farris, a white member of the Fulton County Commission, to win the vice mayor position. Jackson received 58.2 percent of the vote compared to 39.1 percent garnered by Farris. Atlanta's black vote would gain additional leverage in future elections with the significant expansion of the African American population. Black residents increased from 38.2 percent of the population in 1960 to 51.5 percent of the total population in 1970, partly due to white flight. The municipality lost 25 percent of its white residents during the 1960s.[7]

The Massell-Jackson administration (1969–1973), a new model of southern political leadership, governed a city that had undergone significant economic development during the previous decade. Award-winning political journalist Frederick Allen observed in 1970, "The city was like a teenager who gradually outgrew the clothes of childhood and got a new wardrobe, only to experience a sudden, secondary growth spurt that necessitated another complete change. The new airport terminal, finished in 1961, handled 3.5 million passengers its first year; by 1970, traffic had quadrupled to more than 14 million passengers and talk had begun of building a second airport. The new Civic Center had opened in the fall of 1967 and already seemed tight fitting. Its auditorium seated only 4,600 people, adequate for the symphony and opera but too small for major concerts."[8]

During this period, downtown business elites consolidated Atlanta's regional dominance of the transportation, communications, and other corporate sectors in the South, and Atlanta earned the mantle "Capitol of the New South." Atlanta enjoyed a growing reputation as a city with economic prosperity, an international outlook, avid support of the arts, and racial moderation, and racial tranquility was the linchpin. As Allen notes: "Atlanta's growth had been driven in considerable measure by good race relations."[9] The city's economic development required a stable, violence-free landscape. Racial hostilities, unabated anti-black sentiment, and violence were not good for business, especially in a city with a black majority. Meanwhile, white terroristic violence and intimidation prevailed across the rest of the Old South.

Things, however, had not always been so calm in Atlanta. Back in 1906, over the course of September 22–24, groups of white vigilantes roamed the city indiscriminately attacking black Atlantans, killing twenty-five of them.[10] When the Ku Klux Klan reconstituted in 1915, the terrorist organization located its headquarters in Atlanta. During the early 1920s, the Klan basked in civic respectability as a regular participant in the annual Confederate reunion celebration and exercised considerable influence in Atlanta politics.[11] In the 1930s, the city witnessed the rise of the Order of the Black Shirts, a white supremacist organization formed to remove black residents from the Atlanta workforce. During the Depression, racial violence permeated Atlanta, and Ku Klux Klan members were responsible for floggings and beatings of blacks and labor organizers.[12]

Beginning in the 1940s, Atlanta's white governing elites discouraged Klan activities within the city, in light of negative national media coverage, and they unsuccessfully lobbied the state legislature to enact anti-mask ordinances. Frederick Allen writes that shortly after a Klan cross burning atop Stone Mountain in 1946, "one of the city's aldermen, O. B. Cawthon, advised his fellow Klansmen against burning crosses inside city limits, lest they rile up the 'city fathers.'"[13] In a memorandum to the city's police chief, Mayor William Hartsfield warned Atlanta police officers with Klan leanings that "acts of lawlessness will be dealt with sternly."[14] The Ku Klux Klan maintained a visible public presence in the city and frequently engaged in counter-picketing at desegregation actions in the early 1960s. However, the local Klan rarely resorted to the acts of racial violence employed by other Klan chapters across the state and throughout the Deep South. Racial terrorism became a rarity in Atlanta. The last racial lynching occurred on July 15, 1930, when members of the Black Shirts lynched Dennis Hubert, a Morehouse College student, on the unfounded charge of raping a white woman.[15]

Atlanta's officials were equally concerned with black-induced racial discord. To that end, white business elites needed and expected the city's black leaders to function as a safety valve on black militancy. For the most part, Atlanta's black leaders adroitly stifled black direct action and violent racial unrest. Black activist college students initiated sit-in campaigns in 1960 and 1964, and both campaigns were subsequently ended at the behest of the old guard black leaders. During the turbulent sixties, Atlanta remained relatively unscathed by the urban racial upheaval that rocked much of the nation.

Two incidents, minor by national standards, were the only exceptions to Atlanta's racially violence-free milieu. One occurred in 1966 in Summerhill, which Alton Hornsby, longtime chair of the history department at Morehouse College, describes as "one of those poor black neighborhoods in Atlanta that most whites rarely saw and one that the middle class blacks ignored."[16] On September 6, 1966, Summerhill exploded in response to a police shooting of an auto theft suspect. Residents battled the police and attacked white businesses in the area over the course of several days. City officials deployed hundreds of Atlanta police officers and solicited the assistance of black community leaders to quell the racial disturbance, which eventually left one person dead and another twenty injured. Approximately 140 people were arrested.[17] A second outburst of racial unrest occurred the following summer, in 1967. Three days of violence erupted in Dixie Hills, a poor neighborhood in southwestern Atlanta, resulting in the death of one person and the wounding of several others.[18] Again city officials subdued the disturbance with heavy police deployment and assistance from old guard black leaders. Neither of these two incidents produced the magnitude of violence and destruction of the nation's major uprisings of the era—the 1965 Watts revolt in Los Angeles and the 1967 black rebellions in Detroit and Newark. Nonetheless, as Grady-Willis correctly observes, "The Summerhill and Dixie Hills protests challenged the hegemony of the biracial Atlanta regime in ways that no previous occurrence had, including the student-led sit-in movement of the early 1960s and the induction center protests conducted by the Atlanta Project activists."[19]

Atlanta's white business elites and black leaders formed a biracial coalition to enhance their power and influence in setting policy priorities. Such coalitions constituted an essential element in the governing of Atlanta, dating back to the mayoral administrations of William Hartsfield (1937–1961). Atlanta's governing model hinges upon "the informal arrangements by which public bodies and private interests function together in order to be able to make and carry out governing decisions," in the words of political scientist Clarence Stone.[20]

Under the arrangement that was mutually beneficial to both parties of the biracial coalition, Atlanta's white economic elites dictated economic development and maintained power. Atlanta's prominent black leaders delivered critical electoral support and stifled black dissent to ensure racial stability and received gradual desegregation concessions and selective black middle-class benefits. Larry Keating, a city and regional planning scholar, summarizes the salient dynamics of the quid pro quo relationship sustaining the biracial coalition that shaped modern Atlanta politics:

From the late 1940s to the early '70s, the city government was dominated by wealthy, white downtown business leaders. Throughout most of this period the government depended on the support of a biracial coalition. In the '50s, while William Hartsfield was mayor, and the '60s, while Ivan Allen Jr. was mayor, the white downtown business elite managed to hold on to city hall by maintaining an informal political alliance with the city's middle-class African American political leadership. The white elite supported elements of desegregation and the civil-rights struggle, and expansion of housing for middle-class blacks. In return, black, middle-class political leaders secured the African American vote for Hartsfield and Allen, providing the electoral margin the white elite needed to stay in power.[21]

Clearly the black vote played a vital role in the governance of the city.

As late dean of African American politics Hanes Walton observed, "Black Americans have always voted.... Throughout American history blacks have voted in sundry localities, even when the law forbade them to do so. This was because the practices of segregation have from the start been unevenly applied."[22] In the case of Atlanta, African American residents had limited access to the ballot as early as 1919, when they comprised 11 percent of the total registered voters. Two later major judicial rulings significantly enhanced the clout of the black vote in Atlanta's elections. In 1945, a U.S. Supreme Court decision, *King v. Chapman*, eliminated the white Democratic primary as a device to disenfranchise African Americans in Georgia. Shortly after the ruling, massive community voter registration drives in Atlanta increased the proportion of black registered voters in the city from 8.3 percent to 27.2 percent. In 1963, the landmark Supreme Court decision of *Gray v. Sanders* further heightened the impact of the black vote by eradicating the state's arcane County Unit System that severely diluted African American political representation.[23]

In the mid-1940s, Atlanta's African American leaders began to leverage the influence of the expanding black electorate through disciplined and cohesive strategic voting to secure multiple offices and various policy concessions. Hornsby notes that "a decade before the passing of the Civil Rights Act of 1965, black Atlantans had won and were exercising the right to vote and to significantly influence the course of political life in the city unparalleled in the rest of the South."[24] As early as 1953, Atlanta's black voters elected Rufus Clement to the city's school board. Benjamin E. Mays, president of Morehouse College, won a seat on the Atlanta school board in 1961. The following year, 1962, black Atlantans elected Leroy Johnson to the Georgia Senate, and Johnson would be the first African American to serve in the legislature since the turn of the century. In 1965, the same year that the national Voting Rights Act passed, black Atlantans could boast of Q. V. Williamson, the first African American elected to the city council, a feat that preceded such elections in other southern localities. Then in 1966, when African Americans were largely absent from other southern state legislatures, five black lawmakers representing districts in Atlanta joined Leroy Johnson in the Georgia statehouse.[25]

During the 1969 municipal elections, the city council gained four additional African Americans, which increased the total number of black aldermen to five, and the number African Americans on the school board expanded to three with the election of a new black member. In short, black Atlantans exercised unprecedented electoral participation in the South. As observed by one analyst, "At a time when blacks elsewhere in the South were just beginning to escape the poll taxes, literacy tests, and incidents of sheer physical intimidation that kept them from voting, black Atlantans could look back on more than 20 years of political involvement."[26] In 1970, the prospect of the majority-black city electing an African American mayor further accentuated the importance of electoral politics among Atlanta's black residents.

African American electoral ascendancy in Atlanta was undoubtedly linked to the city's role as harbinger of desegregation in the South. City officials first integrated Atlanta's police force in 1948 when eight black patrolmen were hired, albeit with restricted law enforcement powers. In 1957, Hartsfield, with the cooperation of black leaders, integrated city buses without racial turmoil, and Atlanta underwent the peaceful desegregation of its public schools in 1961, also as a result of backroom negotiations between Hartsfield and prominent African American leaders. During the early 1960s, the city hall cafeteria and chamber of commerce were desegregated. In 1963, state senator Leroy Johnson integrated the Commerce Club, a private club that catered to Atlanta's white civic and business elites. City leaders also desegregated municipal swimming pools during the spring of 1963, six months prior to the March on Washington. However, the desegregation of Atlanta's downtown businesses (including department stores, hotels, and restaurants) required more than the unilateral actions of city officials. It was only after the sit-in campaigns of 1960 and 1964, which led to protracted negotiations between white elites, old guard black leaders, and insurgent black activists, that Atlanta's downtown businesses were completely integrated. While the process of removing all vestiges of segregation from its downtown businesses was atypical of Atlanta's desegregation efforts, the city remained in the forefront of racial transformation in the South.[27]

Notwithstanding Atlanta's record of progress in race relations during the two decades preceding 1970, its history as a segregated city rooted in racial inequality and white supremacy is not lost in this analysis. To be sure, segregation was both the law and custom in Atlanta. Black Atlantans encountered the daily indignities of the tripartite system of racial domination defined by sociologist Aldon Morris: "economic, political, and personal oppression [which] was backed by legislation and the iron fist of Southern governments."[28] Manifestations of segregation abounded in Atlanta, particularly in the lives of the black poor. Police mistreatment and brutality frequently occurred in black neighborhoods. Atlanta's African American citizens, like their southern counterparts, faced restricted residential options. Robert Bullard, also a sociologist, reported that as late as 1970, "over 92 percent of Atlanta's blacks lived in mostly black neighborhoods."[29]

Atlanta's black residents also had few recreational facilities and endured substandard housing, poor schools, and inadequate municipal services. Segregation also limited the employment opportunities of black Atlantans, whose unemployment was consistently double that of the city's white citizens. The racial economic disparity was further evident in Atlanta's acute black poverty. In 1970, 25.1 percent of Atlanta's African American families lived below the poverty level, compared to 15.9 percent of all families in the city.[30]

In sum, the black Atlantan experience was one of contrasts and contradictions. On the one hand, the city was a precursor to racial integration in the South, underscored by unprecedented black electoral participation. On the other hand, the city simultaneously maintained segregation and perpetuated systemic racial inequality via its economic development initiatives. Likewise there were two black Atlantas, one comprised of a striving black middle class and the other embedded in abject poverty.

Mack Jones, founder of the doctoral program in political science at Atlanta University and longtime local scholar-activist, unearthed empirical data supporting Atlanta's growing reputation as an emerging black mecca of the New South. In a seminal 1978 essay assessing black political empowerment in Atlanta, Jones first confirmed that black Atlantans possessed a higher family median income than that of black residents in other major southern cities. The $6,450 median income of black families in Atlanta in the 1970s was "slightly above its two southern rivals, Dallas and Houston, but significantly higher than other southern cities." Secondly, he found higher black educational attainment in Atlanta than in other southern localities. Six percent of Atlanta's black populace twenty-five years or older had at least four years of college compared to 5.4 percent of black Houstonians, its closest southern competitor. Finally, Jones concluded that Atlanta's black businesses were more prosperous than their counterparts located in other southern cities.[31]

While Atlanta's burgeoning image as a black haven and the hub of the New South was not without merit, major pockets of poverty and racial inequality persisted in the city. Poor and working-class black neighborhoods such as Summerhill, Buttermilk Bottom, Dixie Hills, the Fourth Ward, Peoplestown, and Vine City suffered from neglect by white city officials and middle-class blacks alike. As Larry Keating has observed, these isolated, poverty-laden black neighborhoods were beset with "a high crime rate, high unemployment, an undereducated, and undertrained workforce, widespread drug use, and high rate of teenage pregnancy."[32] Black Atlantans residing in these blighted communities also encountered rampant police abuse and woeful municipal services. Moreover, Robert Bullard has noted that during the 1970s the black working poor were subjected to nine different urban renewal projects that eliminated thousands of units of low-income housing with little opposition from the city's black leadership.[33] For example, the construction of the Atlanta Civic Center followed the razing of the entire Buttermilk Bottom neighborhood.

These neglected black neighborhoods offered fertile ground for BPP activism. The quid pro quo arrangement between the city's white and black elites often came at the expense of the black working poor. As Clarence Stone astutely observes, "Advocates of the poor and the defenders of the neighborhoods failed to gain an institutionalized place in the city's informal structure of governance."[34] This void provided the Panthers with an opportunity to establish a substantive outpost in the city by addressing the needs and discontent of the "other" black Atlanta. From the party's inception, its leaders saw the BPP as an advocate for the black downtrodden. On another front, the city's significant presence of black protest and radical organizations potentially represented another important lever for successful Panther organizing in Atlanta. James Smethurst underscores this observation in his examination of Atlanta's rich Black Arts Movement legacy. In the late 1960s and the early 1970s, Smethurst notes, "Atlanta was a key site of the radicalization of the civil rights movement and the emergence of Black Power as a social formation."[35] The Southern Christian Leadership Conference (SCLC) and SNCC were both headquartered in Atlanta. SNCC veterans such as Julian Bond, Gwendolyn Robinson, Lonnie King, Bill Ware, and Willie Ricks resided in the city. In addition, Black Power formations such as the Black Workers Congress, All African Youth Party, and the Georgia Black Liberation Front appeared on the Atlanta landscape. The city's white left included the Socialist Workers Party (SWP), the October League, and the Progressive Labor Party. In sum, notwithstanding Atlanta's largely conservative nature, a myriad of radical organizations and entrenched discontent among the black working poor primed the city for effective BPP activism.

1969: War against the Panthers

At the start of 1970, the Black Panther Party was reeling from the onslaught of repression inflicted on the organization by multiple levels of government, from local police to the FBI. The expansion of the scope and intensity of the repression levied against the party during 1969 led Frank Donner to identify the twelve-month period as the "Year of the Panther."[36] Huey Newton's 1980 dissertation, titled *War against the Panthers*, posthumously published as a monograph by Harlem River Press in 1996, aptly captures the adversarial, hostile, and deadly relationship between members of the Black Panther Party and law enforcement officials in 1969.[37] Political repression decimated the party's national and local leadership ranks. All of the party's top three leaders were either jailed or exiled.

Cofounder Huey Newton was serving a two-to-fifteen-year sentence on a manslaughter conviction in the October 27, 1967, shooting death of police officer John Frey. During that time, the organization's other cofounder, Bobby Seale, was extradited to Connecticut and held without bail to stand trial on charges of conspiracy to commit murder following the death of a rank-and-file Panther. The party's minister of information, Eldridge Cleaver, who had gone underground in November 1968 to avoid parole revocation stemming from the April 6, 1968, shoot-out with Oakland police officers, resurfaced in Algiers, Algeria, in July 1969 during the first Pan-African Cultural Festival.[38] On the eve of the festival, Stokely Carmichael, the BPP field marshal since June 29, 1967, resigned from the party. David Hilliard, chief of staff and the highest-ranking officer available to direct the organization, was free on a $30,000 bail bond after a December arrest on charges of threatening the president of the United States.[39]

Government repression also took a toll on the local leadership of Panther affiliates throughout the country. One can argue that party members at the local level encountered even more intense repression than did national BPP leaders. Fred Hampton and Mark Clark, who headed Panther units in Illinois, were killed by police in a December 4, 1969, raid in Chicago. Panther fatalities also occurred in Los Angeles, where the Southern California chapter was constantly under siege.[40]

In 1969, local law enforcement officials, often in coordination with FBI agents, executed approximately twenty-five raids on BPP offices across the nation.[41] Gun battles between Panthers and police officers usually ensued during these raids. One of the most notable incidents was a raid on December 8, 1969, in which Los Angeles Panther members repelled the local police in a five-hour shoot-out at the party's Forty-First and Central office.[42] The Des Moines, Iowa, BPP headquarters was dynamited on April 26, 1969, during a year in which several rank-and-file members lost their lives around the country.[43] During the contentious twelve months of 1969, BPP members were subjected to more than 580 arrests, on charges ranging from the murder of a police officer to failure to have proper identification.[44] This is a grossly disproportionate number of arrests in light of the party's estimated membership of between fifteen hundred and five thousand.

Over the course of 1969, the BPP under the direction of Bobby Seale and David Hilliard adopted several measures to combat the adverse impact of the intense repression. These counter-repression measures sought to enhance organizational discipline and expand the influence of the party. The Panther leaders used a multipronged approach. First, at the beginning of the year, the leaders expanded the number of rules of the organization from its initial ten to twenty-five. The new rules focused on improving the accountability of both individual members and party units. BPP members were now required to attend political education classes, read at least two hours per day to keep abreast of current political developments, and submit daily work reports. At the organizational level, Panther affiliates were now required to submit weekly reports as well as monthly financial reports to headquarters. The new rules also dictated formal operations of the local party units, as indicated by rule 19: "Only office personnel assigned to respective offices each day should be there. All others are to sell papers and do Political work out in the community including Captains, Section Leaders, etc."[45]

Secondly, party officials initiated a moratorium on the admittance of new members and additional Panther units in order to foster organizational discipline. It was during this period, late 1969 through 1970, that Carl Hampton, the founder of People's Party II in Houston, Texas, was denied a charter to establish a Panther unit in the city. Although Hampton spent time volunteering and selling newspapers at the party's headquarters in late 1969, historian Paul Alkebulan noted that "the BPP was not accepting new members at the time, and he [Hampton] was unable to join."[46] Ester King, a Houston activist, recalled that Hampton returned to Houston and attempted to recruit members of Texas Southern University's Organization of Black Student Unity (OBSU) to form a Houston Panther formation but was rebuffed "after an OBSU member called Oakland and reported that Hampton was not authorized to start a BPP chapter."[47]

Purging individual members and sometimes entire Panther units from the organization constituted the third prong for improving discipline within the party. Between March and August 1969, the BPP leadership expelled 250 members for a variety of reasons, ranging from renegade activities to dereliction of assigned duties. Also, national officials disbanded local Panther affiliates in Omaha, Milwaukee, and Detroit.[48] Building a national, multiracial coalition to combat political repression served as the centerpiece of the party's antirepression strategy. BPP leaders organized and sponsored the Revolutionary Conference for a United Front Against Fascism (UFAF), a three-day event held July 18–20, 1969, in Oakland. Multiracial coalition politics was a hallmark of Panther praxis both at the national and local level, and the party's proposed coalition was predicated on the shared experience of government repression. Progressive activists of all hues and ideological dispositions had this in common, and approximately three thousand attended the conference. Although participants were predominantly white leftists, representatives of the major radical racial formations of the time were also in attendance—members of the Red Guards, Young Lords, Brown Berets, and the Republic of New Afrika. Members of more than forty organizations attended the conference, but many Black Power groups failed to participate, which furthered the perception of some that the Panthers were captives of the white Left.[49]

During his keynote address, Seale urged conference attendees to "go forth" and "defend not only BPP political prisoners but... all political prisoners."[50] He also called for "decentralization" of police on a national scale, proposing neighborhood-based police councils of elected community members. Seale introduced the National Committee to Combat Fascism (NCCF), intended to support political prisoners and drum up support for community control of the police. The multiracial NCCF would serve as an organizing arm of the Black Panther Party. NCCF members would provide party leaders with an additional means of assessing an aspiring local Panther unit before they officially sanctioned it. In the period that followed the conference, Ryan Nissim-Sabat notes, "New Panther operations were first given the title of NCCF as a method of screening potential Panthers. Once they proved their worthiness to the party, national headquarters granted a branch or chapter."[51] The NCCF would become the most prevalent organizational structure among party's affiliates through 1970. As the party's national leaders turned their attention to the South, at the behest of Los Angeles Panther leader Geronimo Pratt, who hailed from Morgan City, Louisiana, local Panther formations tended to follow this model. The Winston-Salem, North Carolina, party outpost is a case in point and was officially sanctioned as an NCCF unit in November 1969. The Atlanta Panther affiliate was the exception to this model.

1970-1971

The Black Panther Party's first public recognition in Atlanta occurred as a result of a Panther fund-raising rally held in mid-February 1970 at Georgia Tech, a predominantly white university located in midtown. Former activists of the Georgia Black Liberation Front, who constituted the core membership of the upstart Atlanta BPP affiliate, sold party pamphlets, posters, and buttons at the rally. They also screened two films featuring the exiled Eldridge Cleaver and incarcerated party cofounder Huey Newton.[52] Among the predominantly white audience of approximately three hundred people were two state lawmakers, William Armstrong Smith and Jim Tysinger, both members of the Georgia Senate. During the Senate session of February 16, 1970, Smith pleaded, "Wake America! Wake Georgia! Time is running out."[53] Senator Smith's outrage was directed at the Panthers' presence in Atlanta. His complaints of the BPP speakers' excessive profanity and their advocacy of armed revolution foreshadowed difficulties in establishing a strong BPP chapter in Atlanta.

Contrary to other southern Panther affiliates, which initially organized below the radar of local government officials, the Atlanta party outpost came to the immediate attention of the city's leaders as a result of Smith's statehouse exhortations. Also significant was its official authorization as the Georgia chapter of the Black Panther Party, further distinguishing the local affiliate from its counterparts elsewhere in the South. State chapter status was the highest-level designation assigned to a Panther affiliate by the party's central committee, superseding three other designations: branch, NCCF, and community information center. During the winter of 1970, according to the Committee on Internal Security of the U.S. House of Representatives, "There was apparently local Panther activity in at least 35 different cities in 19 states and the District of Columbia. This activity was conducted under the supervision of 13 chapters and five 'branches,' 20 National Committee to Combat Fascism [units] and two community information centers."[54]

In 1970 the BPP central committee chartered party outposts in five other southern cities besides Atlanta—New Orleans, Memphis, Richmond, Virginia, and Cleveland, Mississippi—but none of these would receive party chapter designation.[55] The Richmond affiliate would be designated a community information center, and the others would be designated as NCCF. As noted, the NCCF served as a mechanism for assessing the organizing efforts of affiliates seeking official recognition from the national leaders. The BPP affiliate in Winston-Salem is a case in point. As Benjamin Friedman observes, "Although the Winston-Salem group began organizing in late 1968, it was not officially sanctioned by the national office as a full-fledged BPP branch until April 1971."[56] In the case of Atlanta, the prospective Panther unit did not undergo any probationary period. It assumed chapter status immediately, which was a rarity for new units during this era.

Atlanta was strategically important to the national party leaders for several reasons. First, it was seen as an anchor for the party's 1970 foray into the South. As a chartered state chapter, it not only had authority and supervision over Panther entities located within Georgia but was also eligible to assume regional responsibilities. Select chapters served as intermediaries for national headquarters in supervising geographically dispersed party units. For example, the Illinois chapter was assigned authority over the party's various Midwest units, which included Des Moines, Detroit, Kansas City, and Omaha.[57] As Grady-Willis notes, "The five offices of the Georgia State Chapter of the Black Panther Party also served as way stations in a manner similar to the Atlanta SNCC office, with Panthers staying in the city en route to offices in New Orleans, North Carolina, and other places throughout the region."[58]

Second, Atlanta was a city with a newly majority black electorate, with attendant expected electoral payoffs. In theory, black control of the city levers of power meant a less repressive environment. Atlanta was home to black elected officials as well as African American radicals, and it offered a vibrant political setting and many potential allies to help advance the goals of the Black Panther Party. Later in 1970, during the Labor Day weekend, three thousand black and Third World activists would come to the city to found the Congress of African People. Historian Komozi Woodard notes, "The Atlanta Congress was ... encouraging because the black nationalists had never before attracted so many black elected officials and civil rights leaders to a Pan-African summit."[59]

The upstart Georgia chapter of the Black Panther Party opened its first office in February 1970 at 18 Ashby Street in a black working-class neighborhood near the Atlanta University Center, west of downtown. Similar to the other southern BPP entities, with the exception of New Orleans, the original leaders of the Atlanta Panther affiliate were indigenous to the state. (In the case of New Orleans, BPP national leaders dispatched a two-member delegation led by Steve Green to establish a party outpost there in the spring of 1970.) Emma Jean Martin, an early Atlanta Panther, recalls that the initial leaders of the chapter were "from the grassroots, born and reared in the state of Georgia."[60] Alton Deville, raised in Columbus, Georgia, and Thomas Freeman, a native Atlantan, both attended the mandatory six-week training period held in Oakland. During this stint on the West Coast, representatives of prospective local party units were introduced to the administrative procedures of the organization, sold copies of the *Black Panther* newspaper, and attended political education classes. After their return from Oakland, Tim Hayes, a former Morehouse College student and one-time member of the Georgia Black Liberation Front based in Atlanta's Vine City neighborhood, would also assume an early leadership role in the Georgia BPP chapter.[61]

In February 1969, one year prior to the founding of the Georgia chapter of the party, black activists from Louisville, Kentucky, who aspired to form a Panther affiliate in that city, had been denied affiliation due to their financial inability to send a local representative to Oakland to attend the required training session. In correspondence from the central committee, David Hilliard wrote, "Brothers, your request will be granted as soon as your real representative arrives. Brothers, this way is necessary because Pigs all over the nation is using the mail to test our strength and attack our local chapters. I will personally give your representative written authorization to begin the Louisville chapter."[62] A party affiliate would not appear in Louisville until 1972.

The Panthers in Atlanta engaged in limited activities during their first year. The Georgia chapter held weekly community political education classes and film screenings on Wednesday and Sunday evenings. During the first year, the Atlanta Panthers did not sponsor any survival programs. Instead, they largely concentrated on selling the party's newspaper and establishing a presence in the city's black working-class and poor neighborhoods. The *Black Panther*, which sold for twenty-five cents, served several key functions for the organization. It published directives from party leaders, material for the political education classes, and information about the activities of the various party units dispersed across the nation. The latter connected the Georgia chapter to other party affiliates and helped foster camaraderie among Panther members.

Most importantly, the newspaper provided a major source of revenue for the national leaders. History professor and former Black Panther Paul Alkebulan observes that the "national headquarters imposed quotas for newspaper sales based on the size of the chapter and required payment for the previous week before a new shipment was sent."[63] Nationwide, each individual BPP member was assigned one hundred newspapers per week to sell. The important task of selling the *Black Panther* was a staple Panther activity, particularly at the rank-and-file level. National leaders would readily suspend individuals and entire party affiliates for dereliction of this critical undertaking. The corner of Broad and Alabama Streets in downtown Atlanta was a popular site for Panthers and other black activists to hawk their respective newspapers.

During its initial year of operations, the Panther affiliate in Atlanta established multiple offices throughout the city. The local party leaders targeted several black, poor, and working-class neighborhoods for their grassroots organizing efforts. One of these neighborhoods was economically depressed Summerhill, the site of one of Atlanta's rare instances of violent racial unrest in 1966. Vine City, a blighted neighborhood beset with deplorable living conditions, also received attention from the local party leaders. Vine City was the setting of SNCC's Atlanta Project, an urban grassroots initiative whose accomplishments, Grady-Willis contends, have been underappreciated by scholars.[64] In 1966, the year of the founding of the Black Panther Party in Oakland, Atlanta Project activists were fixtures in Vine City, and four years later local BPP members became the heirs of SNCC's organizing efforts. The Kirkwood neighborhood on Atlanta's east side, which had become predominantly African American due to the white flight of the mid-1960s, would eventually house the headquarters of the local BPP affiliate.

The Georgia BPP chapter's opposition to police brutality, a defining feature of Panther activism nationwide, was critical to local organizing. Party members rallied the Summerhill community to protest the police shooting death of Andra Moore, a black fourteen-year-old killed in September 1970. In mid-1970 and early autumn, Atlanta's BPP members, along with their comrades across the country, were preoccupied with promoting and preparing to attend the Panther-organized Revolutionary People's Constitutional Convention (RPCC) to be held in early September in Philadelphia for the purpose of rewriting the U.S. Constitution and then a follow-up convention in November. Huey Newton, released from prison on August 5, 1970, after the reversal of his earlier conviction, was billed as the RPCC's keynote speaker. The event would not be as big as planners hoped, however. FBI agents, with the assistance of local law enforcement officials, successfully conspired to prevent members of several southern Panther units from attending. Panther activists from New Orleans were arrested while leaving the city driving rental cars acquired with the assistance of film actress Jane Fonda, while Winston-Salem Panthers were stranded after their charter bus allegedly broke down and the driver mysteriously disappeared.[65]

During much of 1970, members of the Atlanta Panther outpost encountered rough going in their efforts to establish a substantive party chapter. Part of the problem was politically unsophisticated leadership. For example, Tim Hayes, the chapter deputy chairman in late 1970, declared that "there should be no involvement of black people in politics. Politics itself is not a game, but the way it is practiced in the United States it is." He further maintained publicly that organizations such as the NAACP, CORE, and SCLC were "a joke, ineffective and irrelevant to black people at this time."[66] Hayes's blanket indictment of the mainstream civil rights organizations made it difficult to forge coalitions with potential allies in the city. Moreover, his abdication of the electoral arena was certainly contrary to the significance of electoral politics to black Atlantans. A real estate agency owned by Q. V. Williamson, the city's first African American alderman, evicted the upstart Atlanta Panther affiliate from its Ashby Street headquarters on December 1, 1970, for failure to pay rent, which reflected the initial woes of the fledgling organization.

During early 1971, the organizational tribulations of the Georgia BPP chapter continued as a result of negative publicity ensuing from a downtown disturbance. On February 15, a melee occurred when an Atlanta patrolman intervened during an altercation between a local Panther and a member of the Nation of Islam who clashed over selling their organizations' respective newspapers on a popular downtown corner. Several windows of downtown stores were broken when black bystanders annoyed with police intervention in the fight threw rocks and other objects. Approximately one hundred police officers in full riot gear restored order after the arrest of twenty-one individuals.[67]

In some cities, such as Boston, the Panthers and the Nation of Islam enjoyed cordial relations. Both sold newspapers at the Dudley station of the Massachusetts Bay Transportation Authority in Roxbury, a hub for the black community in Boston. Similarly, the Cleveland Panther affiliate and the city's local Nation of Islam members participated in a fund-raising event with other Cleveland Black Power groups. However, there were other instances of conflict between the organizations. The late Manning Marable wrote that "Nation of Islam members in Philadelphia destroyed the city's Black Panther Party headquarters in retaliation for the group's public advocacy of Malcolm X's ideas."[68] The civil unrest in Atlanta triggered by the brawl between a Panther and a member of the Nation of Islam undoubtedly contributed to the Black Panther Party being depicted as a gang by the mainstream media.

The party's central committee sought to reverse the fortunes of the Atlanta affiliate after its headquarters eviction by seeking to acquire property to serve as a new home for the Georgia chapter. Oakland-based leaders attempted to purchase the former SNCC national headquarters building located at 360 Nelson Street in Southeast Atlanta, but the purchase never materialized. FBI operatives in Atlanta viewed negotiations to acquire the building as an opportunity to create dissension with the Georgia chapter. The local FBI office proposed writing a phony letter, a common COINTELPRO tactic, suggesting that the liaison person negotiating the transaction was "receiving a fee for his services which was being withheld" from the local Panther affiliate as well as recommending that the "letter be mailed anonymously with an Atlanta postmark."[69] Although the purchase never materialized, the willingness of national party leaders to purchase a building on behalf of one of its local units accentuates the strategic value of the Georgia chapter. Oakland did not make a practice of providing material support of such magnitude to its local units. Party affiliates were usually left to their own independent means of financial solvency. While the acquisition of the SNCC building did not transpire, the Atlanta Panther outpost would soon benefit from a tactical shift initiated by the Newton-led central committee.

During the spring of 1971, the BPP entered a new stage of its sixteen-year life span. Beginning in May and lasting until Newton's August 1974 departure to Cuba, this phase was one in which the party de-emphasized its early dictum of "picking up the gun." Instead, the BPP leaders now placed greater attention on the survival programs and electoral politics. This demilitarization period—one of five distinct stages in the party's existence—was initiated after a sometimes deadly factional conflict that surfaced shortly after Newton's release from prison in August 1970. Critics of this tactical change asserted that this went against the party's revolutionary essence. Regardless, the party's tactical shift would be expected to produce dividends for the Atlanta Panther affiliate. An Atlanta BPP member explained, "[W]e have dropped the gun in favor of trying to become closer to the [grassroots] citizenry, to try to get closer to them, so that we can work with them, organize them and politicize them so that the community can make a move and not just the Party."[70] However, the positive impact in Atlanta of the party's shift in focus would not be immediate.

In late September 1971, local BPP leaders acknowledged their difficulty in establishing a foothold in Atlanta. In a party communiqué published in the *Great Speckled Bird*, an Atlanta alternative newspaper, the leaders lamented that they had a "hard time forming a chapter of the Black Panther Party, as did all southern chapters."[71] The reliance on a white leftist newspaper to transmit party communiqués reflected the impotence of the local unit. Many Panther affiliates published their own newsletter to disseminate organizational information. After nearly a year and a half in Atlanta, the local Panther affiliate had only sponsored one major survival program. However, it had set up multiple offices in the city. The Georgia BPP chapter's various offices included its headquarters at 2041 Dunwoody Street in the Kirkwood neighborhood, 585 Parkway Drive in the Old Fourth Ward, 607 Rhodes Street in Vine City, and 281 Armond

Street in Summerhill.[72] These offices were located in the heart of poor and working-class communities, a hallmark of BPP practice not only domestically but also abroad. Kathleen Cleaver notes that the initial office of the International Section of the Black Panther Party was "set in the midst of a poor Berber community."[73]

Organizational inroads gained from establishment of multiple party offices throughout the city were further bolstered by a Huey Newton visit in which he announced the move of the national party headquarters to Atlanta. During a press conference on September 8, 1971, held at the local headquarters in Kirkwood, Newton announced that the Oakland headquarters would move to Atlanta in early 1972. Newton explained, "It's only logical that the liberation of black people begin in the South, where their oppression started." He stressed that Atlanta was selected over Dallas and New Orleans "because of the progressive thinking and actions [of] people here."[74] An editorial by national BPP leaders appearing in the *Black Panther* two weeks later echoed Newton's words in Atlanta and said that by relocating to Georgia, "We are returning to the 'Origins of the crime... where the contradiction started,' to the place where our oppression and enslavement in the United States began."[75] Moving the BPP headquarters to Atlanta was an idea that dated back to the eve of the Free Huey Birthday Rally held in Oakland in February 1968, according to David Hilliard, who years later in his memoir recalled that it was then that "Newton raised the possibility of moving the Party to Atlanta."[76]

The Black Panther Party's announced move of its national office to Atlanta triggered a wide range of responses from the city's white and black leaders. Not surprisingly, white politicians expressed their disapproval, even though some remarks were more measured than others. For example, Lester Maddox, an avowed segregationist and then lieutenant governor of Georgia, declared, "I hate to see this thing happen because we've got enough problems already. This group is licensed to steal, destroy, and kill and wage war upon our society."[77] Fletcher Thompson, a member of the US House of Representatives, remarked, "This organization is a group of militant revolutionaries whose history demonstrates that they are intent on causing trouble, and in my opinion, they will only bring trouble and problems to Atlanta. I hope that all Atlantans, both black and white, will rise up and let the Black Panther[s] know that neither they nor their philosophies are welcome in Atlanta."[78] State lawmaker Ben B. Blackburn, whose district housed the Kirkwood headquarters, commented, "They are the most exaggerated force in America[,] an aggregation of first class nitwits. I guess I would hate to have any bunch of nitwits hanging around my district." In a more restrained response, Mayor Sam Massell noted, "We have the Ku Klux Klan with its history of hate and destruction so I guess we can deal with the Panthers as well."[79]

The responses of city's black leaders ranged from welcoming the BPP's relocation to Atlanta to cautionary words with undertones suggesting that the Panthers would do well to remain in Oakland. Ralph Abernathy, the head of the SCLC, enthusiastically stated, "We certainly welcome the Black Panthers. We would be delighted to have our black brothers come to Atlanta, an all-American city."[80] Similarly, two former SNCC leaders—Julian Bond, a member of the Georgia state legislature, and Lonnie King, the president of the local NAACP—supported the move. In contrast, the old guard black leaders expressed reservations. Jesse Hill, CEO of Atlanta Life Insurance Company and civic leader, remarked that the "Panthers could choose a better southern city if they were mainly concerned about problems of housing, employment, and jury duty."[81] Andrew Young, then director of the Community Relations Commission, warned that "the Panthers will either have to conform to the style of operations that is confined to the South or be isolated."[82] Echoing these sentiments, an editorial titled "Are the Panthers Needed?" published in the *Atlanta Daily World*, the city's black newspaper, questioned the purpose of the proposed BPP relocation and warned, "The Negro citizens boast that Atlanta is perhaps the most intellectual city in the nation, and we intend to keep it that way, so if any group plans to bring turmoil and unnecessary strife to our town, then Atlanta is hardly the place to land."[83]

Extensive media coverage generated by Newton's announcement of the planned move raised the profile of the BPP chapter in the city. Newton's visit also enhanced the morale of Atlanta's Panthers and their supporters. Newton inspected the chapter's various offices and talked with local Panthers. Most BPP members only knew Newton as the revolutionary hero on the poster. Few Panthers across the country had actually had personal contact with the organization's cofounder and minister of defense. Newton's presence among Atlanta's party members energized them and reinforced their commitment to the party.

Another benefit of Newton's proposed relocation of BPP national operations to Atlanta was the deployment of Ron Carter, a seasoned Oakland Panther, to lend assistance to the local party outpost. During the fall of 1971, the central committee assigned Carter, who would become the Georgia chapter's most effective and respected organizer, to work on a permanent basis with Panthers in the city. Carter's full-time assignment to Atlanta further underscores the privileged stature of the city's BPP outpost. The Winston-Salem Panther affiliate made numerous requests for assistance from the party's headquarters before Oakland dispatched Doug Miranda, a Boston party member, to North Carolina for a short stint. While Oakland dispatched members to assist with organizing the various Panther affiliates, it was usually done on a temporary basis such as this. June Hilliard recalled, "New Orleans, Winston Salem . . . somebody had to go and try to give them directions on how to put it together, make sure they were structured correctly. I was assistant chief of staff. I would go to the new chapter."[84] Also of note, Carter's deployment did not supersede the Atlanta affiliate's local leadership, which demonstrated Oakland-based leaders' sensitivity in this instance. In contrast, the BPP headquarters assigned Charles Scott, a party member from New York City (Corona, Queens), to New Orleans in a leadership capacity. Scott would lead the Panthers in defending themselves against two violent police assaults on New Orleans BPP offices in the early 1970s.[85]

At the close of 1971, Atlanta's BPP outpost gained additional momentum as it added another office at 578 English Avenue in Northwest Atlanta. After nearly two years of organizing, the Georgia BPP chapter had an impressive infrastructure of five offices in different parts of the city. The Panther affiliate also expanded and diversified its membership, beginning to attract students from the Atlanta University Center, a consortium of four historically black college and universities. In addition, the chapter forged alliances with civil rights organizations such as the SCLC, which it had once lambasted. BPP members in Atlanta solidified relationships with key community activists and Panther sympathizers. In short, at the onset of 1972, the Georgia chapter of the Black Panther Party was poised for its most effective year of activism in Atlanta.

1972: Survival through Service to the People

The Georgia chapter's third year was the heyday of BPP activism in Atlanta. In 1972, the local Panther affiliate amassed its largest membership and developed an extensive network of community supporters, which permitted it to sponsor a number of survival programs. These emanated from an earlier directive issued by Bobby Seale in Oakland. In mid-November 1968, Chairman Seale ordered all BPP affiliates to implement three "serve the people" projects: a free breakfast program, free health clinics, and a campaign to acquire petition signatures for a referendum to "decentralize" local police (and form neighborhood-based elected councils to control law enforcement). In January 1969, a fourth initiative was added: the formation of "liberation schools." This group of projects morphed into the party's "survival program" in 1971, significantly expanding the party's community service activities.[86]

Although the BPP national headquarters move to Atlanta never transpired, despite its having been announced, a second Newton visit to the city within a six-month period further energized local party members and Panther sympathizers. After a black student protest, Georgia State University officials finally relented and permitted Newton to deliver a Black History Month lecture on campus. Earlier, Kenneth England, the dean of students at the university, had refused to authorize the $900 honorarium for Newton. England declared that it was "not university policy to pay racist speakers," and he deemed Newton a racist.[87] Despite the BPP's commitment to multiracial coalition politics, the organization continued to be depicted as anti-white. On February 10, 1972,

Newton addressed an audience of approximately one thousand and discussed recent party developments. He explained that "community organizing[,] not shoot-outs with the police[,] is the central program of the party at the present."[88] Newton also disassociated the BPP from the recent Black Liberation Army activity in the city.[89]

Atlanta's Panther affiliate benefited from a membership surge during the year. Greg Bailey, from the Dixie Hills neighborhood, recalled that "there were not even a dozen members during the early years."[90] In 1972, it claimed its largest membership—approximately two dozen hardcore members. While its membership base was largely grassroots, a contingent of college students joined. Several of the early leaders were college educated, including Tim Hayes and Sam Gilliam, who both attended Morehouse College. The Georgia BPP chapter successfully tapped into the pool of students at the Atlanta University Center (AUC) as a source of members and volunteers for the "serve the people" projects. Panther activists regularly sold newspapers, gave presentations, and recruited students on campuses of the AUC. Emma Jean Martin, a graduate student pursuing a master's degree in French at Atlanta University, was one such recruit.

Martin became a member of the Georgia BPP chapter in 1971 after she and several of her fellow students volunteered for the party's free breakfast program at the Kirkwood headquarters. She explains, "I joined because of the Black Panther Party's sense of community and their willingness to help grassroots people." As a graduate student and experienced activist, Martin was an invaluable addition to the Atlanta Panther delegation. In Clinton, Louisiana, where she was born and raised, Martin's parents had provided shelter for CORE activists who had come to dismantle segregation. As a youngster, Martin wrote to President Kennedy to complain about a policy in her hometown that disenfranchised unwed black mothers. At fifteen years of age she participated in a direct action, joining civil rights activists who picketed a store in Clinton to secure the employment of a black clerk. As a result, Martin was arrested and placed in the West Baton Rouge Parish jail, where she spent time in solitary confinement. Upon graduating from high school, she continued her activism during her undergraduate studies at Southern University in Baton Rouge.[91]

Martin's work in the Georgia Panther chapter diversified the male-dominated leadership. She frequently served as officer of the day (OD) and eventually assumed the position of minister of education of the Atlanta BPP outpost. As OD, Martin supervised the daily activities of the Kirkwood headquarters, monitored the whereabouts of local Panthers, and interacted with the public on behalf of the other leaders. In addition, she logged phone calls and on occasion disciplined party members. While serving as officer of the day, Martin met Newton during his visits to Atlanta. She recalls that Newton and other national party leaders stressed the need for discretion when dealing with party business. Central committee members would often call and test her, she says, explaining, "You don't give out certain information." Contrary to Oakland and other early BPP affiliates, the Atlanta BPP chapter did not rely on "mud-holing," a type of physical punishment to discipline members. Instead, the local Panther leaders required individuals to run laps.[92]

As minister of education, Martin directed several educational outreach programs, including an after-school tutorial program and a Saturday "freedom school." Martin's leadership ascendancy in Atlanta reflected the chapter's commitment to gender-neutral organization. Nicole "Nicky" Bowden, another AUC student, also served as officer of the day on various occasions. Martin remembers that "sometimes the men did not like taking orders from women, but they still [carried out] their assigned duties."[93] Martin, Bowden, and other female Panthers also performed security duties. Greg Bailey reflects: "The women's role in the party—in the Atlanta chapter—was to help not only motivate and to get young women to understand their rights as young women in this society, but also how not to be oppressed by patriarchal relationships. They were feminists in that sense and very forward thinking to empower themselves by being able to be a total human being—not just being seen as a woman or a sistah—with the ability to do the same thing that guys could do."[94] A manifestation of the gender equality prevalent in the Georgia BPP chapter was that both men and women party members were responsible for breakfast program shifts.

During 1972, the Georgia chapter of the Black Panther Party sponsored eight survival programs: a free breakfast program, the Saturday freedom school, the after-school tutorial program, a day-care program, a pest-control program, a free clothing program, a program providing bussing so that people could visit family members in prison, and a mobile medical clinic.[95] Beginning early that year, breakfast programs at three localities in the city were launched in addition to the one started in 1971 at the Kirkwood site. Located in Vine City, Old Fourth Ward, and Summerhill, these fed approximately four hundred children between four and thirteen years of age daily. BPP member Earnest Watts headed the Vine City breakfast program, which served approximately fifty-five kids each day.[96] Atlanta University Center students provided invaluable assistance, and Spelman students volunteered in the program in the Old Fourth Ward. Local party members solicited donations from neighborhood businesses to operate the breakfast programs. They received donations in money and food from Atlanta dairies and other small local businesses but failed to secure support from the city's major grocery chains: Kroger and Colonial Stores. Members of a local white commune also donated fruits and vegetables to the party's breakfast programs.[97]

In her role as minister of education of the local Panther affiliate, Martin coordinated the Saturday freedom school and after-school tutorial program held at the Kirkwood office. She developed lesson plans and class activities that introduced students to Marcus Garvey, Harriet Tubman, and other prominent black historical figures. Martin fondly recalls that she came up with a "black alphabet" that the students enjoyed, assigning an aspect of black history to each letter to heighten awareness and interest in black culture.[98] During field trips, freedom school attendees visited local museums and viewed educational movies. Neighborhood parents and their children attended an open house, replete with balloons and hot dogs, to launch the tutorial program for K–6 schoolchildren. Party members and volunteers assisted students with their homework assignments, particularly reading and math. "The parents were grateful and thanked us for helping their children," Martin recalls.[99]

The Georgia chapter's "People's Free Clothing Program" and the "People's Free Pest Control Program" were community outreach efforts offered by most party affiliates around the country since these required minimal resources. These were among the initial survival programs run by Houston party members, and BPP outposts in Winston-Salem, Dallas, and New Orleans also offered them. However, Atlanta's "People's Free Day Care Center" was not as commonplace. Party members at the Summerhill office operated a day-care center that served thirteen children who received meals and participated in various educational activities. The day-care center was available to neighborhood parents between 6:00 a.m. and 7:00 p.m. during the week. Community residents and students from the various AUC institutions assisted Panthers in staffing the Summerhill day-care center.[100]

In addition, the Georgia BPP chapter provided assistance to families "who had transportation difficulties visiting their relatives incarcerated in Georgia's state prisons" by instituting the "People's Free Busing Program."[101] Martin explains that the program was much needed since "wives and children had a difficult time visiting their family members in prisons . . . in Jackson and Reidsville, Georgia."[102] Both locations were quite a distance from Atlanta. In contrast to the Detroit Panthers, who purchased the vehicle that anchored the Motor City chapter's free busing program, Atlanta party members had difficulty procuring a bus, which delayed the implementation of the program and precluded them from offering the service consistently.[103]

Finally, the Georgia chapter of the Black Panther Party sponsored a mobile health clinic that offered limited medical treatment options. An anonymous donor supplied a van that frequented the neighborhoods of the party's offices. Free medical clinics were arguably the crown jewel of the BPP's survival programs. Only a few Panther affiliates nationwide had the resources and contacts to implement this community service, which required recruiting highly skilled volunteers with health-care expertise, acquiring special equipment and supplies, and securing a facility to house the clinic. BPP members in Houston worked tirelessly to no avail to institute a free health center to commemorate their fallen leader Carl Hampton, who was shot to death by Houston police on July 26, 1970.[104] Sociologist Alondra Nelson's study of the party's health-care activism underscores the uncommonness of the free medical clinics. Only twelve BPP outposts nationwide operated free health centers, none of them in the South.[105] However, in addition to the Atlanta mobile service, in 1971 the Panther affiliate in Winston-Salem initiated the party's sole free ambulance service, named in honor of one of its fallen comrades, Joseph Waddell.

The Atlanta Panther outpost's mobile health clinic administered tests to detect sickle cell anemia, diabetes, and hypertension.[106] Alondra Nelson writes, "In the spring of 1972, the Party's sickle cell anemia initiative was a hallmark of its health politics. This campaign epitomized the Party's social health perspective, highlighting both the biological and the extra-medical circumstances that contributed to the prevalence among African Americans and to the disproportionate burden of disease borne by blacks more generally."[107] A mostly black volunteer medical staff provided critical health-care services to impoverished black Atlantans.

Atlanta's Panther affiliate, like others nationwide, benefited from the national office's tactical shift of emphasizing survival programs because these greatly enhanced the public image of the party. The Georgia chapter's change from revolutionary swagger to pragmatic grassroots community activism expanded the base of party supporters in Atlanta, as local Panthers found allies, some from the city's African American religious community. During 1972, the city's party members solidified relationships with several activist ministers. In Vine City, the Reverend Henry Delaney, pastor of the Butler Street Christian Methodist Episcopal Church, befriended local BPP members because of their commitment to serving dispossessed black people. Pastor W. J. Stafford of the Free All Baptist Church supported the Atlanta party office in the Kirkwood neighborhood, assisted the prison bussing program, and permitted local BPP members to use church facilities.[108]

Party members in Atlanta now forged alliances with traditional civil rights groups that they once scorned, such as the SCLC. In 1972 local BPP activists worked extensively with Joe Boone, the outreach director of the SCLC and pastor of the Rush Memorial Congregational Church. Atlanta Panthers cosponsored a rally with the SCLC and Angela Davis to protest the arrest of Emily Butler, a black IRS employee accused of shooting to death her white supervisor in Georgia's Dekalb County. While the Georgia BPP chapter worked with the Black Federated Alliance, Black Workers Congress, and other African American radical groups, it never developed a multiracial rainbow coalition in Atlanta, although it did occasionally organize with the Socialist Workers Party.[109]

Other key party allies included the Atlanta-based Institute of the Black World, which donated educational materials to the party's freedom school and after-school tutorial programs. Al Horn, a white civil rights lawyer, furnished legal counsel for local party members and was a founding member of a law project in Atlanta that represented political defendants and other clients on a pro bono basis. Attorney John Jenkins, a colleague at the project, described Horn as "one of those rare people who was not only somehow larger than the surrounding landscape, but unstintingly and outspokenly dedicated to criminal law practice for a higher purpose than financial gains."[110] BPP members across the country depended on politically conscious lawyers such as Horn, as they were sometimes arrested on specious charges.

As the Georgia BPP chapter proceeded into the summer of 1972, it enjoyed unprecedented organizing success. The Panther affiliate sponsored an extensive slate of survival programs and expanded its base of supporters. With five offices dispersed throughout the city, the party's outpost appeared firmly entrenched. However, this success was short lived. By the end of the year, a confluence of external and internal factors stymied and then dissipated its momentum.

Reversal of Party Fortunes

During the remainder of 1972, extensive negative media coverage, governmental repression, and unprincipled local BPP leadership contributed to the reversal of the fortunes of the Georgia BPP chapter. Beginning in late August, the chapter was subjected to a barrage of unflattering media attention. Within a few months, over a dozen news articles would appear in the city's two leading newspapers, the *Atlanta Journal* and the *Atlanta Constitution*, framing the Atlanta Panthers as anti-white, violence-prone black extremists. In her study of the elite national media coverage of the BPP, Jane Rhodes defines framing as the process by which "subjects are placed within a formal frame that focuses attention on selected aspects of a visual or verbal text, or subjects are set up to be something they are not," and she writes that the "Panthers were framed as a threatening entity to be feared, particularly by whites."[111] Atlanta's two mainstream newspapers did just this, publishing unfounded accusations, innuendo, and unsubstantiated allegations that demonized the members of the city's Panther outpost.

The onslaught commenced with a front-page story in the *Atlanta Constitution* on August 24. The article accused Atlanta party members of demanding $50,000 in money and supplies from executives of the city's major grocery stores. Representatives of the Colonial, Kroger, and Big Apple supermarkets complained of the party members' less than courteous demeanor, but none confirmed the $50,000 demand. As an example of the paper's use of innuendo, it quoted Ernest Boyce, president of Colonial Food stores: "Last year there were five attempts at arson against us, but we don't have any proof who did it."[112] By placing this in a story about the Panthers, the newspaper implied that they might be involved in arson. The following day the newspaper published an article reporting that Police Chief John Inman had initiated an investigation of the party's solicitation practices in order to ascertain whether extortion charges were warranted.

A week later, the Georgia BPP chapter was linked to death threats against Dr. Clayton Powell, a local black Republican Party operative, who claimed that the Panthers had placed a $1,500 contract on his life. Although Powell eventually accepted the party's denial of involvement in alleged death threats against him, the Georgia BPP chapter remained marred by the accusation.[113] In September the *Constitution* went to the new acting FBI director, featuring Patrick Gray III as the source. In a front-page article headlined "FBI Eyeing Panther Money Demand Here," Gray raised the issue of "whether or not [the Panthers] were actually financed by sources external to this country. Their financing is not really clear." He also remarked that the FBI was "more concerned with [the party's] violence and violent plans as expressed in their rhetoric."[114] September would close with yet another front-page story that linked local Panthers to the murder of an Atlanta police officer allegedly killed by members of the Black Liberation Army. The local press's negative portrayal of the Georgia BPP chapter would continue during the remainder of 1972, leading Ron Carter to complain, "They want to vilify us as cop killers and dope pushers in the community, then, when they feel we are isolated, victimize (us)."[115]

Atlanta was no exception. In every locality throughout the nation with a BPP outpost, party members coped with active government repression, although the tactics and impact varied. Political scientist Robert Goldstein calls repression "government action which grossly discriminates against persons or organizations viewed as presenting a fundamental challenge to existing power relationships or key governmental policies, because of their perceived political beliefs."[116] Sociologist Alan Wolfe identifies three broad categories: legalistic, covert, and violent. Legalistic repression entails stifling political dissent by invoking and enforcing a broad array of laws in a way that is exclusionary and amounts to harassment. Covert repression involves use of informers, agents provocateurs, and other clandestine tactics to disrupt organizational activities, while violent repression entails overt actions such as police raids and shootings.[117]

In the case of the Georgia BPP chapter, multiple levels of government officials, federal and local, primarily used legalistic and covert repression to neutralize Panther activism. City officials adroitly avoided acts of violent repression that could have increased public sympathy and support for the Panthers. Increased police attention did not involve the shoot-outs characterizing many of the other BPP southern outposts. There were no documented incidents of gunfire exchange between police officers and party members during the four-year tenure of the Georgia Panther chapter. However, on June 14, 1971, two patrolmen did fire a shotgun blast into the unoccupied Kirkwood office.[118] Only three police raids on party facilities occurred during the tenure of the Atlanta BPP affiliate.

On November 9, 1972, a thirty-member contingent of local police officers and federal agents, led by Lieutenant W. W. Holley, a member of the intelligence division of the Atlanta Police Department (APD), stormed the party's office on English Avenue, allegedly in search of a .45 caliber pistol thought to have been used in a sniper shooting of a patrolman on October 26 during traffic accident investigation near the BPP headquarters. While the police did not find the pistol, eight Atlanta Panthers were arrested on charges of illegal possession of explosives and possession of stolen goods. The raid was free of gunfire, and the law enforcement officials declined to arrest a pregnant female party member, underscoring the relatively genteel character of local repression. Deborah Johnson, a Chicago Panther and the pregnant fiancée of Fred Hampton, had not been as fortunate, arrested in the aftermath of the same raid that resulted in the deaths of Mark Clark and Fred Hampton on December 4, 1969.[119] After the November 1972 raid in Atlanta, judicial proceedings supported Panther attorney Al Horn's contention that the eight Panthers were arrested "for political prosecution and no other reason." Charges would soon be dismissed against all but the two primary leaders, Alton Deville and Ron Carter, whose cases were bound over to the Fulton County Grand Jury, and their original bail was increased from $1,000 to $10,000 and $15,000 respectively. All charges against Deville and Carter were eventually dropped as well.[120]

In early December 1972, Atlanta police officers, acting on a tip from an informant, staged a raid on the party's Parkway Drive office, during which they discovered approximately a pound of marijuana. Six individuals were arrested, including three BPP members. An Atlanta police spokesperson declared the raid a simple drug bust, but Horn noted the presence of members of the APD's intelligence division during the execution of the search warrant.[121] The third and final raid of the Georgia BPP chapter occurred in June 1973. Nine police officers surrounded the East Point apartment of Ron Carter, who was wanted in New Jersey on charges of possessing a concealed firearm.[122] As in the two prior raids, police arrested Carter without violence. City officials did not have to resort to frequent raids due to the effectiveness of covert and legalistic repression.

Both the Atlanta Police Department and the local FBI office closely monitored Panther activities in the city. Lieutenant Holley frequently attended party rallies and organizing events wearing his well-known sombrero, easily identifiable. Holley reported that during his surveillance of the local BPP chapter activities he had often witnessed Carter "call for the overthrow of the U.S. government and making threats of a conspiratorial nature."[123] On one occasion, Holley covertly entered the party's English Avenue headquarters without a search warrant when he accompanied a building inspector examining the facility.

An edition of *Signal 39*, a newsletter of the APD, offers additional evidence of police monitoring members of the local BPP outpost. The newsletter published names and addresses of nine of the city's so-called extremist militants. Five were Atlanta Panthers: Samuel Lundy, Ronald Carter, Ernest Watts, Charles Lundy, and Kouson Oliver. Police Chief Inman warned his officers that "caution should be used when arresting these subjects or a call is received to these addresses. When approaching these addresses and individuals, request assistance and use extreme caution."[124] Atlanta's police officers were also instructed to contact Holley or Captain J. R. Spence, both of the APD's intelligence division, for any "further information concerning subversive individuals and addresses."[125] Local FBI agents also engaged in covert operations against the Georgia BPP chapter. Under the auspices of COINTELPRO, FBI director J. Edgar Hoover instructed all FBI offices with Panther outposts to devise strategies to neutralize BPP activism. COINTELPRO tactics were largely conducted in secret, away from public awareness and accountability. As noted, FBI officials had attempted to cause disruption between BPP headquarters and the Atlanta party affiliate during the former's negotiations to purchase SNCC's former national office building. After the February 1971 Panther-Muslim melee, FBI officials sought to foster additional dissension between the BPP and the Nation of Islam, a strategy that proved successful in stimulating the internecine BPP-US conflict in what the FBI deemed "Black Propaganda" operations.[126]

In their seminal *Agents of Repression: The FBI's Secret Wars Against the Black Panther Party and the American Indian Movement*, Ward Churchill and Jim Vander Wall explain that "Black Propaganda" refers to the fabrication and distribution of publications (leaflets, broadsides, etc.) "in behalf of targeted organizations/individuals designed to misrepresent their positions, goals, and objectives in such a way as to publicly discredit them and foster intra/inter-group tensions."[127] The FBI proposed that its Atlanta office send a fabricated letter to Elijah Muhammad, the leader of the Nation of Islam, in Chicago, "complaining of the attack by BPP members upon NOI members indicating that the NOI has been selling newspapers on this street corner for years and now [its members] are being attacked by BPP members."[128]

FBI agents were particularly active in preventing the Georgia Panther chapter from establishing BPP outposts elsewhere in the state besides Atlanta. Alton Deville—a Columbus, Georgia, native and founding member of the Atlanta BPP outpost—had the goal of forming a party unit in his hometown, but this never materialized due to covert FBI intervention. Bogus letters were mailed to Panther sympathizers in Columbus and Augusta, Georgia, to circumvent

BPP activism in the two cities. The FBI director, Hoover, suggested to his agents in Georgia, "You may desire to consider preparing an anonymous letter to various local businessmen indicating that funds contributed to the BPP are not used for the black community but for personal escapades, thereby creating local opposition to the Panthers and drying up any source of funds."[129]

Perhaps the most egregious FBI-implicated covert repression involved Sam Gilliam, an early member of the Atlanta Black Panther Party affiliate. The *Black Panther* reported that in June 1971 Gilliam went to Greensboro, North Carolina, to attend to his sick mother. During his stay in North Carolina, Gilliam organized with the Winston-Salem Panther affiliate and was arrested and convicted on public disorder charges. Released pending an appeal of his conviction, Gilliam returned to Greensboro to check on his mother. After a short visit, he disappeared in late June upon leaving for his new assignment to work with the BPP community information center in High Point, North Carolina, near Winston-Salem. Party officials declared in August, "That was the last that anyone . . . saw or heard from Sam." BPP leaders had contacted "all the jails and prisons, hospitals, etc. in North Carolina and Atlanta, Georgia—with no success."[130] Two months later, in late August, Gilliam was discovered in New York. An August 21, FBI correspondence from San Francisco alerted the Atlanta FBI office that an informant had reported that "Sam had been beaten in the head and was in a daze and was not talking since."[131] Greg Bailey, one of Gilliam's Atlanta comrades, later lamented, "thinking back to some of the things that they have done to people in order to stop the movement—Sam Gilliam a brilliant, brilliant man—he was driven crazy. He was never the same—basically, he had lost it."[132]

Government officials implemented a legalistic repression tactic to undermine the Georgia BPP chapter's free breakfast program and other survival programs. This tactic rested upon harassment laws. According to Alan Wolfe, a harassment law is "a simple law that was originally passed with no political purpose [but] is used to repress."[133] As mentioned above, *Atlanta Constitution* accounts of Panther $50,000 demands from the city's major grocery store chains triggered an investigation of the BPP's solicitation practices. Police Chief Inman announced that he had instructed the investigator of the aldermanic police committee to ascertain whether the BPP chapter had obtained the required permit to seek donations. The aldermanic police committee was but one of several municipal entities whose permission was needed to acquire a city permit to solicit funds and other donations.[134]

An affirmative vote from the Atlanta Fund Appeals Review Board, the city council's police committee, and the full city council were necessary for approval of a solicitation permit. Atlanta police officials made it clear that party members risked arrest if solicitations were made without the permit. At the initiation of Police Chief Inman, Panther leaders Sam Lundy, Ron Carter, and

Kouson Oliver met with him concerning the need to obtain a permit in order to solicit donations. After the meeting Inman remarked, "We told them we meant to enforce the law."[135] Although the local Panthers were aware of the slim likelihood of securing approval of their permit, they submitted a formal application. The permit was never approved. The enforcement of the ordinance in question, Ordinance 13–28, represented a classic usage of the harassment law. It is difficult to imagine that violation of the ordinance would ordinarily garner such police attention.

Law enforcement officials on several occasions threatened BPP members with extortion charges for the manner in which they solicited funds. Fulton County District Attorney Lewis Slaton declared, "I cannot say to a certainty that they have ever threatened anyone." Nevertheless, Slaton expressed his concern that party members were engaged in "the old mob business of selling protection."[136] Acting FBI director L. Patrick Gray expressed similar sentiments, which illuminated the coordination between actors at multiple levels of government to disable Panther activism. In a front-page *Atlanta Constitution* article in September 1972, Gray noted that the FBI had completed a preliminary investigation of alleged extortion committed by the local BPP outpost. He explained, "It is alleged that they have used some strong-arm tactics on black businessmen who have not contributed what the Panthers thought was adequate."[137] Gray nevertheless failed to disclose any findings that confirmed extortion.

Besides negative media coverage and political repression, the Atlanta BPP chapter's reversal of fortunes can also be attributed to ineffective leadership. Atlanta's BPP leaders engaged in detrimental actions that further exacerbated the adverse impact of governmental repression. In mid-October 1972, Alton Deville traveled to Oakland to lodge charges against Atlanta Panther leaders Sam Lundy and Kouson Oliver. Deville informed members of the BPP's central committee that Lundy and Oliver had committed numerous transgressions that undermined Panther organizing efforts in the city. Among the most serious of the forty charges leveled by Deville were physical abuse of rank-and-file members, misuse of party funds, inattentiveness to administrative duties, mistreatment of community supporters, and drug possession while performing party duties.[138]

Deville reported that Oliver frequently physically abused party members and "was known to attack brothers in the office for not jumping quick enough on his order." On one occasion, Oliver had struck a party member and "kicked him out on the street," according to Deville. During another incident occurring on Broad Street in downtown Atlanta, Oliver had physically attacked a party member who questioned his leadership authority. Oliver allegedly "grabbed him by the throat, threw him against a brick building and struck the brother in the face and left him on the street." Regarding misappropriation of organization funds, Deville recounted that Lundy had secured monetary contributions from Rev. Stafford, a key Panther supporter, on the pretense of emergency party business, but had kept the money for personal use.[139]

According to Deville, leadership malfeasance was hampering local BPP operations. He cited neglect to pay bills in a timely manner as well as failure to properly supervise the collection and dissemination of food and supplies donated to the party's survival programs. On October 20, 1972, BPP members under the leadership of Oliver were evicted by their landlord from their office on Parkway Drive in Vine City. *Black Panther* sales in the city declined from 2,200 to 1,100 per shipment. Deville also complained to Oakland leaders that the Atlanta leadership had failed to follow up on collecting food donations: "We came over to [the Kirkwood office] [and] realized by looking at the board that... there was a great amount of donations that was overdue for pick up. People were calling every day when we went there concerning donations pick up." This dereliction of responsibility, claimed Deville, led to the spoilage of meat donated to the party. He told central committee members that he "observed the staff throwing out plastic bags. The large plastic bags that go in large garbage containers[,] full of meat."[140]

Undoubtedly these leadership transgressions impeded party activism in Atlanta and greatly enhanced the repression by government officials. What started as a promising year for the Panthers in Atlanta became a time of organizational disarray. To no avail, members of the party's local collective such as Alton Deville, Ron Carter, and Emma Jean Martin persistently criticized the Lundy-Oliver leadership clique. It would take the March 1973 dispatch of national BPP representatives to Atlanta before Ron Carter, arguably the chapter's most effective and respected member, assumed sole leadership of the affiliate. However, the much-needed leadership change would prove insufficient to rejuvenate the chapter.

1973: Atlanta's Party Is Over

The beleaguered BPP chapter staggered into 1973 as its organizational woes continued. It remained beset with internal problems at the same time as it continued to by harassed by police. In March 1973, as a result of the charges lodged by Deville against Lundy and Oliver, national BPP officials deployed June Hilliard and John Seale to Atlanta to investigate operations of the Georgia chapter. Carter told a news reporter that Hilliard and Seale came to Atlanta and "checked out each party member to see whether the individual met with the criteria of the Party. We had to rid ourselves of a lot of individuals. And we had to close down a number of offices."[141] The March 1973 purge triggered a split among the remaining members, some of whom joined with Oliver to form the People's Liberation Party, a black radical party modeled after the Panthers.

Ron Carter rose to the leadership position of the Georgia BPP chapter as one of its most seasoned and widely admired members. Scholar-activist Mack Jones recalls, "Ron Carter was a serious, committed young brother. I was impressed by him. However, I did not have a good vibe about the other leaders."[142] Atlanta novelist and playwright Pearl Cleage was similarly impressed with Ron Carter's activism. Cleage wrote after Carter's untimely death in April 1979: "I was not a close friend of Ron Carter's, but I knew him and admired his courage, his strength and his unwavering commitment to what I believe to be true and just."[143] Unfortunately, Carter's assumption of the leadership mantle came too late to reenergize the BPP chapter.

Carter's leadership made him a likely target of government repression. In June 1973 he was arrested twice in one week. First, police officers raided Carter's East Point apartment on June 23 to arrest him on a New Jersey warrant for a firearm violation. They confiscated a .44 magnum Ruger rifle and one hundred rounds of ammunition. Incredibly, police suggested the rifle was linked to the 1972 New Year's Eve police sniper shootings by Mark Essex in New Orleans.[144] Within the week, the police detained Carter for "aggressive acts toward the general public while selling the paper."[145] He incurred minor injuries during a brief scuffle with the arresting Atlanta police officers and received medical treatment at a local hospital.

A harrowing incident also occurring in June would cause the local chapter to lose one of its most talented and long-time party members. Emma Jean Martin left the Atlanta BPP chapter after "renegade Panthers" previously purged from the party attempted an armed robbery of the Dunwoody office. Martin's former comrades held her hostage with a gun aimed at her head, demanding money used for the breakfast program. She vividly recalls, "That was the scariest thing I ever experienced; even Louisiana was not like that when they put me in solitary confinement." Community residents began to gather outside the party's office after one of the neighborhood kids told adults that "men with guns had the Panther lady." Rebecca Maltise, a white radical volunteer, had the presence of mind to call Oakland, which led Huey Newton to order the renegade Panthers to release Martin, who resigned from the party soon after the incident. Martin laments that by the latter part of 1973, the Georgia BPP chapter "was nothing but the name—the police had destroyed it."[146]

During the fall of 1973, the prospect of electing Maynard Jackson, the city's first African American mayor, called for a show of black unity, which engulfed black radical activism in Atlanta. In fact, the local BPP affiliate endorsed Jackson's candidacy. Ron Carter recommended that the black community mobilize to elect Jackson as mayor and "as many good black city council candidates as possible."[147] The Georgia BPP chapter's impotence during this period is evident in its absence from a September 12, 1973, protest march against the increasing number of police homicides in Atlanta, an event organized by the broad-based

Anti-Repression Coalition.[148] While the problem of police brutality had long been one of the signature organizing issues of the Panthers, the party's absence from the coalition was conspicuous and reflected its waning influence. In accordance with the BPP central committee directive that ordered all chapters to cease operations and deploy their members to Oakland, the Atlanta affiliate terminated its now skeletal operations. The remaining local party members relocated to the Bay Area in California, and the Georgia state chapter of the Black Panther Party officially closed its doors in December 1973.[149]

Conclusion:
Remembering the Atlanta Panthers

Atlanta had long held special significance to the national Panther leaders. The local party affiliate was the first sanctioned BPP chapter in the South. The allure of Atlanta to national party leaders is evident in Huey Newton's consideration on two occasions to relocate the party's Oakland headquarters to the capital of the New South. After the Atlanta outpost ceased operations in 1973, the Oakland BPP leaders continued to show a keen interest in the affairs of the city. For example, in 1975, a Newton-authored letter to Reginald Eaves, commissioner of public safety in the Maynard Jackson mayoral administration, expressed the party's concern with vandalism of the building housing the Institute of the Black World and with racist threats lodged against staff members of the institute.

The Georgia state chapter of the Black Panther Party had limited success during its four years. At one point, the local party unit operated multiple offices in various neglected black neighborhoods across the city. The chapter also sponsored eight community service programs, anchored by a free breakfast program at four different Atlanta locations. While acknowledging these notable accomplishments, this essay demonstrates that the activism of the Atlanta party affiliate did not meet the threshold criteria to constitute a substantive BPP outpost. As stated, a substantive party unit lasts more than a year, sponsors survival programs during multiple years, and affects the politics of its local setting. While the Atlanta BPP affiliate operated over four years, only one of its survival programs was implemented for more than a year. The majority of the programs were short lived, during its heyday of activism in 1972. Moreover, the Panther affiliate was not a significant actor in Atlanta politics. The city proved inhospitable for a BPP outpost due to negative media framing, police harassment, and missteps by chapter leaders.

This conclusion does not intend to diminish the dedication and sacrifice of the unheralded members of the George BPP chapter. Local party comrades such as Phillip Lester, Jennifer Lemons, Charles Lundy, Columbus Ward, Frank Scruggs, Frank Jones, Jerome Bussey, Bobbi Harrison, Patricia Scruggs, Ron

Porter, and Donald Calhoun, as well as the other Atlanta Panthers mentioned in this essay, all worked against great odds in the face of intense political repression to advocate on behalf of the "forgotten" black Atlanta.

NOTES

1. Winston A. Grady-Willis, *Challenging U.S. Apartheid: Atlanta and Black Struggles for Human Rights, 1960–1977* (Durham, N.C.: Duke University Press, 2006), 174–76; Benjamin R. Friedman, "Picking up Where Robert F. Williams Left Off: The Winston-Salem Branch of the Black Panther Party," in *Comrades: A Local History of the Black Panther Party*, ed. Judson L. Jeffries (Bloomington: Indiana University Press, 2007), 44–88; Arend, *Showdown in Desire*; Orissa Arend and Judson L. Jeffries, "The Big Easy Was Anything But for the Panthers," in *On the Ground: The Black Panther Party in Communities Across America*, ed. Judson L. Jeffries (Jackson: University of Mississippi Press, 2010), 224–72; Charles E. Jones, "Arm Yourself or Harm Yourself: People's Party II and the Black Panther Party in Houston, Texas," in Jeffries, *On the Ground*, 3–40.

2. Grady-Willis, *Challenging U.S. Apartheid*.

3. Judson L. Jeffries and Ryan Nissim-Sabat, "Painting a More Complete Portrait of the Black Panther Party," in Jeffries, *Comrades*, 1–14; Jeffries, *On the Ground*.

4. Gene Ferguson quoted in Winston A. Grady-Willis, *Challenging U.S. Apartheid*, 177.

5. FBI COINTELPRO memoranda and Atlanta Police Department materials were used in this analysis. The author interviewed Emma Jean Martin and Greg Bailey, both members of the Georgia BPP chapter, as well as Dr. Mack H. Jones. Archives consulted included the Dr. Huey P. Newton Foundation Inc. Collection, Department of Special Collections, Green Library, Stanford University, Palo Alto, California; Sam Massell papers, MSS695, Kenan Research Center, Atlanta History Center, Atlanta; William Collection, Auburn Avenue Research Library on African American Life and History, Atlanta-Fulton Public Library System, Atlanta; and the Black Panther Party files, Martin Luther King, Jr. Center for Nonviolent Social Change, Atlanta. Mainstream newspapers *Atlanta Journal* and the *Atlanta Constitution* as well as alternative newspapers including the *Atlanta Voice*, *Atlanta Daily World*, *Great Speckled Bird*, and the *Black Panther: Black Community News Service* were also used. The author wishes to acknowledge the invaluable research assistant of Grace Gipson, currently a doctoral student in the Department of African American and African Diaspora Studies at University of California, Berkeley, and Kamontá Heidelburg, psychology major and Putting Retention 1st in the Zest for Excellence (PR1ZE) mentee at the University of Cincinnati.

6. Robert A. Holmes, *Maynard Jackson: A Biography* (Miami: Barnhardt and Ash, 2009), 50–52.

7. Ibid., 51; Robert D. Bullard, "Atlanta: Mecca of the Southeast," in *Search of the New South: The Black Urban Experience in the 1970s and 1980s* (Tuscaloosa: University of Alabama Press, 1989), 77.

8. Fredrick Allen, *Atlanta Rising: The Invention of an International City 1946–1996* (Atlanta: Longstreet Press, 1996), 168.

9. Ibid., 136.

10. Gregory Mixon, *The Atlanta Riot: Race, Class, and Violence in a New South City* (Gainesville: University of Florida Press, 2004).

11. Donald L. Grant, *The Way It Was in the South: The Black Experience in Georgia* (Secaucus, N.J.: Carol Publishing, 1993), 325–28.

12. Ibid., 18–19.

13. Allen, *Atlanta Rising*, 19.

14. Ibid.

15. Grant, *The Way It Was in the South*, 328.

16. Alton Hornsby Jr., *A Short History of Black Atlanta, 1847–1990* (Kennesaw, Ga.: Advance Printing, 2003), 83.

17. Grady-Willis, *Challenging U.S. Apartheid*, 114–27; Clayborne Carson, *In Struggle: SNCC and the Black Awakening of the 1960s* (Cambridge, Mass: Harvard University Press, 1981), 225; Grant, *The Way It Was in Georgia*, 427.

18. Grady-Willis, *Challenging U.S. Apartheid*, 129–33; Ronald H. Bayor, *Race and the Shaping of Twentieth Century Atlanta* (Chapel Hill: University of North Carolina Press), 142–45.

19. Grady-Willis, *Challenging U.S. Apartheid*, 133.

20. Clarence N. Stone, *Regime Politics: Governing Atlanta 1946–1988* (Lawrence: University of Kansas Press, 1989), 6.

21. Larry Keating, *Atlanta: Race, Class, and Urban Expansion* (Philadelphia: Temple University Press, 2010), 2–3.

22. Hanes Walton Jr., *Black Politics: A Theoretical and Structural Analysis* (Philadelphia: J. B. Lippincott, 1972), 33.

23. Bayor, *Race and the Shaping of Twentieth Century Atlanta*, 18; *King v. Chapman* 62 F. Supp. 639 (1945); *Gray v. Sanders* 37 U.S. 36 (March 18, 1953).

24. Hornsby, *A Short History of Black Atlanta*, 74.

25. Holmes, *Maynard Jackson*, 53.

26. Allen, *Atlanta Rising*, 161.

27. Ibid., 70–71; 96–98; 122–24;162–63; Grady-Willis, *Challenging U.S. Apartheid*, 33–55; Stone, *Regime Politics*, 52–54.

28. Aldon Morris, *The Origins of the Civil Rights Movement: Black Communities Organizing for Change* (New York: Free Press, 1984), 3.

29. Bullard, "Atlanta," 78.

30. Mack H. Jones, "Black Political Empowerment in Atlanta," *Annals of the American Academy of Political Science and Social Science* 439 (1978): 95.

31. Ibid., 95–96.

32. Keating, *Atlanta*,

33. Bullard, "Atlanta," 79.

34. Stone, *Regime Politics*, 73.

35. James Smethurst, "The Black Arts Movement in Atlanta," in *Neighborhood Rebels: Black Power at the Local Level*, ed. Peniel E. Joseph (New York: Palgrave Macmillan, 2010), 176.

36. Frank Donner, *Protectors of Privilege: Red Squads and Police Repression in Urban America* (Berkeley: University of California Press, 1990), 180.

37. Huey P. Newton, *War against the Panthers: A Study of Repression in America* (New York: Harlem River Books, 1996).

38. Kathleen Neal Cleaver, "Back to Africa: The Evolution of the International Section of the Black Panther Party (1969–1972)," in *The Black Panther Party Reconsidered*, ed. Charles E. Jones (Baltimore: Black Classic Press, 1998), 216–20.

39. "Executive Mandate No. 2: June 29,1967," in Huey P. Newton, *To Die for the People: The Writings of Huey P. Newton* (1972; repr., New York: Writers and Readers, 1995), 9–11. Also see "Carmichael Quits Post in Panthers," *Los Angeles Times*, July 4, 1969; Carmichael Condemns Panthers, Resign Post," *Washington Post*, July 4, 1969.

40. See Scot Brown's insightful account of the BPP–US conflict, *Fighting for Us: Maulana Karenga, the US Organization, and Black Cultural Nationalism* (New York: New York University Press, 2003), 91–99, 107–40; Roy Wilkens and Ramsey Clark, *Search and Destroy: A Report by the Commission of Inquiry into the Black Panthers and the Police* (New York: Metropolitan Applied Research Center, 1973); Peter L. Zimroth, *Perversions of Justice: The Prosecution and Acquittal of the Panther 21* (New York: Viking Press, 1974); Donald Freed, *Agony in New Haven: The Trials of Bobby Seale, Ericka Huggins and the Black Panthers* (New York: Simon and Schuster, 1973); Joel P. Rhodes and Judson L. Jeffries, "Motor City Panthers," in Jeffries, *On the Ground*, 157.

41. See "Chronology of the Black Panther Party," in *Still Black, Still Strong; Survivors of the U.S. War against Black Revolutionaries Dhoruba Bin Wahad, Mumia Abu-Jamal, and Assata Shakur*, eds. Jim Fletcher, Tanaquil Jones and Sylvere Lotringer (Brooklyn: Semiotext, 1993), 221–42; "Chronology of the Black Panther Party," in Kit Kim Holder, "The History of the Black Panther Party, 1966–1971: A Curriculum Tool for Afrikan American Studies," PhD diss. (University of Massachusetts, 1996), 208–48.

42. Bloom and Martin, *Black against Empire*, 223–25.

43. For additional discussion of the deaths of John Savage and Sylvester Bell, see Curtis J. Austin, *Up against the Wall: Violence in the Making and Unmaking of the Black Panther Party* (Fayetteville: University of Arkansas Press, 2006), 232–34.

44. "Harassment of Members of the Black Panther Party," May 2, 1967, through November 11, 1969, complied by Charles Garry, lead counsel for the Black Panther Party, Black Panther Party Collection, Southern California Library for Social Studies and Research, Los Angeles.

45. A complete list of the additional rules adapted by the BPP leaders first appeared in *Black Panther*, January 4, 1969. See G. Louis Heath, ed., *Off the Pigs: The History and Literature of the Black Panther Party* (Metuchen, N.J.: Scarecrow Press, 1976), 123–25.

46. See Heath, *Off the Pigs*, 125; Paul Alkebulan, *Survival pending Revolution: The History of the Black Panther Party* (Tuscaloosa: University of Alabama Press, 2007), 51.

47. Ester King, interview by Charles E. Jones, August 5, 2003, Houston.

48. Heath, *Off the Pigs*, 127.

49. Ibid., *Off the Pigs!*, 93–96; Bloom and Martin, *Black against the Empire*, 299–301.

50. Chairman [Bobby] Seale, "Sums Up Conference," *Black Panther*, August 2, 1969.

51. Ibid., 17; Ryan Nissim-Sabat, "Panthers Set Up Shop in Cleveland," in Jeffries, *Comrades*, 104.

52. "Sen. Smith Lashes Tech Panther Rally," *Atlanta Constitution*, February 17, 1970.

53. Ibid. Also see Grady-Willis, *Challenging U.S. Apartheid*, 174; Scottie Lowe, "Eyes on the Prize: The Rise and Fall of the Atlanta Chapter of the Black Panther Party", unpublished paper in author's possession, 5.

54. Heath, *Off the Pigs!*, 117.

55. An excellent discussion of the party's organization structure is found in Holder, "The History of the Black Panther Party, 1966–1971, 16–26; Heath, *Off the Pigs!* 120–21.

56. Friedman, "Picking up Where Robert Williams Left Off," 71.

57. Holder, "The History of the Black Panther Party 1966–1971," 19.

58. Grady-Willis, *Challenging U.S. Apartheid*, 177.

59. Komozi Woodard, *A Nation within a Nation: Amiri Baraka (LeRoi Jones) and Black Power Politics* (Chapel Hill: University of North Carolina Press, 1999), 164.

60. Emma Jean Martin, interview by Charles E. Jones, May 9, 2013, Atlanta; Greg Bailey, telephone interview by Charles E. Jones, October 1, 2013.

61. Boyd Lewis, "Black Panther Center to Resist Eviction in Courts," *Atlanta Voice*, December 6, 1970; Robert W. Widell Jr., "'The Power Belongs to Us and We Being to the Revolutionary Age': The Alabama Black Liberation Front and the Long Reach of the Black Panther Party," in *Liberated Territory: Untold Local Perspectives on the Black Panther Party*, ed. Yohuru Williams and James Lazerow (Durham, N.C.: Duke University Press, 2008), 148.

62. Cecil Blye, "Black Panthers to Organize Here?" *Louisville Defender*, February 27, 1969.

63. Alkebulan, *Survival pending Revolution*, 49.

64. Grady-Willis, *Challenging U.S. Apartheid*, 84.

65. Friedman, "Picking up Where Robert F. Williams Left Off," 68; Arend, *Showdown in Desire*, 125–26.

66. Tim Hayes quoted in Lewis, "Black Panthers Center to Resist Eviction in Courts."

67. "Two Blacks Come to Blows: A Melee Flares in Atlanta," *New York Times*, February 16, 1971; "21 Blacks Arrested in Atlanta Meleé, *Houston Chronicle*, February 16, 1971.

68. Manning Marable, *Race, Reform and Rebellion: The Second Reconstruction in Black America, 1945–1982* (Jackson: University of Mississippi Press, 1984), 178.

69. Memo to Washington DC from SAC, Atlanta, to FBI Director, February 10, 1971.

70. Ron Carter quoted in "Panthers Leave Atlanta," *Atlanta Voice*, December, 17–31.

71. "Panthers in Atlanta," *Great Speckled Bird*, September 20, 1971. Also see "Why Is the Black Panther Party in Atlanta?" *Great Speckled Bird*, July 26, 1971.

72. Flyer of Georgia State Chapter Black Panther Party Intercommunal Survival Centers, no date, in author's possession.

73. Cleaver, "Back to Africa," 227–28.

74. Aaron Taylor, "Panthers Moving HQ to Atlanta—Newton," *Atlanta Constitution*, September 9, 1971.

75. "Black Panther Party Headquarters Moving to Atlanta," *Black Panther*, September 18, 1971.

76. David Hilliard and Lewis Cole, *This Side of Glory* (Boston: Little Brown, 1993), 171.

77. Harmon Perry and Hugh Merrill, "Guarded Words, Welcomes Meet Planned Panther Shift, *Atlanta Journal*, September 9, 1971.

78. "Panthers Stay in Calif. Rep. Thompson Advises," *Atlanta Daily World*, September 15, 1971.

79. Taylor, "Panthers Moving HQ to Atlanta—Newton."

80. "Abernathy Welcomes Panthers," *Atlanta Constitution*, September 11, 1971.

81. Perry and Merrill, "Guarded Words, Welcomes Meet Planned Panther Shift."

82. Taylor, "Panthers Moving HQ to Atlanta—Newton."

83. "Are The Panthers Needed?," *Atlanta Daily World*, September 12, 1971.

84. June Hilliard quoted in Hilliard and Cole, *This Side of Glory*, 246.

85. Arend, *Showdown in Desire*, 64–66, 71–72.

86. Daniel J. Willis, "A Critical Analysis of Mass Political Education and Community

Organization as Utilized by the Black Panther Party as a Means for Effecting Social Change," PhD diss. (University of Massachusetts, 1976).

87. Mike Raffauf, "Georgia State and the Panthers" *Great Speckled Bird*, February 7, 1972.

88. "Panthers in Transformation Newton Tells GSU Students," *Atlanta Voice*, February 19, 1972; "Newton Sees Milder Future for Panthers in Talk Here," *Atlanta Constitution*, February 11, 1972.

89. The BLA was a group of underground militants, many of them former members of the Black Panther Party, who carried out much of their purportedly revolutionary activity in clandestine fashion.

90. Bailey interview.

91. Martin interview.

92. Ibid.

93. Ibid.

94. Bailey quoted in Lowe, "Eyes on the Prize," 16.

95. People's Survival Programs, Sam Massell Papers, box 66, folder 6, MSS 698, Kenan Research Center, Atlanta History Center, Atlanta.

96. Ibid. Also see Harmon Perry, "Black Panthers Feed Kids Here," *Atlanta Journal*, in Black Panther Party Files, Special Collections, Robert W. Woodruff Library, Atlanta University Center.

97. Martin interview; Perry, "Black Panthers Feed Kids Here"; Grady-Willis, *Challenging U.S. Apartheid*, 177.

98. Martin interview.

99. Ibid.

100. People's Survival Programs.

101. Ibid.

102. Martin interview; People's Survival Programs.

103. Rhodes and Jeffries, "Motor City Panthers," 148.

104. Jones, "Arm Yourself or Harm Yourself," 26.

105. Alondra Nelson, *Body and Soul: The Black Panther Party and the Fight against Medical Discrimination* (Minneapolis: University of Minnesota Press, 2011), 92–93. Nelson identifies thirteen BPP affiliates that operated free health clinics, including Winston-Salem. However, Winston-Salem did not sponsor a health center but rather a free ambulance service, which is noted by Nelson. See Friedman, "Picking Up Where Robert Williams Left Off"; Evans Hopkins, *Life after Life: A Story of Rage and Redemption* (New York: Free Press, 2005).

106. Martin interview; People's Survival Programs.

107. Nelson, *Body and Soul*, 116.

108. Lowe, "Eyes on the Prize, 8–9; "Pastor Asserts Panthers Work in Black Discontent," Black Panther Party Vertical Clipping File, Martin Luther King, Jr. Center for Nonviolent Social Change, Atlanta; Grady-Willis, *Challenging U.S. Apartheid*, 179; People's Survival Programs; Martin interview.

109. "GSU Blacks to Aid in Kids' Breakfast," *Atlanta Journal*, March 15, 1972; Martin interview.

110. "Champions: James Jenkins, Atlanta, GA," *Champion* (National Association of Criminal Defense Lawyers), September/October 1990, 54.

111. Rhodes, *Framing the Black Panthers: The Spectacular Rise of a Black Power Icon* (Urbana: University of Illinois Press, 2017), 5–6.

112. Jim Stewart, "Store Chains Get Demands of Panthers," *Atlanta Constitution*, August 24, 1972. Other news articles appearing in the city's two major papers, *Atlanta Journal* and *Atlanta Constitution*, included Keeler McCartney, "Police Will Investigate Black Panthers' Demand," *Atlanta Constitution*, August 25, 1972; "Chief Says Panthers Need Permits to Solicit Funds," *Atlanta Constitution*, August 29,1972; Nick Taylor, "Panthers Deny Threat against GOP's Powell," *Atlanta Constitution*, September 3, 1972; "Panthers to Continue Efforts," *Atlanta Constitution*, September 6, 1972; Nick Taylor, "FBI Eying Panther Money Demand Here," *Atlanta Constitution*, September 15,1972; Keeler McCartney and Tom Linthicum, "Shoot-to-Kill Intent Is Denied by Inman," *Atlanta Constitution*, September 15, 1972; "Black Panthers Editorial," *Atlanta Constitution*, September 16, 1972; "Black Panther Suspect Held," *Atlanta Journal*, September 28, 1972; Keeler McCartney, "Policeman's Murder a Militant Ceremony," *Atlanta Constitution*, September 30, 1972.

113. Nick Taylor, "Panthers Deny Threat against GOP's Powell," *Atlanta Constitution*, September 3, 1972.

114. Taylor, "FBI Eying Panther Money Demand Here."

115. Joe Cole, "Atlanta Panthers Describe Cop Harassment," *Militant*, January 12, 1973.

116. Robert Goldstein, *Political Repression in Modern America* (New York: Schenkman, 1978), xvi.

117. Alan Wolfe, *The Seamy Side of Democracy: Repression in the United States*, (New York: David McKay, 1973), 93–124.

118. Acting Captain Claude Dixon Police Report: Gun Shot at Black Panther H.Q., 2041 Dunwoody, June 28, 1971, document in author's possession.

119. Interview with Deborah Johnson, Eyes on the Prize II Interviews, October 19, 1988; Washington University Digital Gateway Texts, http://digital.wustl.edu/e/eii/eiiweb/joh5427.0255.082marc_record_interviewee_process.html.

120. Barry Henderson, "Arms Seized by Police in Panther Raid," *Atlanta Constitution*, November 10, 1972; "Panther Hearing This Afternoon," *Atlanta Daily World*, November 11, 1972; "Explosives Found [in] Raid on Black Panther Headquarters," *Atlanta Daily World*, November 12, 1972; Barry Henderson, "2 Are Bound in Panther Case," *Atlanta Constitution*, November 15, 1972.

121. Barry Henderson, "Six Arrested in Drug Raid," *Atlanta Constitution*, December 6, 1972.

122. Jim Gray, "Black Panther Leader Jailed," *Atlanta Constitution*, June 26, 1973; "Black Panther Arrest Ridiculous, Stupid," Black Panther Clipping File, William Collection, Auburn Avenue Research Library on African American Life and History, Atlanta.

123. "Two Black Panthers Bound Over to Grand Jury," *Atlanta Daily World*, November 16, 1972.

124. John F. Inman, "Survival Information," *Signal 39* (APD newsletter), 1972, 4.

125. Ibid.; Keeler McCartney and Tom Linthicum, "Shoot-to-Kill Intent Is Denied by Inman," *Atlanta Constitution*, September 15, 1972.

126. Austin, *Up against the Wall*, 230–40.

127. Ward Churchill and Jim Vander Wall, *Agents of Repression: The FBI's Secret Wars against the Black Panther Party and the American Indian Movement* (Boston: South End Press, 1988), 42.

128. Memo to Atlanta from FBI Director to SAC Atlanta, February 22, 1971.
129. Memo to Savannah from FBI Director to SAC Savannah, February 22, 1971.
130. "Where Is Sam Gilliam?" *Black Panther*, August 14, 1971.
131. Memo to Washington DC from SAC, San Francisco to FBI Director, August 21, 1971.
132. Bailey quoted in Lowe, "Eyes on the Prize," 18; Bailey interview.
133. Wolfe, *Seamy Side of Democracy*, 98.
134. McCartney, "Police Will Investigate Black Panthers' Demands."
135. "Chief Says Panthers Need Permits to Solicit Funds," *Atlanta Constitution*, August 29, 1972.
136. Jeff Nesmith, "Panther Tactics Questioned," *Washington Post*, September 5, 1972.
137. Taylor, "FBI Eying Panther Money Demand Here."
138. "Report from Atlanta Georgia, Alton Deville, October 16, 1972," M864 Series 6, box 10, no. 18, Dr. Huey P. Newton Foundation Inc. Papers, Department of Special Collections, Green Library, Stanford University, Palo Alto, California.
139. Ibid.
140. Ibid.
141. "Panthers Leave Atlanta."
142. Mack H. Jones, telephone interview by Charles E. Jones, September 10, 2013.
143. Pearl Cleage Lomax, "In Memory of Ron Carter, the Unwavering Activist," *Atlanta Constitution*, April 14, 1979.
144. Gray, "Black Panther Leader Jailed."
145. Henderson, "Police Seize Panther Here." Also see "Atlanta Party Member Arrested Twice in One Week," *Black Panther*, July 28, 1973; "Panthers Harassed by Atlanta Police Raids," *Muhammad Speaks*, January 19, 1973.
146. Martin interview.
147. B. Norwood Chaney, "Ron Carter Extradited, Discusses Campaign Issues," *Atlanta Voice*, September 1, 1973.
148. "Citizens Protest Police Homicides," *Great Speckled Bird*, September 10, 1973; "Atlanta Anti-Repression Coalition," *Great Speckled Bird*, September 24, 1973.
149. "Panthers Leave Atlanta." For a detailed discussion of the directive that closed BPP affiliates, see Ollie Johnson, "Explaining the Demise of the Black Panther Party: The Role of Internal Factors," in Jones, *The Black Panther Party Reconsidered*, 403–6.

Exceptional Headwinds
The Black Panthers in D.C.

JOHN PREUSSER

The Black Panthers in Washington, D.C., had little chance for success. Entrenched hostile groups within the city's black community, combined with local and federal law enforcement, made the establishment of a chapter difficult. Nevertheless, from a hotbed of black militancy and radicalism emerged an important message of empowerment and unity focused on community. The D.C. Panthers sprouted in the District during a period in which many wealthy D.C. blacks moved to the suburbs, and it became a transitional organization to run programs needed but not provided by the government. It inspired city government projects like neighborhood spending programs and neighborhood citizen oversight boards that gave blacks greater control over their communities. The Panthers would also inspire food banks, public transportation expansion in poor neighborhoods, and clothing donations to help the underprivileged.

The Panthers and their community worker supporters assisted the city's poor people as dedicated community activists rather than as revolutionaries bent on the overthrow of the system. Forget the popular image of the shotgun, beret, and leather jacket. The focus should be on consciousness raising and the compassion and dedication of those helping people in need.

The Washington, D.C., chapter can be viewed through a number of lenses. How society and academia have viewed the Panthers has varied tremendously. Some have divided Black Panther Party (BPP) historiography into three different periods, the first being participant accounts and friendly academic works emphasizing the role of the federal government in the Panthers' downfall.[1]

The negative and highly successful 1994 book *Shadow of the Panther*, by Hugh Pearson, polarized matters by focusing on Panther criminality and drug use.[2] A more dramatic nineties production, *Forrest Gump*, highlighted the fears of conservative white America in its depiction of the D.C. chapter of the Panthers as militant revolutionaries.

The more recent examinations of the Panthers, creating a third period of

Panther historiography, have followed Pearson's lead in focusing on Panther misdeeds while others have come to opposite conclusions. Participant narratives and papers on local chapters and branches of the BPP have delved into the Panthers' community service programs and de-escalated political rhetoric by refocusing on poor urban communities. Each local Panther branch had unique factors affecting them, and Washington was no different. The local and national significance of the Panthers in D.C. was slight compared to that of some other branches and chapters of the BPP. The D.C. chapter was launched in 1970, after the period of heavy national media coverage of the party in the late 1960s. The militant exterior diminishing, the party's focus nationally was turning away from militant talk of revolution to local politics, as in Oakland. Some media had begun to show Panthers as hardworking community organizers. The BPP was not as radical as it had once been, and for many of the less dedicated members any radical chic posturing disappeared.

Narratives of the Black Panther Party continue to be vilified by the ascendant Right. The experience of BPP members, their motivations, and their contributions should not be cast aside in the post-Obama years. Instead their actions and writings should be recognized as representing a stand against imperialist war, poverty in the midst of plenty, and oppression based on race and class.

Communications scholar Jane Rhodes views the Panther experience through their images in the *Black Panther* newspaper and examines how the mainstream media and pop culture depicted Panther militancy as the vanguard of a revolution, which the Panthers used to spread their message. Rhodes also describes how the mainstream media played both sides, helping the government engage in disinformation, as well as creating a celebrity culture of the Panthers, particularly their leaders.[3] Historian Curtis Austin argues that the Panthers' move from revolutionary rhetoric to community-focused work actually slowed the party's momentum and diminished its relevance in urban black communities.[4] Judson L. Jeffries, in his edited works about the BPP, has led the charge in investigating local branches and chapters of the party, while focusing on the social dynamics unique to each city in which those branches were founded. This essay parallels all these studies and examines the unique circumstances opposing a vibrant Panther chapter in the nation's capital.

Washington, D.C., hosted many civil rights movement activities during the 1960s, when the passage the Civil Rights Act of 1964 and the Voting Rights Act of 1965 eliminated *de jure* segregation in the United States. Yet blacks in D.C. as elsewhere still confronted *de facto* segregation, institutional racism, police brutality, and limited political representation, while U.S. participation in the Vietnam War continued to result in a disproportionate number of black casualties.

By the mid to late 1960s, the hardened discontent among many black urbanites erupted in violence, and across the country black neighborhoods lashed out at police brutality. Rebellions in Los Angeles, Newark, Detroit, Cleveland, and other cities were widely covered in the national media. Washington, D.C., remained relatively tranquil until April 4, 1968, with word of Martin Luther King Jr.'s assassination. Insurrection in the District's black neighborhoods destroyed white- and black-owned stores, homes, and cars, and fires burned for a week. The rebellion of D.C.'s black population increased the influence of Black Power groups in the nation's capital. Militant rhetoric increased, and many people embraced the ten-point program of the now famous Black Panther Party. Panther leaders Huey P. Newton, Bobby Seale, Eldridge Cleaver, and Howard University alumnus Stokely Carmichael inspire revolutionary visions in many.

The Washington, D.C., black community has played a prominent role throughout the city's history. D.C. became a major stop for runaway slaves before and during the Civil War, and after the Union victory large numbers of blacks migrated to the city. Founded in 1867, Howard University, black America's most prestigious institution of higher learning, attracted great talents. Anchored by Howard and federal jobs, D.C.'s black community developed a large and prosperous middle class, and by 1900 Washington had the largest percentage of African Americans of any city in the nation. This strong middle class became the backbone of churches, and church leaders exhibited a major influence in the community.

By the end of the 1950s, Washington's African American population surpassed 50 percent of the city's total, making it the first predominantly black major city in the country. The March on Washington in 1963, where Dr. King gave his famous "I have a dream" speech on the steps of the Lincoln Memorial, was a pinnacle of the modern civil rights movement and the culmination of years of nonviolent protest. King's assassination in 1968 would trigger massive revolt in black communities throughout the country, and many of Washington's black residents would rebel against continued racism, injustice, and what they saw as the federal government's abandonment of the poorer sections of the city. Demands for justice would push the federal government to take steps toward "home rule" by appointing African American Walter E. Washington as mayor-commissioner in 1967.[5] A Howard graduate with a long career in public housing, Washington would be palatable not only to Lyndon Johnson, the Democratic president who appointed him, but also to the Republican Nixon administration that followed. Agitation by D.C. residents would lead to the 1973 District of Columbia Home Rule Act, and in 1974 Walter Washington would be elected D.C.'s first mayor.

The burning and looting that followed King's assassination devastated D.C.'s black commercial districts of Georgia Avenue and U Street and contributed to the rise of Black Power in the city. One instantiation can be seen in activist Robert Rippy, a former member of the Student Nonviolent Coordinating Committee (SNCC) who founded the Black Defenders, the first group to mimic the Black Panthers in Washington.[6]

Robert Rippy and Cultural Nationalism in D.C.

Robert Rippy's Black Power group had begun with a mere four members in December 1967. Eager to become Panthers, they met with a representative from the established New York state chapter of the BPP sometime in 1968 and were told that they had to meet Panther standards of membership and indoctrination and go through Panther training before using the name. Rippy promptly named his group the Black Defenders. Rippy worked as a supervisor for the United Planning Organization, a nonprofit that provides community services to D.C. residents, but he wanted to do more. Intending Black Defenders to be for youths aged fourteen and up, Rippy wanted to train recruits to deal with all types of crime but especially those committed by outsiders and the police. Applicants for his group had to own a gun, as the use of guns for self-defense was central to Rippy's vision.[7]

In 1969 Rippy again sought to become a Panther, and he traveled to Oakland to attend the United Front Against Fascism conference, hoping that his willingness to travel three thousand miles might illustrate just how serious he was. At the conference Huey Newton read a quote by Chinese Communist Party leader Mao Zedong. "'We are advocates of the abolition of war. We do not want war, but war can only be abolished through war. In order to get rid of the gun it is necessary to pick up the gun.' POWER TO THE PEOPLE!"[8] After the speech Newton and central committee members met with Rippy but denied him a charter because Rippy disapproved of the Panthers' coalitions with white radical organizations such as the Students for a Democratic Society (SDS).[9]

Later that year, back in D.C., Rippy opened a wig shop on the 3100 block of Georgia Avenue NW, where he held meetings of the United Black Brotherhood. This organization was created out of the core of the Black Defenders, and members of the brotherhood were cultural nationalists who said that "you couldn't look to your oppressor for salvation" and who detested the alliances the Panthers made with white radical groups.[10] Students from Howard University would come to Rippy's business, and Rippy would hold court using *The Autobiography of Malcolm X*. The United Black Brotherhood was militant in its rhetoric but held a vastly different philosophy on white America than the Panthers. Snubbed by the Panthers, Rippy's United Black Brotherhood would become rivals of the official D.C. branch when the latter formed in the spring of 1970, and they would compete for new recruits.[11] With the formation of the local Panther branch, David Hilliard, the party's chief of staff, addressed Rippy's organization in the *Black Panther* as "bootlickers," perhaps wanting to paint the United Black Brotherhood as a group subservient to authorities—"the man"—which by all accounts was the farthest thing from the truth.[12]

A champion of pan-Africanism, Rippy believed, like many black nationalists, in voluntary separation of blacks and whites, and in that regard followed the likes of Stokely Carmichael and US leader Maulana Karenga. Many black militant groups, especially nationalistic ones, considered the Black Panther Party's decision to ally with white radicals counterrevolutionary. The Panther alliance with the SDS and the establishment of the first "rainbow coalition" of radicals of all races opened the Panthers to criticism by black nationalists who saw the Panthers as revolutionaries first, black defenders second. Rippy and his cohorts abandoned black berets and leather jackets in favor of dashikis and overalls, and they joined the D.C.-based cultural nationalist Black United Front.[13]

More Background on D.C.

From its founding the District of Columbia had been almost fully dependant upon the U.S. Congress for everything from its annual budget to criminal ordinances. In 1970 Washington, D.C., had over eight hundred thousand residents—over 70 percent of whom were African American—and was at the mercy of legislators from across the country whose various interests (including segregationist constituencies back home) had little to do with the District's pressing needs.[14]

The 1970 U.S. Census described Washington as 71.1 percent black and 27.7 percent white. The white population in the western portion of the District was quite well off. According to the Census Bureau, 81,678 black residents, 17 percent of the black population, lived below the federally mandated poverty level in D.C.[15] This percentage was much lower than in other U.S. cities, with the most extreme example of black poverty being Newark, New Jersey, with over 41 percent of its mostly black population living below the poverty line. Over a third of Detroit's black residents lived under the poverty level, and the black populations of Chicago and New York had close to 30 percent living in poverty in the 1970s.[16] Inner cities throughout the country dealt with white flight to the suburbs, but in Washington, D.C., the economic effect was lessened by an entrenched black middle class. The violence that followed Dr. King's assassination, however, spurred some in the black middle and upper class to migrate to adjacent Prince George's County, Maryland.

Black unemployment in D.C. according to the 1970 Census was 43,848, or 12 percent of the black workforce of 360,048. Young black males (sixteen to twenty-nine years of age) had the highest unemployment rate, 16.4 percent. White unemployment was much lower for city residents, with only 7.3 percent of white workers unemployed. As with blacks, the great majority of unemployed whites were in the young adult bracket, ages sixteen to twenty-nine.[17]

Employment opportunities for blacks in professional administration or white-collar jobs were greater in the 1960s in Washington than in previous decades. The drive of President Lyndon B. Johnson's administration to increase racial diversity increased African American employment in civil service positions, and the 1970 Census identified 151,486 black residents employed in white-collar positions in the District. Jobs with the federal or district government, academia, and private industry together meant much greater opportunity to blacks in D.C. than elsewhere.[18] This relatively well-off black community made it difficult to organize the disaffected and oppressed. Malik Edwards, a Vietnam veteran and former marine who was central to the D.C. Black Panther chapter, describes a city unreceptive to Panther recruiting and its message.[19]

From June 1969 to June 1970, the D.C. area was without an official Black Panther presence, and because of Washington's situation as a locus of wealth and government repression, some leaders of established black nationalist groups believed that a Panther branch would never be established there. Mindful of the Chicago murders of Fred Hampton, deputy chairman of the Illinois state chapter of the BPP, and Peoria Panther leader Mark Clark in January 1970, the Reverend Douglas E. Moore, a civil rights movement veteran and leader of the Black United Front, said that it would be suicide for the Panthers to establish a Washington branch. Moore knew of the intense persecution of Black Panthers by law enforcement across the nation, and he regarded the notoriety surrounding the Panther image as "detrimental."[20] It is not clear whether by this he meant detrimental to the Panthers or to Black Power groups generally seeking to alter the redistribution of power and resources in Washington.

Party Branch Founding

Toward the end of 1969, the BPP central committee dispatched a loyal and dedicated Panther, Charles Brunson, from Oakland to D.C. to help establish and oversee a branch office of the National Committee to Combat Fascism (NCCF). Washington activists Maxine Schoop and Willie Lee Dawkins began commuting to the Baltimore branch of the Black Panther Party in late 1969 and early 1970 to pick up newspapers to sell in D.C. The Baltimore branch was founded in 1968 and was the closest branch to D.C.

The NCCF branch was located in Shaw, near Adams Morgan, a neighborhood filled with Howard students and many young activists. The NCCF headquarters was close to the headquarters of Marion Barry's organization Pride, Inc. As the office was attempting to find its footing, the war in Vietnam continued to rage.

The May 4, 1970, National Guard killing of students at Kent State University inspired hundreds of thousands of the country's college students to openly revolt against U.S. involvement in Southeast Asia.[21] Richard Nixon had been elected president in 1968, many viewed his administration as fascist and imperialist, and support for revolution increased nationwide. With the national reputation of the Panthers preceding them, the establishment of the D.C. Panther chapter in June 1970 attracted significant police attention, especially during its first six months. Composed of young, idealistic, and fairly well-educated black men and women, the Washington chapter never had the membership or influence of the larger East Coast BPP chapters in Baltimore, Boston, Philadelphia, and New York. A number of original D.C. Panthers were transplants dispatched by the Party's central committee or people who had recently migrated to the D.C. area, but others were D.C. natives.[22]

The unique conditions of D.C. molded the D.C. chapter into one that, for the most part, downplayed confrontational revolutionary rhetoric and focused on community service. Eventually the D.C. Panthers realized that they could assist the community more effectively by working within the system and influencing the newly formed city government.

The turning point for the D.C. Panthers would be Thanksgiving weekend in 1970. The branch failed to secure a venue for the highly publicized follow-up to the Revolutionary People's Constitutional Convention held in Philadelphia that September. This led to a slight estrangement with central headquarters in Oakland. From this juncture, however, the chapter's defense captain and coordinator Jim Williams and other local party members transformed the D.C. Panthers into an effective community support organization. They embraced new opportunities provided by the creation of self-rule in D.C. but did not disavow the overarching goal of revolution and followed the directives of Oakland.

Civil Rights Groups in D.C. in the Late Sixties

Conservative civil rights organizations such as the NAACP, National Urban League, and Southern Christian Leadership Conference (SCLC) all had offices in Washington, D.C., and lobbied the government for programs to help the disadvantaged. The Congress of Racial Equality (CORE) fractured as conservative members willing to work with white liberals couldn't come to terms with CORE's black nationalist cadre that demanded that only blacks participate in the organization. Black Power also splintered the youthful SNCC.[23] SNCC created several groups in the District, primarily focusing on black nationalism. Some groups in Washington, like the Nation of Islam, advocated religious black nationalism, while other groups like the Black United Front decreed a cultural nationalism. Black cultural nationalist groups in Washington included the Black United Front, the United Black Brotherhood, the Blackman's Volunteer Army of Liberation (more about this below), and Stokely Carmichael's

All-African People's Revolutionary Party. Embracing African culture—including dress (dashikis), cuisine, and languages—these groups stressed community building, pushed for educational and employment opportunities, and supported anticolonial struggles, especially in the newly independent nations of Africa. After the Black Panthers began to ally with white radicals to form a revolutionary vanguard, these groups charged the Panthers with looking to the oppressor for salvation, and their entrenchment in D.C. would make it difficult for Panthers to recruit.

The city's residents were under the jurisdiction of the federal government, and only with the 1961 passage of the Twenty-Third Amendment were they allowed to vote for president. Civil rights organizations began to use the demand for home rule as a recruiting tool and a way to expand their influence in the District's black communities. From 1967 to the establishment of limited home rule in 1973, the issue of political representation of city residents helped swell the number of civil rights groups in the nation's capital. D.C.'s status (it had first been an unincorporated territory) meant administration by appointees. City council members were appointed by the powerful District Committee, presided over by influential conservative southerners in the U.S. House of Representatives, many of whom supported segregation. So it was with the chair of the committee from 1958 to 1969, Senator Alan Bible (D-NV). Bible supported Alabama's racist George Wallace during his days as governor and during his 1968 presidential campaign. Wallace became a symbol of segregation by physically blocking two black students from classes at the University of Alabama in June 1963.

In the 1950s, D.C. had become the first major city with a black majority, and many of those in Washington's powerful black middle class enjoyed job security from the federal government.[24] The black community had lost many wealthy and powerful residents, however, after 1948, when the Supreme Court declared restrictive housing covenants illegal. The decision facilitated the flight of the black elite to more affluent, predominantly white neighborhoods. Continued destabilization of D.C.'s black community and ghettoization of neighborhoods followed the 1964 Civil Rights Act and the 1968 Fair Housing Act, both of which hastened the flight of the black middle class to suburban neighborhoods in Maryland and Virginia.[25] Areas east and north of the Capitol became poorer and less stable, rife with crime, the same conditions that the Black Panthers condemned nationwide and worked to rectify.

SNCC had attracted younger recruits than more conservative and religious-based civil rights groups, its membership included many liberal or Marxist white youth, and its orientation was more toward direct action than that of more conservative groups. SDS leaders Tom Hayden and Mark Rudd had been SNCC volunteers and registered black voters in the 1964 Mississippi Freedom Summer, and thousands of returning SNCC students made campuses fertile activist recruiting grounds.[26] This formative period, before the escalation in Vietnam and assassination of black and liberal leaders, established a pattern of whites and blacks working together for change. Conversely, in 1966, SNCC elected nationalist Stokely Carmichael (later renamed Kwame Ture) as chairman, and H. Rap Brown, another nationalist, would follow Carmichael in this role. Under their leadership SNCC purged white members from its ranks under the subterfuge that they were being sent to university campuses and white neighborhoods to recruit among their own people.[27]

In Washington, D.C., segregated until the 1950s, racial barriers were not as distinct as the rigid segregation of the South, but racism and bias permeated the mentality of judges, police officers, real estate agents, and small business owners. The one thing the Panthers and black nationalists did agree on was that the white power structure was engaged in a conspiracy to keep blacks oppressed.[28] Black leaders slain prior to the shift to black militancy include Medgar Evers and Malcolm X. SNCC, under the leadership of Carmichael, began preaching armed resistance to racist police and a racist society. This gained resonance with the 1968 assassinations of Martin Luther King and Robert Kennedy. The outbreaks of violence in urban areas—rebellions or riots, depending on one's point of view—continued to grow in intensity, and black communities were increasingly seen as colonies dominated by the nation's capital, with white police as an "occupation army."[29] Frustration with the Vietnam War and the stalled civil rights movement provided additional momentum to the Black Power groups.

Divergence from civil rights movement goals of equality and integration is the hallmark of the Black Power movement. In 1967 Carmichael dismissed the civil rights movement, stating, "Integration is irrelevant. Political and economic power is what black people have to have."[30] In Washington black militants described the "white world" as a giant conspiracy and a "fascist" state arising.[31] The focus shifted from a problem of caste (in the South) to a problem of class (in the industrial cities of the North), and the enemy was no longer the Klan or southern sheriffs but institutional racism. Hostility shifted to the economic and political elites who perpetuated racism. Many younger black activists embraced Black Power and approved of meeting violence with violence and arming for self-defense.[32] Northern cities dealt with rebellions, open housing marches, and confrontations over school busing during the late 1960s, with hostilities seemingly intensifying each summer. After Carmichael stepped down from SNCC chairmanship in June 1967 and not long afterward became aligned for a time with the Black Panther Party, SNCC's new leader H. Rap Brown supported armed tactics, declaring violence "as American as cherry pie." Other black militant leaders besides Carmichael began shifting to the Panthers.[33]

Led by cultural nationalists and religious leaders of the District, the Black

United Front (BUF) was formed after the 1965 assassination of Malcolm X and included many militant cultural nationalist groups composed primarily of ex-SNCC activists. Curiously, they believed in revolution, as long as it took place within the context of a capitalistic system. The BUF disavowed the tactics of the Maoist Panthers and felt private enterprise was central in securing equality with whites. Led by the Reverend Douglas E. Moore, a SNCC veteran from North Carolina, the BUF eschewed the idea of working with white organizations. Moore stated that "the policy not to participate in coalition with white groups is because we believe you cannot look to your oppressor for salvation."[34] Like Rippy, Moore was a believer in pan-Africanism, and he was not only a former member of SNCC but also a longtime member of the NAACP, CORE, and the SCLC. He claimed his civil rights background proved his commitment to D.C.'s black community, unlike some "instant militants," a comment presumably revealing his contempt for the Panthers.[35]

Another radical militant black group with a presence in Washington was the Blackman's Volunteer Army of Liberation, led by Colonel Hassan Juru-Ahmed Bey. Juru-Ahmed Bey's small group of militant Muslims had a strong presence in the District as well as at the Lorton Reformatory, a prison located twenty miles south in the Virginia countryside. Juru-Ahmed Bey lived in a high-crime neighborhood of D.C., and he organized a small group of followers to patrol the local streets at night. Drug addicts committed the overwhelming majority of street crime, and Juru-Ahmed Bey and two others incorporated their headquarters (the Blackman Development Center) as a nonprofit public drug treatment program in May 1969. Juru-Ahmed Bey claimed that his group mushroomed in D.C. to over seven hundred volunteers by 1971, and they wore black berets and uniforms and vowed to smash D.C.'s heroin trade.[36]

The Panthers had entrenched militant groups to contend with, and Rippy, by 1970 a member of the Black United Front, stated that he didn't "believe that the police and the FBI would allow a Black Panther Party to exist here in the form which they exist in other cities."[37] Panthers may have scoffed at Rippy's comment, but some had to know that he was not totally off-base, even if they were unwilling to admit it.

A set of barriers unique to Washington prevented the formation of a BPP chapter in the city for nearly four years after the organization's Oakland founding in 1966. The second-class status of the District encouraged many black Washingtonians to ignore local politics entirely. In D.C.'s poorer communities there was a palpable sense of political apathy. In stable middle-class neighborhoods there were steady paychecks. Combined with hostile cultural nationalist groups, these made the delay of a Panther branch founding understandable, even though most major cities in the United States had a Panther presence by 1970.[38]

The growth of Black Power, the antiwar movement, and the aggressive policing of the Nixon administration made D.C. a focal point for demonstrations. A small group of District activists turned their attention to addressing the political apathy that had been ingrained for generations, and slowly many black residents began to support self-determination and backed the D.C. statehood movement. The statehood goal and the idea of black government combined into one cause. The city's more conservative blacks wanted national representation of the District and agreed on the home rule desired by progressives and Black Power advocates.[39]

Marion Barry's Influence on the Black Community

President Johnson's administration (from November 1963 to January 1969) changed the way the District would be administered. Johnson used his power to do away with the three-commissioner system, replacing it with a council and a mayor, appointing black career bureaucrat and moderate Walter Washington to the latter office. For the first time in a hundred years, local residents could vote, and the city gained an elected school board.[40] One of those elected to the board was Marion Barry.[41] Barry had moved to the District in 1965 at the request of SNCC and worked with and was close to Carmichael, H. Rap Brown, such Panthers as Fred Hampton and Kathleen and Eldridge Cleaver, and other leaders of Black Power organizations.[42]

In July 1969 Barry was operations director of his self-help organization Pride, Inc., and he asked blacks not to take part in a national day of celebration to honor the Apollo 11 moon landing that month. Barry stated, "Why should blacks rejoice when two white Americans land on the moon when white America's money and technology have not even reached the inner city?"[43] In May 1970 Barry had stunned many when he called on city residents to shoot any police officer entering their homes unannounced under the controversial "no knock" provision of a new crime bill. This bill allowed police to burst into suspected criminals' houses unannounced.[44]

Barry also labeled the Metropolitan Police an occupation army and preached against the white dominance of businesses in the inner city after the 1968 revolts. "White (business) people should be allowed to come back only if the majority of the ownership is in the hands of blacks," he said.[45]

Barry enjoyed a close relationship with the D.C. branch of the Black Panthers. In fact, Panthers Dawkins and Schoop were members of Pride, Inc. The Office of Economic Opportunity financed what was first called Youth Pride in the immediate aftermath of the 1968 rebellion, as a self-help "public rights organization," Barry says.[46] Soon shortened to Pride, Inc., it set up headquarters at Sixteenth Street Northwest and Florida Avenue, right across from Meridian Hill Park (also known as Malcolm X Park) between the Adams Morgan and the Shaw neighborhoods. These neighborhoods were home to many young black activists and Howard University students.[47] Pride's headquarters building was about seven blocks from the future Panther community center at 1732 Seventeenth Street and close to the future Panther branch headquarters on Eighteenth Street. When asked about the closeness of these organizations, Barry stated that many Panthers took part in Pride's programs and activities.[48] The friendships that evolved in that neighborhood in 1970–72 pointed many participants to a lifetime of community involvement, and revolutionary idealism prevailed in this area.

SNCC's Black Power turn with the election of Stokely Carmichael as its chair in 1966 caused Barry to distance himself from SNCC so that he could apply for federal monies to establish poverty programs under Johnson's Great Society initiatives. Despite this politically expedient move, Barry still supported views on self-determination and community control of police.[49] He found many people their first job in the District, and Barry transformed Pride, Inc. into a political machine that helped him get elected to the school board in 1971.

Interest in Panther Politics Grows

An inspired rally caught the attention of the central committee of the BPP. A group calling itself the Coalition against Racism and Fascism (CARF) formed to serve as an umbrella for the area's diverse black and antiwar organizations. CARF sponsored a protest rally at the Unitarian All Souls Church on Sixteenth and Harvard Streets Northwest on December 21.[50] The BPP central committee sent Charles Brunson, a trusted Panther from Oakland, to reconnoiter the nation's capital. The rally's main purpose was to support the cause of the Black Panthers, even though no branch yet existed in the District. The event did lead to the founding of the National Committee to Combat Fascism (NCCF) in the spring of 1970, an organization created to raise funds, spur sympathy, and organize. One of the major differences between an NCCF branch and a full-fledged branch of the BPP was that whites could join local NCCFs. Jim Williams, a D.C. activist who eventually headed both the NCCF office and the Panther chapter, stated at the time (February 1970) that some progress had been made in late 1969 and early 1970, but he was very disappointed in what he called the "bourgeois attitude" of Washington blacks.[51]

Williams was quoted as saying that "the government has been able to control the black people in this city through jobs and poverty programs, and has virtually silenced so-called community leaders by putting money into their pockets."[52] Organizations like Pride, Inc., and similar antipoverty groups made it difficult to build a revolutionary party in D.C. Black nationalist groups were already entrenched in Washington's black neighborhoods, especially those around Howard University.

In addition to the predominantly white Metropolitan Police Department, the capital was home to headquarters of the FBI, Secret Service, Alcohol Tobacco and Firearms (ATF), and other federal law enforcement agencies, all of which were charged with rendering the Panthers ineffective. The Central Intelligence Agency was also headquartered in nearby northern Virginia and tasked with surveillance of the BPP. FBI director Hoover was quoted in 1968 in the *New York Times*: "Schooled in the Marxist-Leninist ideology and the teaching of Chinese Communist leader Mao Tse-tung, [BPP] members have perpetrated numerous assaults on police officers and have engaged in violent confrontations with police throughout the country. Leaders and representatives of the Black Panther Party travel extensively all over the United States preaching their gospel of hate and violence not only to ghetto residents, but to students in colleges, universities and high schools as well."[53]

Police nationwide viewed the Panthers as a grave threat and used the FBI's counterintelligence program (COINTELPRO) to divide and destroy the leadership of the party. COINTELPRO tapped phones, spread rumors and disinformation, and instigated violence among Panthers and black nationalist groups nationwide. In addition, the FBI and local police placed informants and agents provocateurs inside the Panthers as a way to destroy the party.[54] Malik Edwards, a D.C. Panther, speaks of police infiltration of the D.C. branch. In the late 1970s, Edwards saw an ex-Panther known as Jeru on television describing his role as an informant for the Metropolitan Police Department and the FBI. Edwards states, "We were focused on survival programs for the community, programs that demanded so much that we didn't have time to plot against the government. We were glad that he showed up to help feed the children."[55]

Police informants and agents provocateurs infiltrated various BPP branches and chapters, and by 1969 the Panthers instituted a moratorium on accepting affiliates as a way of stemming this. Panther members were under surveillance and had to be secretive about activities seen as threatening by government agencies. The constant police pressure made Panthers fortify safe houses, safeguard information, and be vigilant about vetting recruits.[56]

The Panthers' growth from a chapter in Oakland in 1966 to reportedly more than forty chapters and branches nationwide by the early 1970s made the Panthers a prime target. J. Edgar Hoover hyperbolically declared the Panthers the "number one domestic threat." Bobby Seale was awaiting trial for murder in New Haven, Connecticut. Newton was still imprisoned for the alleged murder of a police officer (having been convicted on manslaughter charges), and with Eldridge Cleaver in exile in Algeria, individual chapters and branches operated with much more autonomy and independence from the central committee than they had earlier.[57] One Panther leader not dead, imprisoned, or in exile was David Hilliard, and he was jailed briefly in April 1970 following a speech in which he recklessly threatened the life of President Nixon.[58]

The D.C. NCCF office became quite busy fielding inquiries about the Panthers and took direction from the nearby Baltimore branch of the party. Sherry Brown, the lieutenant of finance for the Baltimore branch, described how activists of the D.C. NCCF were excited about Hilliard's arrival in June 1970, and rumors were circulating that the NCCF was to be declared a full Panther branch. A rally was scheduled for June 19, 1970, on the steps of the Lincoln Memorial. Four years after Huey Newton and Bobby Seale founded the Black Panther Party for Self Defense, Hilliard, Sherry Brown, and Jim Williams, the leader of the Washington NCCF, agreed that a Panther outpost should be official.[59]

D.C. Panthers Fight the System

In May 1970 over one hundred people were killed or wounded nationwide by the police and National Guard, George Katsiaficas notes. "Besides the four murdered and ten wounded at Kent State on May 4 and the two people murdered and twelve wounded at Jackson State on May 14, six black people were murdered and twenty were wounded in Augusta, Georgia; eleven students were bayonetted at the University of New Mexico; twenty people suffered shotgun wounds at Ohio State; and twelve students were wounded by birdshot in Buffalo."[60] All these events were unified by the protest of the Cambodian invasion ordered by the Nixon administration. Revolution seemed imminent to many radicals in the United States, and many envisioned the Black Panther Party leading the charge. A top-secret special report written by the FBI for President Nixon described the Black Panther Party as "the most active and dangerous black extremist group in the United States." It continued describing the appeal of the Panthers: "A recent poll indicates that approximately 25 percent of black population has a great respect for the BPP, including 43 percent of blacks under 21 years of age."[61]

The violent month of May 1970 actually hastened the formation of the Panther branch in D.C. Leftists worldwide looked to the Panthers to lead a revolution in the United States. Panther chief of staff David Hilliard came Washington in June ostensibly to deliver a statement at the 107th anniversary of the Emancipation Proclamation, a Black Panther Party event to be held on the grounds of the Lincoln Memorial. On June 19, 1970, with over a thousand in attendance, Hilliard declared that the District's National Committee to Combat Fascism had graduated to a Black Panther chapter, with the full backing of the Central Committee. He stated that the group had grown enough to be a full chapter, and the agreement was that the D.C. Panthers would be responsible for organizing and hosting the follow-up Revolutionary People's Constitutional Convention in November 1970, an event that promised to be a huge gathering of New Left organizations. Hilliard's speech, on the same spot where Martin Luther King delivered his "I have a dream" speech in August 1963, railed not only against the Nixon administration and white colonization of black neighborhoods, but also against competing militant Black Power organizations. Hilliard warned Nixon that the forthcoming new constitution, offering a guarantee of true freedom and justice to all, was the only alternative to revolution in America.[62]

The pressure placed on the branch rubbed some D.C. Panthers the wrong way, turning them against the guidance and authority of the party's central committee. Relations became even more strained when efforts on the part of the D.C. Panthers to secure a site for the November convention kept coming up short, embarrassing the Panther central committee, who placed all the blame on the D.C. chapter.

The headquarters of the BPP's thirty-eighth branch, previously home of the six-month-old NCCF, was in an Adams Morgan row house at 1822 Eighteenth Street Northwest. The predominantly black neighborhood was also home to the Blackman's Volunteer Army, the Black United Front, and Pride, Inc. In the center of this neighborhood was the three-block-long Meridian Hill Park. In 1969 black nationalists called for it to be renamed Malcolm X Park, due to the numerous times Malcolm had spoken there in the early 1960s. A renaming bill was introduced in the city council but failed. Still, many would refer to it as Malcolm X Park, and it served as a venue for rallies, and the area around it was known as a hotbed of activism.[63]

As decreed by the Party central committee, the Washington Panther branch excluded white members of the NCCF, who formed a new party, the Patriots. The Patriots, along with representatives from the Young Lords, a revolutionary Puerto Rican group based on the Panther model, formed an alliance with the D.C. Panthers and lived collectively in adjoining town houses in Adams Morgan for four years.[64]

D.C. Panthers versus Law Enforcement Agencies, 1970

The chapter's first major undertaking was the late June opening of a community center on Seventeenth Street, less than two blocks from the Metropolitan Police Department's Third District headquarters. As temperatures rose that summer, so did tension between the police and the Panthers. The party's publications calling for the blood of police and chants like "Off the Pigs!" naturally got the attention of the Third District officers.

On July 4, at approximately 10:30 p.m., the police responded to a noise ordinance violation at 1932 Seventeenth Street Northwest. Osa Massen, then a fifteen-year-old member of the party, later recalled "the one time that there was a police raid just because we were singing 'Off the Pigs.' The police came up the stairs like storm troopers breaking cement on the stairs. Their justification was that someone threw a brick and hit a cop in the face. No one knew of that happening."[65]

Two different stories of the incident emerged. The branch was less than two weeks old, and members believed that the police were trying to intimidate them. The police, on the other hand, contended that "they were in hot pursuit of a felon," who had assaulted a peace officer. On July 5 the *Washington Evening Star* reported that the incident had begun after the group would not stop singing "We Shall Overcome" and chanting "Power to the People!"[66] Conflicting with the *Star*, the *Washington Daily News*, whose readership was predominantly black, stated that the group was not singing "We Shall Overcome" but quoted a Panther saying, "Who sings that anymore?—We were singing 'Power to the People—Off the Pigs.' Are the papers afraid to print that?"[67]

Regardless of intent, the warrantless raid was violent and chaotic. Several said the Panthers had taunted the police and thrown rocks and bottles at the first officer who arrived. They said that someone had hit Officer John Robinson in the face with a brick, busting his scalp open. At that point, Panthers stated that more officers had arrived and that one had charged into the crowd, flailing a nightstick. According to this version of the story, most of the Panthers had retreated inside the community center, but some had stayed out on the steps and porch, taunting the officers. A third group of police had arrived, and the rest of Panthers retreated inside. The police had then proceeded to break the door down and arrest everyone inside, taking them to Third District headquarters.[68]

Maurice Laurence, information officer for the Panther branch, told the story this way, according to a *Washington Post* article two days later. "The people were so stimulated by the songs, so they sang louder. Then the pigs moved in and we went into the house. Then they kicked in the door and started beating everybody." A police official said there was "some struggling" as arrests were made.[69] Laurence also stated that over eight hundred dollars in cash had disappeared during the police raid. The raid coincided with the theft of the monies targeted for a free breakfast and clothing program. Another newspaper, the *Washington Afro-American*, also quoted Laurence: "These Fascist fools with wrecking hammers and axes in their hands started chasing children, women, and men all over the house like mad slave catchers. It took five or six for every brother. They handcuffed the brothers, threw them on the floor and began their mad terrorist act of beating, stomping, and kicking."[70]

Throughout Panther literature and interviews, accusations of government fascism are rife. The July 4 raid led to more. All the Panthers arrested posted the $10 bail and were released from jail on Sunday, July 5. Word of the confrontation spread through the community and led to a march on the Third Street police station from the Panther community information center on July 5, 1970. People in the crowd of about two hundred, many of whom had witnessed the raid, were hostile toward the police and wielded rocks and beer bottles. The police set up extra guards and called for backup. Tension between police and

Panther supporters continued, but the crowd eventually dispersed by early Sunday morning when all the Panthers were released.[71]

The *Evening Star* covered the raid with a story on July 6 and noted that some of the guns taken by police from the Panther community center were not registered. Two rifles, a shotgun, and a pistol, along with over two hundred rounds of ammunition, were seized. For this article the police had declined to comment on charges that arresting officers destroyed personal property, including clothing, furniture, and tape recordings. James Heller, a lawyer for the D.C. Panthers, told the *Star*, "It was an unbelievable mess. The place was completely ransacked." A Panther named Maxine told the paper that one daughter, eight years old, was knocked downstairs and that her sixteen-month-old baby had received a bump on the head.[72]

In the *Daily News* on July 7, Officer Tilmon O'Bryant, director of training and personnel for the Metropolitan Police department, was quoted: "I don't regard the Black Panther[s] as something exceptional. They do not warrant special concern. What may be considered a threat to other departments is not what we consider a threat here. We deal with demonstrations differently from other departments." Much of the Panther notoriety, he said, came from the publicity. "They need confrontation and they're not going to get it here." O'Bryant's comments on the raid were geared to deflate Panther claims of special persecution. O'Bryant did set up an investigation of the allegations of beatings and theft of the Panther free breakfast program funds. Maurice Laurence, spokesman for the branch, called this useless and said that this happens "every time a pig takes an oppressive act against the people."[73]

Marion Barry in 1970 was chairing the Citizens' Board of the experimental Pilot District Project, in which citizens of the Third Police district were given a voice in law enforcement policies. Quoted in the *Washington Daily News*, Barry announced, "The July 4 incident has come to our attention and we are going to find out what happened." Barry said the Panthers had indicated that they would cooperate with his investigating committee. A report was to be submitted to the citizens' board on July 30. "We'll decide what to do from there," Barry said. "We just want to make sure the police department is doing its job and that our people are cooperating with them."[74]

The incident landed Willie Dawkins a television interview. On WMAL's *Newswatch* show that aired Sunday, July 26, 1970, Dawkins asserted that the government was "taking away the constitutional rights of black and white people instead of enforcing them." Speaking these "fascist tendencies," he referred to "Chicago, not only... the conspiracy trial but [also] the Democratic Convention where they said they would not give their children a voice in the decision-making of the country. In fact, we'll prosecute and murder them if we have to."[75] This sort of rhetoric, from Dawkins and others, only resulted in more intense surveillance and persecution of the Panthers.

Dawkins, Jim Williams, and Charles Brunson provided the local leadership that oversaw the NCCF transformation into an official Black Panther Party branch that summer. Some Baltimore Panthers also helped. According to Baltimore Panther Steve McCutchen, John Clark, head of the Baltimore branch, would drive over to D.C. to check on his comrades there—he was the main liaison between Baltimore and D.C.[76] Hilliard placed Brunson, originally from Sacramento, in charge of organizing and securing the follow-up constitutional convention site. Says Esutosin Omowale Oaunkoya (formerly Charles Brunson), "If I remember correctly, it was the latter part of 1969 . . . Hilliard dispatched me to D.C. . . . I get to D.C. and contact Jim Williams who had grown up in D.C. . . . We immediately started working together."[77] Brunson had his hands full as he was directed to organize the Panthers' Richmond, Virginia, information center in 1970. In August 1970, Brunson was charged for the unregistered weapons confiscated by the police on the July 4 raid. The police department, the U.S. Attorney's office, and lawyers for the Panthers worked together to avert a potentially explosive situation. They allowed Brunson to surrender voluntarily to the Court of General Sessions rather than issue an arrest warrant. The U.S. Attorney explained, "Experience in other cities indicates they have had major confrontations." So "when we have a viable alternative, we should use it."[78]

A D.C. Panther chapter press release quoted New York Panther Zayd Shakur on the matter. If a warrant was issued, Shakur said, police will be allowed to search Panther offices or homes "as long as they are accompanied by members of the community, namely the Citizens' Board of the Pilot Precinct Project and our attorneys." He said that "the person that the police are looking for is not in any of our offices or homes," and he also commented, "Judging from the repressive history meted out against our party and black people here in Babylon, we think it would be stupid and absurd for us to turn over one of our members to barbaric tortures."[79] Shakur had come to the D.C. branch from New York after the July 4 raid, and he would guide the response of the Panthers for the next few months.

The height of publicity for the D.C. Panthers came in its first months, from June to November 1970. Photos of the Panthers were plastered across every newspaper in D.C., and the branch gained new recruits among local black radicals. After the Panthers' confrontation with the Metropolitan Police Department (MPD) within two weeks of its formation, the branch's leadership felt it was necessary to publicly explain to the community and others why it had not shot it out with the police. The Panthers' rival Black United Front meanwhile questioned the tough talk of the Panthers and used the raid as an example of Panther bluster and cowardice.

In an open letter to the community, the D.C. Panthers responded to the Black United Front. On one side of the letter was drawn an armed Panther holding a bloody machete and a pig's head with a police officer's cap, while the other side declared the branch's position on the raid. Under the heading "Death to the Fascist Pigs," the letter was distributed with *Black Panther* newspapers and outside the community information center and branch headquarters. It challenged the rumor that the Panthers feared the police: "Some of our peoples that weren't on the scene are wondering if we violated our principles by not wiping out the first of those gangsters that crashed through our door. Then some of our comrades who weren't at the scene are questioning the order that was given to 'hold our fire until we're fired upon.'" The letter went on: "We'll kill anybody that stands in the way of our freedom. And because they were able to take four of our weapons and beat us after we didn't shoot, they still can't stop us. How can they? We will take a hundred beatings as long as it educates our people on the necessity of arming themselves. Every attack the pigs make brings them closer to their DOOM!"

The open letter was meant to assure D.C.'s black community that the Panthers were not going to back down or capitulate. Its violent tone did nothing to diminish Panther scrutiny by the MPD and the FBI. Law enforcement agencies continued surveillance and worked on infiltration and building a network of informants to destabilize the D.C. Panthers.[80]

Revolutionary People's Constitutional Convention

On September 5, 1970, the plenary session for the Revolutionary People's Constitutional Convention began in Philadelphia. Plans were finalized to hold a follow-up convention in D.C. on Thanksgiving weekend.[81] Members of D.C.'s Black Panther Party chapter continued looking for a location that could accommodate over five thousand people. Local members, in cooperation with other groups in the city, had already requested permission to rent the National Guard Armory. But a three-person civilian board, composed of a Montgomery County businessman, a National Guard general, and a representative of Mayor Washington, had reviewed the Panthers' application and turned it down—the convention was said to conflict with prearranged activities at the armory. Representatives of the party went back to the Armory Board and asked specifically whether the convention could be held at the armory on Thanksgiving weekend. On October 6, armory head administrator Arthur Bergman responded that the armory was no longer to be used for "rock concerts or organizations such as yours."[82] The powers that controlled the armory were steadfast in their refusal, and the Panthers had little chance lease other large convention halls because of their militant rhetoric and perceived communistic platform.

The same day the Panthers' application was turned down, Elbert "Big Man" Howard, editor of the *Black Panther* newspaper, was dispatched from Oakland to D.C. Once there he called a press conference to discuss the Armory Board's action. "Why should the black people of D.C., which is 80 percent of the population," he said, "pay their tax dollars for a facility that exists primarily for the use of white people who live outside the community?"[83] Although Howard exaggerated somewhat the size of D.C's black population, his point was not without merit. Indeed, the establishment's subsequent silence on the matter reinforced the feeling among the Panthers that there was little chance to secure the needed large hall for the convention.

Following the denial, the Panthers and their lawyers filed a lawsuit on the grounds that one of the stated uses of the National Guard Armory was "conventions" and that to refuse permission for its use for the Panthers' convention was a violation of the constitutional right to freedom of assembly. The D.C. Superior Court denied the suit, presumably because the Panthers could not prove that a large hall was necessary for their convention.[84] An example of court bias against the Panthers, the ruling reflected the Washington elite's fears of the Panthers and showed that they would use all means necessary to sabotage the convention.

At the same time that the Panthers were working on getting the armory for the convention, students representing the Democratic Radical Union of Maryland (DRUM) at the University of Maryland and the school's Student Government Association began to negotiate with the University of Maryland administrators to use Cole Field House for the convention activities. Despite the administrators' growing support for use of the field house by other student groups, use of the field house was denied.[85] According to the decision makers, the Panthers were refused because of the potential for violence associated with the party.

Even though a convention venue had not been found, groups in Washington went ahead in organizing housing, food, and transportation for convention participants. Antiwar GIs, women's liberation and gay liberation activists, the Youth International Party (Yippies), and numerous campus organizations made arrangements for their particular workshops. The Panthers envisioned high school students, college students, workers, street hustlers, and welfare recipients working to perfect a vision of a new America.[86] This new vision included participatory democracy, socialist programs, ending imperialism, racism, and social classes, and a more open society with new personal freedoms. It might have been easy to envision, but implementation was another matter.

Jim Williams and "Big Man" Howard scrambled to find a convention hall. The Panthers complained of "a large machine designed to destroy all revolutionary movements in the United States, the Black Panther Party in particular" and the mainstream press noted that "police harassment of the local Branch of the Black Panther party has become heavier as the opening date of the Convention move[s] closer."[87]

The police began to arrest Panthers leaders and used information from the FBI and their own intelligence section to go after Panthers with the greatest visibility. Willie Dawkins and D.C. Panther Robert Schoop, who had traveled to New Orleans, were listed on warrants charging "Criminal Anarchy" and "Flight to Avoid Prosecution" issued on September 17, 1970, by the district attorney of New Orleans. The warrants became public one day after a raid of the New Orleans NCCF, which resulted in the arrest of fourteen members of that group. Both Schoop and Dawkins had important duties in organizing the November convention and now had to defend themselves in court, represented by attorneys of the American Civil Liberties Union (ACLU).[88] The ACLU took the case because it felt the Panthers were being targeted for their political views.

In addition to legal pressure, there was financial pressure on the D.C. BPP branch. The city's gas, electric, and phone companies sent notice that if bills were not paid immediately on the date due, the utilities would be disconnected and a two-hundred-dollar deposit would be required to reconnect them. This was a much different policy than for other customers, who often had a two-month window to pay late bills before services were shut off. The pressure on the Washington branch just continued to increase.

The FBI's COINTELPRO used eavesdropping, forged letters and other disinformation, and harassment arrests to foster ill will between groups and create animosity between Panthers themselves. The FBI and local police put intense pressure on the D.C. Panthers, especially by manufacturing threats from rival black revolutionary groups. The FBI used *agents provocateurs* and infiltrators to sow dissent among the leadership of Panthers and advocate violence that often ended in arrest or death.[89]

In 1970 the *Black Panther*'s national circulation was reaching its height, and the Panthers continued to use the paper to fund the party.[90] D.C. Panthers pounded the pavement hawking the paper. Osa Massen recalled selling papers on Fourteenth and H in front of the Waxie Maxie record store, a popular hangout where "everyone" went. "I can remember having conversations with people going in and out of the record store. It really was a good feeling to sell all of them." She states, "We also had an information table in front of the house where we would sell books or give out information, and I would sometimes sit out there to speak with the people in the community."[91] The dedication and devotion of some members began to change the perception of the Panthers as violent militants.

Sherry Brown describes competing cultural nationalist organizations in the District, including Stokely Carmichael's All-African People's Revolutionary Party (AAPRP). The position of AAPRP, the Black United Front, and other pan-Africanist organizations was that the Black Panthers should not associate with the SDS and other white leftists. They felt black activists should not look to white activists for help, Brown says, adding, "D.C.'s cultural nationalists had a more nationalistic line about black community, exclusively black police, businesses, government." Brown notes that the Panthers had a coalition-building and international approach and took a great deal of criticism in the black community for their cooperation with white radicals.⁹² By the fall of 1970 Black Panther Party leaders supported coalitions with groups working for female and gay liberation, and cultural nationalists in the Shaw/Cordozo/Columbia Heights neighborhoods of D.C. used these unpopular issues to deter potential recruits from joining the D.C. Panther branch and steer them to other organizations.

When asked about the paucity of recruits in D.C., Brown states, "It was a very white-collar, very bourgeois city. D.C. was more of a middle-class city, unlike the Baltimore and Philly branches that had many more members and had a lot more going on. Baltimore and Philadelphia were blue-collar, were more lumpen-proletariat folks, and they were the primary recruiting target. Panthers would work with the poorest of the poor. Washington had more government jobs here and had a more bourgeois orientation."⁹³

In the fall of 1970 Panther lawyers filed a $1 million lawsuit against the MPD for the July 4 raid, and a week later, on October 17, all charges against those arrested in the confrontation were dropped, including the charges against Brunson for possession of illegal weapons.⁹⁴ The Panthers were sure that they would be raided again, though, and they desired greater firepower. Brunson, one of the primary organizers of the November convention, was again jailed on weapons charges after a traffic stop on Interstate 95 in Virginia.

Brunson's path to imprisonment began with the theft of a Chinese submachine gun and a Russian light machine gun from the residence of a Richmond, Virginia, gun collector in September. In Richmond, contacts with the Black Panthers in Washington had been told of the collector's cache. Apparently Brunson traveled to Richmond to appropriate arms for the D.C. branch. With him was Jacob Bethea, a fellow D.C. Panther. After they successfully acquired the stolen weapons, the car they were traveling in was stopped by Virginia state troopers. Five were arrested and charged for the crime of transporting stolen weapons. These Panthers were soon dubbed "the Richmond Five." A trial would ensue on May 21, 1971, and Bethea, Brunson, and one other man, Albert D. Moore of Richmond, would be convicted, with Bethea and Moore given eight years and Brunson four years.⁹⁵ Albert Moore's brother Howard C. Moore was scheduled to be retried at a later date, and Junius A. Underwood Jr. faced similar charges and was also to be tried at a later date. Waverly Patrick Allen Jr., an undercover FBI operative who had acquired the weapons, was an unindicted co-conspirator.⁹⁶

The D.C. Branch presented its case to the media and published a press release in the *Black Panther* in November 1970 denouncing the criminal charges against the Richmond Five:

> Here in Richmond Virginia, they're using a known dope addict, who is also a police informer, in an attempt to railroad these five courageous brothers who only fought to serve the oppressed people of this community. These brothers and those people who have openly supported them have been harassed and intimidated daily by Federal agents... now the Richmond Five and countless other political prisoners reaffirm our position that there will never be justice in the American courts until the people are the judges.
>
> ALL POWER TO THE PEOPLE! FREE ALL POLITICAL PRISONERS!
>
> Black Panther Party
> Washington D.C. Chapter[97]

Brunson and Bethea were arrested two months before the constitutional convention. Panther leaders Willie Dawkins and Robert Schoop were also in jail, and less experienced Panthers were pressed to find a hall. On the first week of November, the Panthers were once more officially denied access to the armory. They had only three weeks to find a venue.[98]

Their last choice was the campus of Howard University. University officials were not inclined to offer its facilities but reluctantly agreed. The university was planning to charge the Panthers $10,823.06 for the use of the facilities—with payment in advance.[99] The branch did not have the funds to pay a fee that large and pleaded with the university to donate the use of the campus "to the people." A Black Panther Party spokesman told the *Washington Daily News* that the Panthers were willing to pay $1,000 in advance and the rest later, but the university rejected the offer. The Panthers were back to square one.

At the last minute, the Panthers received a permit from the National Park Service to hold a rally at Malcolm X Park in order to tell the delegates that the convention was off.[100]

But still people came. Hundreds of delegates from around the nation converged on Washington on November 27, 1970, to attend the follow-up Revolutionary People's Constitutional Convention. D.C.'s Malcolm X Park (Meridian Hill) was filled with representatives from the Socialist Party, the Youth International party, the Young Lords, representatives of the gay and women's liberation movements. And instead of telling people to go home, that the convention was off, the Panthers' deputy minister of information, "Big Man" Howard, announced that they would stay in Washington for three days—or three months if necessary, until they could find a suitable convention hall. Sympathetic ministers in the Shaw and Cardozo neighborhoods opened their doors to the visiting activists, many of whom were white. After registering at the All Souls

Church on Sixteenth and Harvard Street and St. Stephen's Episcopal Church and the Incarnation Church near the Panther headquarters, the delegates were told to canvass Washington's inner city. By mid-afternoon, the delegates organized into workshops, divided up by region. They concentrated on important issues and grappled with social policies to create a better society.[101]

Newton, freed from prison in August, made a rare public appearance at the convention and gave a speech at St. Stephen's on Saturday, November 28. He declared that the Black Panthers' immediate goal was "revolutionary intercommunalism, under which oppressed communities around the world would cooperate to destroy capitalism."[102] Newton informed the delegates that they would get a "rain check" on writing a new constitution. The Panther leaders, however, gave the delegates a draft of the proposed constitution written by the participants of the Philadelphia convention in September.[103]

Many of the young activists who had descended on Washington hoped for massive, revolutionary change, and some no doubt came with the intent of enjoying the festivities. Given the circumstances, it is unsurprising that the convention was marked by confusion. The strife continued when the gay liberation movement and the women's movement threatened several times to split from the convention because of perceived homophobic and misogynistic comments by speakers. The lack of sufficient public space made it impossible for participants to effectively meet and discuss issues. These logistics made it impossible to draft new documents and mandates, and the convention ended having made little progress. Delegates to the Panther-sponsored convention left Washington with a draft constitution that was mostly unchanged and little else to show for two days on the sidewalks along Sixteenth Street Northwest. Between three thousand and five thousand predominantly young white people had arrived from across the United States, but the workshops they had planned to attend never developed because Panther organizers had been unable to obtain an indoor convention site.[104]

The event, intended to give blacks a bigger role in government, was an unequivocal flop. Some delegates started leaving almost immediately, while many of those who stayed through the last night left angry and disappointed at the Panthers' disorganization.[105] These delegates felt that the Panthers should have solved the logistical problems somehow. In retrospect the failed convention highlights the struggle of integrationists and liberationists, such as the Panthers, against black nationalists and pan-Africanists. The majority white turnout for the Panther convention in D.C. reinforced the idea that the Panthers were working in partnership with whites. Panther rivals like the All-African People's Revolutionary Party and Douglas Moore's Black United Front used cooperation with white radicals as an issue to isolate the Panthers from the Washington, D.C., African American community.

A New Approach

To review, the Panthers were not in altogether friendly territory. The federal and city government were D.C.'s biggest employers, and a fair number of blacks were solidly middle class. African Americans in the district were reported to be among the wealthiest in the country, second only to the black community in Los Angeles.[106] "This town has always had an appeal to the black middle class," says demographer George Grier. "Even when this town was segregated that held true. There were more, good, decent jobs here for blacks than most anywhere else."[107] Uncle Sam was hiring African Americans for jobs more or less commensurate with their training long before the private sector adopted even the rhetoric of equal opportunity. The presence of Howard University also helped. It was the first historically black university to offer a full complement of professional schools, from law to dentistry to medicine, to go along with its broad range of graduate and undergraduate programs. This strong black middle class in D.C. resisted revolutionary change and supported conservative politicians and ministers.[108]

Howard University's famous alum Stokely Carmichael was drafted into the Black Panther Party and given the title of prime minister in 1968. In July 1969, however, Carmichael broke with the Panthers, later terming the party "dogmatic" and its tactics "dishonest and vicious."[109] The Panther coalition building with whites rubbed many pan-Africanist Howard students the wrong way.

Newton referred to these differences in the D.C. black community in his speech at St. Stephen's during the Revolutionary Peoples Convention. Located about five blocks away from Malcolm X Park, St. Stephen's was known as a diverse and progressive parish. Newton decried the Panthers' you-can't-go-home-again attitude about Africa and said that the party was internationalist rather than nationalist. Newton said a cadre of Panthers would go into the black community to organize and mobilize, especially against the "ruling class" at Howard.[110]

To add to the failure of the convention, fourteen Panthers were removed from American Airlines Flight 75 to Los Angeles on Sunday, November 29, 1970, allegedly for being "boisterous and unruly" as the plane prepared to take off from D.C.'s Dulles International Airport. The *Washington Post* reported the next day that a flight attendant had not wanted to fly with the swearing and shouting Panthers, and the fourteen had been removed and issued refunds.[111] This last bit of bad press added insult to injury for the D.C. chapter, and the party's central committee heaped criticism on the branch.

The convention proved a turning point for the D.C. chapter, a nadir from which things would improve. Initial energy had worn off, and the work of grassroots social service took center stage. The need to deal with congressionally appointed city officials made it difficult to organize or serve the urban poor through government structures. The D.C. Panthers evolved into an independent community support organization that would operate until party members were called to Oakland in 1972.

D.C. newspapers described the Panthers in starkly different terms, with the *Post* and the *Evening Star* often siding with law enforcement sources and rival militants when reporting about Panther activities during June to November 1970. Black papers like the *Washington Daily News* and the *Washington Afro-American* were sympathetic to the Panthers' views and interviewed members of the D.C. Panther branch. After the chaotic first half-year of the branch's existence, with all of its problems and persecution, its leaders toned down the rhetoric and aimed to change their image as troublemakers. Continued pressure from police and rival black nationalist groups, combined with criticism from the BPP national headquarters, modified the local Panthers' actions and their focus.

After the failure of the follow-up constitutional convention, membership in the branch steadily decreased during the winter of 1970–71, but those who stayed were committed and initiated several community survival programs, of which residents took full advantage.

Community Survival Programs

The Panthers set up free breakfast programs in D.C.'s poor neighborhoods of Shaw, Cardozo, and Anacostia. The Panther community center on Seventeenth Street was home to the first such program in the city. The feeding of children before school gained the party credibility in the eyes of the black press and the community. In 1971 the Panthers expanded the program to other disadvantaged neighborhoods in Northeast Washington and helped out in the neighborhoods, doing odd jobs and running errands. Their goal was to win over the community, and in this respect the Panthers were successful. They also set up a free busing program that allowed those without a car to visit incarcerated friends, loved ones, and relatives incarcerated in Lorton, Virginia, twenty miles south. The District's churches were helpful in allowing their facilities and parking lots as gathering spots for those participating in the busing program. Churches also helped the Panthers' "Angela Davis People's Free Food Program," a food bank that began in 1971.[112]

The focus on community programs and the pragmatic, problem-solving activism displayed by the Panthers inspired the admiration of many D.C. blacks, and women played a significant role in these community programs. Malik Edwards states, "If it wasn't for women, there wouldn't be a Black Panther Party. The guys would be just scratching their asses." The women were responsible for organizing, and mostly they were much better educated than their male counterparts. The changing role of women throughout wider culture made many male Panthers come to see women as liberated, confident, and competent, exemplified by Elaine Brown's rise to the chair of the central committee by 1974. Maxine Schoop was described by Edwards as the glue that kept the branch unified, and Edwards describes Linda Wilson as another hardworking and essential member of the D.C. Panthers, supervising the free breakfast programs.[113]

People's Free Health Service

In 1971 the D.C. Panthers established a clinic in Anacostia, located in Southeast D.C., and created an outreach program that screened residents for sickle cell anemia and hypertension. This was in collaboration with Howard University's Community Medicine program. Dr. Jean Linzau and others recruited medical students at Howard to be part of the People's Free Health Service. The university's Medical Student Association also assisted in recruiting for the program and trained D.C. Panthers to take blood pressure readings and samples for sickle cell testing.[114] Howard students were enthusiastic and involved, and D.C. community members responded positively, appreciative of the program, which would run for several years.

The Panthers and the medical students from Howard would focus on challenged neighborhoods in all four quadrants of the District. The Panthers would set out on Saturdays, knocking on doors and speaking with residents, signing up those interested and returning the next day, Sunday, for testing. The tests were collected and sent to Howard University Hospital for analysis. Longtime Panther Anita Stroud states that the Panthers and the medical students dressed in white jackets and carried identification cards to promote trust and an image of high-quality service. After a week, results of the tests were delivered in person, and the hypertensive and those who tested positive for sickle cell were referred to the People's Free Health Clinic in Southeast.[115] In the course of the door-to-door surveys, if the Panthers or the students noticed other medical concerns they would refer residents to local hospitals if the People's Health Clinic was ill equipped to address them. Panthers from the Baltimore branch also came to help with the canvassing and testing.

By 1972, the D.C. Panthers had set up a second clinic, the People's Free Health Clinic in the basement of the Johenning Baptist Center at 4025 Ninth Street Southeast. At this time the membership of the party had decreased from a high of one hundred members in 1970 to thirty-five or forty members. Health coordinator Catherine Showell described the clinic for a *Washington Post* reporter, stating, "We aren't going to shoot anybody." Linzau was the physician in charge.[116]

"I was working on setting up free health clinics in Mississippi, working as the medical director of the Howard University Mississippi Project," states

Linzau. "I returned late in 1971 and was contacted by the Panthers to see if I would help set up a free health clinic in D.C. I volunteered and looked at the new home of the free clinic. The basement was filthy and had to be remodeled for the clinic. The medical equipment was mostly donations and old rejected stuff. Several doctors volunteered."[117]

"The worst part of the clinic was that we never had the right drug for the disease. We would get our drugs from pharmaceutical companies that would hand out promotional samples. Therefore we were always in desperate need of drugs. The clinic did help out people that would've gotten sicker if there was no place to go if you had little or no money."[118] The Panthers' free health clinic represented their commitment to the community, but members did much more. From clothes to rides, from breakfast to baby sitting, the Panthers established a survival network for some of the District's poorest residents. The Black Panthers were credited for understanding people's needs and lived in the communities they helped support. Ron Clark, a young supporter of the Panthers, describes the leader of the D.C. Panthers, Jim Williams, as a "Marxist guru" who always viewed society in class terms. He says that Williams practiced what he preached, living communally with other Panthers.[119] Williams was remembered by Clark as wise and sensible, a man with quiet brilliance. He would often let Willie Dawkins lead the meetings and speak to the press, and Maurice Laurence and Charles Brunson were also public representatives of the D.C. branch. Clark states that it was Williams who kept the branch together, on a mission to defeat racism, end the violence perpetrated on the black community, and educate D.C.'s poorest citizens. Clark recalled that he didn't parrot the rhetoric from the BPP central committee, and that caused the committee to expel him from the party for a while in 1972, if not on more than that one occasion. Clark also stated that Williams always was able to ingratiate himself back into the good graces of those at national headquarters. Elbert "Big Man" Howard remembers Williams as "a man who was able to get a lot of things done in D.C. in a short period of time ... he was a hard worker.... I admired him, had a lot of respect for him."[120]

Despite Williams's leadership, the chapter was not without internal dissension. Hullabaloo over supporting the women's movement, gay liberation, and drug decriminalization led to some members obeying the central committee and moving to Oakland in December 1972. Other members continued the community work in D.C., but allegiance to the party wavered with each new controversial pronouncement of Huey Newton, Edwards says.[121] Despite disagreements between members, including those in leadership roles, the Panthers remained committed to one another.

When asked about the Panthers' living conditions, Linzau replies, "They did take care of each other. They lived in an enormous building on Fourth Street, and all of them lived together. They didn't use hard drugs and asked for complete secrecy with their medical histories, for fear of government agents accessing them. Therefore all their medical records were labeled by a code [for] which only I had the master key."[122] The government continued its war on the Panthers, and the secrecy of Panther medical records was just one of the precautions they took against government intrusion. Panthers tried to weed out government agents and informers and had little trust of outsiders. They continued to focus on community organization and services but knew that a police raid was an eventuality and so fortified their living space and headquarters with metal doors and reinforced windows.

Linzau states, "I never got paid, but they invited me to their complex on Fourth Street to eat and talk. I would go over to their complex and enjoy relaxing conversation and meals with them. I never saw weapons but was sure they were there." The D.C. Panthers were certainly paranoid about the government and even about the party's own central party, and after the split between Newton and Cleaver (and their respective followers), the group was rife with purges. Linzau says, "They never knew who was going to report you to whom." Linzau also notes that the D.C. branch was very interested in the idea of "communalistic capitalism"—ventures in which they could make some money for the group as a whole. They wanted to "empower the poor people of society." He says he enjoyed the Panthers' company and knew they would always protect him if necessary. "They were really trying to make a difference in this community."[123]

Revolutionary Politics

In keeping with the national BPP leaders' understanding of the importance of coalition politics, the D.C. chapter, despite competition with black nationalist groups, supported other radical groups in Washington and became involved in a high-profile radical takeover in October 1972. The American Indian Movement (AIM), champions of Red Power, took over the Bureau of Indian Affairs (BIA) building in D.C. for six days, beginning immediately before Nixon's re-election in November 1972. By the fifth day of the occupation, Election Day, federal officials were troubled by a rumor that the four-story building was wired with explosives. The rumor gained traction when the leaders of the takeover held a news conference on the steps of the BIA building on November 6. Jim Williams, there representing the Black Panthers, stated that the Panthers supported the Indian demands but declined to say whether or, if so, how many Panthers were being added to the Indian forces. Standing next to him was AIM leader Russell Means who boasted, "If we go, we're going to take this building with us. If we go, this building is not going to be here—there's going to be a helluva smoke signal." Tension eased, however, because the Nixon administration tried to avoid a confrontation on the eve of the election. The Indians abandoned the building after being given money and being allowed to leave unmolested. Before they left, however, they ransacked the building and caused over $2 million in damage.[124]

In 1972 a synopsis of the local Panthers' story was published in the *Washington Evening Star*, and it described how the branch had metamorphosed into a group with less militant proclamations and more involvement in securing the party's goals of education and political and economic freedom for black people. For example, in June 1973 the Panthers had initiated a program to provide free rides for the elderly to and from local banks on the first of each month, when welfare and Social Security checks arrived. They initiated this program because many poor and elderly people were otherwise without transportation. By 1973 Charles Brunson had been freed from prison, and he stated, "While the Panthers nationally were doing great things politically, here in D.C. we were producing a new image for the Panthers."[125] This new image was one of community activism, with volunteerism the main focus of the local Panthers.

Anita Stroud explains, "Those who left the party did so because all the romanticism disappeared when we stopped making headlines, and the military dress disappeared, and the flame died."[126] She also describes the inner workings and day-to-day routine of Washington's remaining Panthers. "On school days we would work serving the children breakfast until they went off to school, then sell newspapers throughout the city, [and] attend political education classes, and by evening we would often work on other survival programs, the clothing program, and the food bank until bed. This would be repeated each school day. On the weekends, we would be part of the bussing to prison, for visitation, and participate in the People's Free Health Service, testing those for hypertension and sickle cell."

Although Steve McCutchen was not a member of the D.C. chapter, he remembers well the political education classes that took place there because he taught a few of them. "I went over there a few times to teach P.E. [political education] classes.... They were an NCCF then... this would have been early 1970, probably.... Mostly I would use articles from our newspaper as a point of discussion.... I might pose a question to the entire group rather than singling any one person out.... I wanted to generate discussion without putting any one particular person on the spot.... From those classes I could tell that the cadre there in D.C. was on solid ground." McCutchen makes clear that his experience was limited, saying, "Other Baltimore comrades, such as Anita Stroud and Chaka Zulu [Ed Martin], had much more contact with the comrades over there than I did."[127]

Stroud says that what stands out from her experience was the commitment, the dedication of her fellow Panthers. "It was like being in the army," she says. As with indoctrination of army recruits, the Panther ideology and philosophy transformed a number of members from extremely different backgrounds and gave them common ground. Unlike the original ten-point program, D.C. Panther leaders demanded that members be willing to change; being a Black Panther required discipline and the ability to lead and to follow.[128]

The smaller and more dedicated D.C. Black Panther Party branch of 1972 differed significantly from the confrontational group that had fought off police officers with bottles and bricks in 1970. The Panther programs continued after publicity of the first six months quieted down and after the failed follow-up constitutional convention. Local Panthers' support of AIM's takeover of the BIA building was their last major militant display. The D.C. Panthers' last appearance in the local media was when national Panther leaders told the branch leaders in mid-1972—as they did other branch leaders—to shut down their office and move to Oakland.[129] Linzau describes the end of the D.C. Panthers as inevitable, and he remembers thinking that the clinic would stay open for only a few months more. He was right. "It was open for a few months and closed that winter [1972–73]." The branch's community programs were slowly dismantled, and needy D.C. residents looked to other groups to help out where the party left off.[130]

About a dozen of the twenty remaining members of the D.C. branch moved to Oakland just in time for Bobby Seale's mayoral campaign and Elaine Brown's city council campaign in 1973, leaving behind the struggles in the nation's capital. Panthers blamed D.C.'s strong law enforcement agencies and the city's burgeoning black middle class, which had for three years thwarted efforts to form a BPP branch. A strong contingent of other radical black nationalist groups in D.C. had added to the difficulties of starting a branch.

In the 1971 and 1972 the Panthers made numerous attempts to change their fierce image by focusing on community programs, but the leadership of the Panthers came primarily from the national headquarters in California. This leadership was stricken by dissension—with confrontations and purges often instigated by the dirty tricks of the FBI, and many members became disillusioned by the infighting. Jim Williams, the loyal captain of the D.C. Panthers, had a dim view of the experience and said of the branch even then, in 1972, "We had no real influence in raising the consciousness of the black community; that is the point where we, the Panthers, failed."[131]

Retrospect

The Black Panthers of Washington, D.C., fell short in recruiting for the revolution, and they also failed in securing a convention hall for a potentially historic meeting where a new version of the U.S. Constitution was to be ratified. The success of the Panthers in D.C. was in their community activism and service to poor families. The militaristic rhetoric that the Panthers had spouted in their first months of existence as a party branch in D.C. shifted to grassroots educational, political, and social programs. These programs had much more of an impact on D.C. as a whole than any inflammatory bluster from a press release or interview, and the legacy of the Panthers in the city is community service, which many surviving members still practice.

Elbert "Big Man" Howard says that he "visited the Washington branch often back in the day. I worked with the leadership as well as members of the rank and file. Jim Williams was in charge of the branch. He has passed on. I can tell you the branch was very strong and made an impact on the community."[132] Black Power activists such as Marion Barry and Ron Clark, while not members of the Panthers, had sympathized with the branch, and after 1972 they represented Washington's disadvantaged. Despite drug and tax-related prosecutions, Barry would continued to be reelected to office in D.C., serving four terms as mayor (with an interruption) and later as city council member, in part because of the antipoverty work he had piloted during the years of the neighboring Panther branch and because of his longtime support of the city's poor black community. Barry described his antipoverty work as his great passion.

Robert Rippy, the founder of the cultural nationalist Black Defenders, would serve three terms in federal prisons for drug-related offenses. In 1998 Rippy lived in Upper Cardozo, where he joined a program that trained public housing residents to help their neighbors protect their health. "The city government now ain't nothing but a bunch of consultants," he was quoted by the *Post* as saying. "Anybody can evaluate something and see the problems. We need to see the solutions."[133]

Many D.C. Panther members and sympathizers continued community activism and local volunteer positions to stay true to the motto of the Black Panther Party, "Power to the People." That the tenure of the Panthers in D.C. was short was the result of exceptional headwinds and obstacles. But their legacy lives on, with community activists and struggles for freedom against oppression.

NOTES

1. See Joe Street, "The Historiography of the Black Panther Party," *Journal of American Studies* 44, no. 2, 351–75, May 2010.

2. Hugh Pearson, *The Shadow of the Panther: Huey Newton and the Price of Black Power* (Reading, Mass.: Addison-Wesley, 1994).

3. Jane Rhodes, *Framing the Panthers: The Spectacular Rise of a Black Power Icon* (New York: New Press, 2007).

4. Curtis J. Austin, *Up Against the Wall: Violence in the Making and Unmaking of the Black Panther Party* (Fayetteville: University of Arkansas Press, 2008).

5. Walter Washington was appointed by Lyndon Baines Johnson after Roy Wilkins had turned down the job.

6. Sherry Brown, lieutenant minister of information and finance for the Baltimore chapter of the Black Panther Party, interview by author, February 20, 2006.
7. "No to Panthers," *Washington Evening Star*, January 22, 1968.
8. "Field Marshal Don Cox at the Conference," *Black Panther*, July 26, 1969.
9. Sherry Brown interview.
10. Sherry Brown interview.
11. Michael A. Fletcher, "Reflections on Chocolate City: The Structure of Change," *Washington Post*, February 1, 1998.
12. "Washington Chapter Official," *Black Panther*, June 26, 1970.
13. Joseph D. Whitaker, "Black Panther Drive Falters in D.C.," *Washington Post*, February 1, 1970. The Black United Front was a D.C.-based organization composed of veteran civil rights leaders.
14. U.S. Census Bureau, *1970 Census of Population: General Social and Economic Characteristics, District of Columbia* (Washington, D.C.: Government Printing Office, 1972).
15. U.S. Census Bureau, *1970 Census of Population: Poverty Status in 1969 and Ratio of Family Income to Poverty Level for Persons in Families and Unrelated Individuals, by Family Relationship, Age and Race, District of Columbia* (Washington, D.C.: Government Printing Office, 1972).
16. Johnnie Dee Swain Jr., "Black Mayors: Urban Decline and the Underclass," *Journal of Black Studies*, 24, no. 1 (September 1, 1993): 22.
17. U.S. Census Bureau, *1970 Census of Population: Labor Force Status and Year Last Worked of Persons Not in the Labor Force by Age, Race, and Sex: 1970* (Washington D.C.: Government Printing Office, 1972).
18. Ibid.
19. Malik Edwards (member and artist of the Washington, D.C., Black Panther Party chapter, 1970–72), interview by author, May 15, 2007.
20. Whitaker, "Black Panther Drive Falters in D.C."
21. On May 4, 1970, on the campus of Kent State University in Ohio, four students were killed and nine others wounded by members of the Ohio National Guard. Some of those shot had been protesting the U.S. invasion of Cambodia, which President Richard Nixon announced on April 30. In response to the killings, universities, colleges, and high schools closed, some for the duration of the spring, due to a strike by students. The Kent State killings further divided the United States along political lines.
22. Edwards interview.
23. By 1967 SNCC had changed its name to the Student *National* Coordinating Committee, an indication of the change in tactics of the group that opposed integration and the Vietnam War, reflecting abandonment of nonviolence.
24. U.S. Census Bureau, *1960 Census of Population: General Social and Economic Characteristics, District of Columbia* (Washington, D.C.: Government Printing Office, 1962).
25. Fred Harris, *Locked in the Poorhouse: Cities, Race, and Poverty in the United States* (New York: Rowman and Littlefield, 1998), 35–39.
26. Nancy Zaroulis and Gerald Sullivan, *Who Spoke Up? American Protest against the War in Vietnam 1963–1975* (New York: Doubleday, 1984), 30–31.
27. Hugh Pearson, *The Shadow of the Panther: Huey Newton and the Price of Black*

Power in America (New York: Addison-Wesley, 1994), 48; H. Rap Brown, *Die Nigger Die!* (New York: Dial Press), 1969.

28. Charles E. Jones, "Reconsidering Panther History," in *The Black Panther Party Reconsidered*, (Baltimore: Black Classic Press, 1998), 39.

29. "Activists Decry White Police Presence," *Washington Post*, May 5, 1969.

30. Kwame Ture (Stokely Carmichael); Charles V. Hamilton, *Black Power: The Politics of Liberation* (New York: Vintage Press, 1992), 71–74.

31. Pearson, *Shadow of the Panther*, 48.

32. Ture, *Black Power*, 76–82.

33. *Justice in Time of Crisis*, District of Columbia Committee on the Administration of Justice under Emergency Conditions Report (Washington, D.C. Government Printing Office, 1969).

34. Whitaker, "Black Panther Drive Falters in D.C."

35. Alma Robinson, "Moore Squares off Again," *Washington Evening Star*, March 15, 1971.

36. "Three Men Form 'Army' to Help Fight Drug Addiction," *Chicago Tribune*, January 18, 1971.

37. Whitaker, "Black Panther Drive Falters in D.C."

38. Ibid.

39. Howard Gillette Jr. *Between Justice and Beauty: Race, Planning, and the Failure of Urban Policy in Washington, D.C.* (Baltimore: Johns Hopkins University Press, 1995), 217–23.

40. U.S. Census Bureau, *1970 Census of Population: General Social and Economic Characteristics, District of Columbia* (Washington, D.C.: Government Printing Office, 1972).

41. Jonathan I. Z. Agronsky, *Marion Barry and the Politics of Race* (New York: British American Publishing, 1991), 167.

42. Marion Barry, interview by author, January 26, 2006.

43. "Barry Nixes Celebration," *Washington Post*, July 22, 1969.

44. "Barry Fights 'No Knock' Crime Bill," *Washington Daily News*, May 14, 1970.

45. Quoted in Agronsky, *Marion Barry*, 150.

46. Barry interview.

47. Paul K. Williams, *The Neighborhoods of Logan, Scott, and Thomas Circles* (Columbia, S.C.: Acadia, 2001), 16–20.

48. Barry interview.

49. Ibid.

50. Michael Anders, "D.C. Activists Marked, Pro-Panther Rally Told," *Washington Evening Star*, December 22, 1969.

51. Whitaker, "Black Panther Drive Falters in D.C."

52. Ibid.

53. "FBI Views Panthers as Threat," *New York Times*, September 8, 1968.

54. "The FBI's Covert Action Program to Destroy the Black Panther Party," Supplementary Detailed Staff Reports on Intelligence Activities and the Rights of Americans, Final Report of the Select Committee to Study Governmental Operations in Intelligence Activities, U.S. Senate, 94th Cong., 1st sess., April 23, 1976.

55. Edwards interview.

56. Jean Linzau, MD (head of the D.C. Panther People's Free Health Clinic, 1972–74), interview by author, April 12, 1996, Washington D.C.

57. Jessica Christina Harris, "Revolutionary Black Nationalism: The Black Panther Party," *Journal of Negro History* 85, no. 3 (Summer 2000): 162–74; Peniel E. Joseph, *Waiting 'til the Midnight Hour: A Narrative History of Black Power in America* (New York: Henry Holt, 2006), 252.

58. Joanne Grant, *Black Protest: 350 Years of History, Documents, and Analyses* (New York: Fawcett Columbine, 1974), 493–95.

59. Sherry Brown interview.

60. George Katsiaficas, *The Imagination of the New Left: A Global Analysis of 1968* (Boston: South End Press, 1987), 120.

61. *Gun-Barrel Politics: The Black Panther Party, 1966–1971, Report by the Committee on Internal Security, House of Representatives, 92nd Congress, First Session* (Washington D.C.: Government Printing Office, 1971), 7–8.

62. David Hilliard, *This Side of Glory* (Chicago: Lawrence Hill Press, 2001), 143–45.

63. "Meridian Hill Park up to Be Renamed Malcolm X Park," *Washington Evening Star*, June 22, 1969.

64. Linzau interview; Sherry Brown interview.

65. Osa Massen, "My Experience as a Community Worker in the BPP," Black Panther Party Alumni, *http://www.itsabouttimebpp.com/Chapter_History/pdf/Washington_D.C. /Osa_Massen.pdf*, accessed December 16, 2016.

66. Donald Lott and Harvey Kabaker, "D.C. Policeman Critically Hurt, Panthers Hit," *Washington Evening Star*, July 5, 1970.

67. Ben McKelway III, "Police vs. Panthers: Two Views," *Washington Daily News*, July 6, 1970.

68. Donald Lott and Harvey Kabaker, "D.C. Policeman Critically Hurt, Panthers Hit," *Washington Evening Star*, July 5, 1970.

69. Ivan C. Brandon, "Panthers Dispute Charges by Police," *Washington Post*, July 6, 1970.

70. "20 Arrested at Center; Officer Hurt," *Washington Afro-American*, July 7, 1970.

71. McKelway, "Police vs. Panthers." The community information center served as a distribution point for the Panther paper.

72. "Seized Black Panther Guns Unregistered, Police Report," *Evening Star*, July 6, 1970.

73. "Panthers Say Police Took Their Money," *Washington Daily News*, July, 7, 1970.

74. "Probe Panther Incident," *Washington Daily News*, July 14, 1970.

75. Willie Dawkins, interview by Vivian Hunt, July 26, 1970, *WMAL-TV Newswatch*, Washington D.C., transcript, National Archives, Washington.

76. Steve McCutchen, conversation with Judson L. Jeffries, December 4, 2016.

77. Esutosin Omonale Oaunkoya, conversation with Judson L. Jeffries, November 7, 2011.

78. "Cooperation Averts Panther Confrontation," *Washington Daily News*, July 22, 1970.

79. Washington D.C. Chapter of the Black Panther Party, "From Washington D.C. Concerning Pig's Plans for Genocide," press release, July 20, 1970, Senator James Eastland files, chairman of the Commission of the Internal Security of the United States, National Archives.

80. Citizen Pilot Precinct Board, "Community Intelligence Report about the BPP," August 1970, Eastland files, National Archives.
81. Flyer for the Revolutionary Peoples Constitutional Convention, November 27–29, 1970, Eastland files, National Archives.
82. "Armory Board Denies Panthers," *Washington Post*, October 8, 1970.
83. Washington Chapter of the Black Panther Party, "Big Man" [Howard], "Why Should D.C. Blacks Pay Taxes?," October 6, 1970, Eastland files, National Archives.
84. "Armory Board Denies Panthers."
85. "U MD Dismisses Panthers," *Washington Post*, August 22, 1970.
86. Flyer for the Revolutionary Peoples Constitutional Convention.
87. "Two Panthers Wanted in Connection with New Orleans NCCF," *Washington Daily News*, September 20, 1970.
88. Ibid.
89. Ward Churchill and Jim Vander Wall, *Agents of Repression: The FBI's Secret Wars against the Black Panther Party and the American Indian Movement* (Boston: South End Press, 1990), 41–53.
90. Yohuru Williams, *Black Politics/White Power: Civil Rights, Black Power, and the Black Panthers in New Haven* (New York: Brandywine Press, 2000).
91. Massen, "My Experience as a Community Worker in the BPP."
92. Sherry Brown interview.
93. Ibid.
94. "All Charges Dismissed in Panther Case," *Washington Post*, October 17, 1970.
95. "Three Convicted in Panther Weapon Case," *Washington Evening Star*, July 7, 1971.
96. "Three Convicted," Virginia News Briefs, *Danville (Va.) Register*, July 7, 1971.
97. "Statement to the Press on the Richmond, Virginia Five," *Black Panther*, November 19, 1970.
98. Richard E. Prince, "Panthers Press Armory Bid," *Washington Post*, October 9, 1970.
99. "Black Panthers Want Howard University to Cancel Fee," *Washington Post*, November 22, 1970.
100. Phil Hilts, "Panther Convention Has a Time but No Place," *Washington Daily News*, November 28, 1970.
101. Ivan C. Brandon and Jim Mann, "Panthers Hold Rockfest, Meet Today," *Washington Post*, November 28, 1970.
102. Ivan C. Brandon and Jim Mann, "Panthers End D.C. Convention," *Washington Post*, November 30, 1970.
103. Hugh Wyatt, "Unconvened Panthers Go Home," *Washington Daily News*, November 30, 1970.
104. Brandon and Mann, "Panthers End D.C. Convention."
105. Ibid.
106. Ben-Chieh Liu, *The Quality of Life in the United States, 1970, Index, Rating, and Statistics* (Kansas City, Mo.: Midwest Research Institute, 1973), 23.
107. Quoted in Michael A. Fletcher, "The Structure of Change," *Washington Post*, February 1, 1998.
108. Ibid.

109. Stokely Carmichael, *Ready for Revolution: The Life and Struggles of Stokely Carmichael (Kwame Ture)* (New York: Scribner, 2005), 78–83.

110. Paul Delaney, "Panther Parley Failure: Problems at Convention in Washington Reflect Philosophical Rift among Blacks," *New York Times*, November 30, 1970.

111. Stephan D. Caplan, "Fourteen Removed from Plane as 'Unruly,'" *Washington Post*, November 30, 1970.

112. Jim Woodson, "Helping Out in Face of Fascist Oppression," *Black Panther*, June 17, 1972.

113. Edwards interview.

114. Linzau interview.

115. Anita Stroud, interview by author, May 31, 2009.

116. John Saar, "Health Clinic Is Opened by Panthers," *Washington Post*, 21 May 21, 1972.

117. Linzau interview.

118. Ibid.

119. Ron Clark, interview by author, February 5, 2006.

120. Elbert "Big Man" Howard, conversation with Judson L. Jeffries, January 3, 2017.

121. Edwards interview.

122. Linzau interview.

123. Ibid.

124. *Trail of Broken Treaties: BIA, I'm Not Your Indian Anymore* (Rooseveltown, N.Y.: Akwesasne Notes, Mohawk Nation, 1974), 77–85.

125. Jacqueline Bolder, "Panthers Shelve Militant Image," *Washington Evening Star*, July 9, 1973.

126. Ibid.

127. Steve McCutchen, conversation with Judson L. Jeffries, December 4, 2016.

128. Stroud interview.

129. Sherry Brown interview.

130. Linzau interview.

131. Bolder, "Panthers Shelve Militant Image."

132. Elbert "Big Man" Howard, editor of the *Black Panther*, email interview by author, February 27, 2006.

133. Quoted in Michael A. Fletcher, "The Structure of Change," *Washington Post*, February 1, 1998.

The Black Panther Party and Community Development in Boston

DUNCAN MACLAURY, JUDSON L. JEFFRIES,
AND SARAH NICKLAS

Eighteenth-century revolutionary activity in America began in Massachusetts, and at the center of it all was Boston. Though not known for its revolutionary activism after the Revolutionary War, Boston has been a site of major political activity from the founding of the United States to today. Boston is a major metropolitan hub, not quite akin to New York City, Los Angeles, or Chicago but important for New England and historically for the United States. The history of African Americans in Boston is as enthralling as that for any major city. The segregation experienced by Boston's black community in the twentieth century was comparable to that of other urban ghettoes around the country. Like other major U.S. cities, Boston also has a rich tradition of African American activism. Although in the nineteenth century the African American population of Boston was a mere 2 percent, African Americans were a vocal minority. On the surface Massachusetts had some of the most liberal laws (comparatively) regarding African Americans in the middle of the nineteenth century because there was no "clearly defined" citizenship for whites only. This legal equality meant that the African American community could easily appeal to the language of freedom. However, "black people found their public worlds governed by white people's preferences," and segregation and inequality persisted despite—and because of—the informal establishment of equality. The term "Cradle of Liberty" was often used to describe Boston in the nineteenth century, but, as pointed out by nineteenth-century orator William Wells Brown, "The term Cradle of Liberty, as applied to Boston, was a mockery.... If it ever was the cradle of liberty, the child had been rocked to death."[1]

The second wave of the Great Migration saw a sizeable increase in the number of African Americans entering Boston.[2] The African American population increased 70 percent in the 1940s, to approximately 40,000 in 1950, and 57 percent in the 1950s, to 63,000 by 1960. And by 1970 the city was 16 percent African American.[3] Despite this growth, the percentage of African American males employed in labor and service jobs in Boston dropped from 65 to 27 percent following World War II.[4] And the community was segregated: in 1970 Boston's black population would be concentrated in a small corridor in the South End, Roxbury, Dorchester, and Mattapan.[5] This segregation, compounded with the reduced job opportunities, meant that many blacks were forced to suffer harsh conditions.

By 1950 Boston was mired in an economic slump, and the city was decaying. Commercially Boston was dying a slow death. Its port was no longer competing with New York, its textile mills were moving south, and the well-off were fleeing to the suburbs. Consequently, the city became "the primary guinea pig for faddish federal experiments."[6] Throughout the 1950s and 1960s, Boston embarked on urban renewal programs and was affected by suburbanization. While urban renewal aimed to improve the city, it had a negative effect on the African American community and was often referred to as "black removal."[7] Former Panther Cappy Pinderhughes concurs: it was "urban renewal equals Negro removal."[8] As suburbanization increased, the city suffered a loss of tax income and jobs.[9]

The demographic makeup of the city was segregated, and certain ethnic groups (Irish and Italians) gained political power and experienced social and upward economic mobility while others did not. The African American population was gerrymandered in a way that limited black accumulation of political power.[10] And this inequality created a hostile environment.

The area of Boston most associated with African Americans in the 1960s was Roxbury. In the early twentieth century, it had been a middle- and upper-middle-class white neighborhood. Between World War I and World War II, its increasingly dilapidated apartments were rented to blacks. Upper Roxbury and Lower Roxbury developed out of a class divide among African American Bostonians.[11] Upper Roxbury was more upper and middle class—sometimes called Sugar Hill in reference to the exclusive section of Harlem—toward Franklin Park and the higher elevations of Roxbury. This section of Roxbury was home to Melnea Cass. Known as the First Lady of Roxbury, Cass was the vice president of the Harriet Tubman Mother's Club and secretary of the Sojourner Truth Club. Lower Roxbury by contrast was much poorer. In the 1940s and 1950s, Lower Roxbury's population pushed "upward" past Dudley Station, followed eventually by an almost total white flight of residents and businesses. Neighboring Dorchester also began to attract more African Americans in the middle of the twentieth century, and Blue Hill Avenue began to compete with the Dudley Station area as a center of African American community and business life in Boston. By the 1960s, Blue Hill Avenue had become a commercial strip, a center for social gatherings, and a place for political and community activism. However, "No one with money or influence cared about Roxbury any more, and the suburb which had been pulled out of the nineteenth century countryside had become a twentieth century slum. The well-tended refuge of the upwardly mobile minority merchant and professional classes was now the neglected and confining black ghetto."[12]

Roxbury became increasingly segregated, turning into a distressed community for the majority of African Americans in Boston. Social services and job opportunities left the neighborhoods, and the community was ignored by the Boston power structure. Such conditions produced an array of unyielding movement that included both militant and nonviolent elements that was as robust as any liberation struggle found on the East Coast. The Black Panther Party of Boston emerged in this urban landscape.

Despite the mountain of literature on the Black Panther Party, surprisingly little has been written about the Panthers in Massachusetts. Even when one scours the Panther historiography, one is likely to find only slivers of evidence of the Panthers' existence in Boston: mentions of Doug Miranda's and Audrea Jones's leadership and the mention in the *Black Panther* of Boston as an official party chapter. In 2008 Jama Lazerow's essay "The Black Panthers at the Water's Edge: Oakland, Boston, and the New Bedford 'Riots' of 1970" was published in *Liberated Territory: Untold Local Perspectives on the Black Panther Party*. While this is the longest scholarly work on the Boston chapter, most of it does not cover the Boston Panthers' history, instead focusing on the role that Boston Panthers played in the New Bedford, Massachusetts, disorders of July 1970. Lazerow writes, "The Panthers there [Boston] were remarkably successful at organizing and sustaining themselves and others in the region, but not at drawing the kind of fire from local authorities that brought national, even international fame—or infamy, depending on one's perspective—and, thus, they have drawn little attention from historians."[13]

One can find a superficial (and at worst erroneous) description of the Boston Panthers in Michael Newton's *Bitter Grain: Huey Newton and the Black Panther Party*. In it Newton writes, "The Panther Party sought to put down roots in Massachusetts' hallowed ground, without success."[14] Nothing could be further from the truth. The Panthers in Boston were effective organizers. They helped empower the African American community and built a solid base of support. Furthermore, their style and substance point a way forward for Panther historiography. It is essential to understand how the Boston Panthers were revolutionaries who simultaneously established social service programs and worked to bring about a caring community in Boston.

Black Panther Party cofounder Huey P. Newton believed that the state had a responsibility to provide for the citizenry—that it was ingrained in the social contract—but there was a disconnect between Boston's African American community and government agencies. In the Boston Panthers' eyes the government had failed in its basic duty and was thus illegitimate. Following Newton and other Panther chapters, the Boston Panthers recognized the lack of needed services and worked within the community to provide food, education, and health care. Consequently, they came to be seen as a group that could serve as a platform for citizens to voice their grievances.

The Boston chapter of the Black Panther Party is a unique case study. There was no mass arrest event, no horrific police raid on party offices, and no shootouts with police.[15] It is possible that the city's authorities did not prioritize the Panthers as a major threat. Publicly acknowledging the Panthers in that way might have engendered sympathy for the Panthers and garnered them more members, and harassing them might have had the unintended consequence of making martyrs out of them. For five years the Black Panthers were a revolutionary force in Boston, defying the odds stacked against them. They organized, rallied, sold the *Black Panther*, provided free breakfasts, opened a free medical clinic, and partnered with other African American organizations in the city. Their members were no less radical in motivations and ideology than Huey Newton or any other Panther, but the Boston Panthers were less ideologues than activists intensely focused on the welfare of their community and providing services to it. The Boston Panthers strove, for themselves and their community, to make their own history rather than to be pawns and perpetuate an oppressive system.[16] Instead of entailing violent clashes with police, the story of the Boston chapter of the BPP is one of community service work and establishment of alternative institutions such as the Franklin Lynch People's Free Health Center, named in honor of an aspiring soul singer who was killed by a Boston police officer.[17]

During the summer of 1967, relations between Roxbury residents and some government agencies, especially the Boston Police Department (BPD), were hostile, to say the least. In the first week of June, a group of organized mothers conducted a sit-in against the welfare department, demanding changes to its policies and practices. When police arrived and carried out the heavy-handed physical removal of the mothers, things escalated into a large melee in the street outside the office. As hundreds of police officers descended on the Boston neighborhood, many youths took to the streets to fight them, and three days of upheaval ensued. After things finally quieted, a sense of unease and disgruntlement continued to simmer in the community.[18]

In the aftermath of the June disorders, many Roxbury residents witnessed an increase police presence. Echoing African Americans nationwide, they argued that the police were not stationed in Roxbury to protect the citizens but to control them. These individuals had come to view themselves as a colonized population. Rather than despairing, some young people mobilized, organizing political groups, many of which identified with the Black Power movement and aspired to generate social and economic change. One of the most prominent of these groups was the Boston chapter of the Black Panther Party. The Boston Panthers would not only work on the ground to provide community services, they would aim to make the community more class-conscious.

The story of the Boston Panthers demonstrates societal conditions that contributed to the mobilization and growth of Black Power and other activist groups in the city. The June 1967 Roxbury disorders are a case in point. The backstory begins in 1965 with the formation in Roxbury of Mothers for Adequate Welfare (MAW). Saying that the welfare department distributed food in a poor manner, the group led a sit-in on April 26, 1965, at the welfare office on Hawkins Street in Roxbury. After two hours, government officials promised to improve the food distribution, and the protesters dispersed. While the group was momentarily appeased, it did not disband. In July 1966 MAW marched on the statehouse, calling for an increase in rental allowance and for the ability to earn a higher income while still receiving welfare. And on May 26, 1967, MAW conducted a sit-in at the Grove Hall welfare office on Blue Hill Avenue in Roxbury, but the group's demands were not even acknowledged by officials.

So it was that on June 2, 1967, MAW led a silent sit-in of fifty mothers inside the Grove Hall welfare office. The mothers' argument was that the welfare system did not meet the basic needs of the community and did not assist recipients in developing skills to join the workforce. They demanded representation on welfare boards as well as an increase in stipends and the development of work-training programs. At about 4:20 p.m. on June 2, the mothers locked themselves—and fifty-eight government employees—inside the building. At 4:45 p.m., police and firefighters responded to reports that a woman was having a heart attack at the welfare office. Finding doors locked, the police forcefully entered the building.[19] Discovering what was actually going on inside, the police attempted to disperse the crowd and reportedly exercised excessive force in removing the mothers. In the *Boston Globe* the next day, a reporter wrote, "Tension mounted in the crowd outside when police tried to remove protesting women from a city-owned building. A woman screamed. Glass shattered. Physical contact followed. In a flash disorder broke out."[20] Police officers would claim that protesters had attacked them and obstructed the door of the office.[21] Other articles asserted that the police had acted with excessive force and incited the disturbance by beating protesters. Individuals participating in the protest-turned-riot affirmed that police had been aggressive with the women, using "vulgar language" including the word "nigger."

The rioting did not cease on June 2 but continued for three days. Businesses were looted and two buildings were burned. Community leaders attempted to quell it, but thousands of residents took to the streets expressing opposition to the police action and racial inequality. On June 3, in front of the Grove Hall office building, MAW leaders gave an account of the previous day's events and described the police use of force. Listeners were enraged, police broke up the gathering, and people began to vent their frustrations on the streets. The city dispatched seventeen hundred police officers, and police fired between eighty and a hundred rounds of ammunition into the air. This did not pacify the crowd but instead further enraged it. The following night, June 4, was noted as the most violent night of rebellion: individuals threw rocks, bricks, and Molotov cocktails and addressed sniper fire toward police officers. The city increased the police presence to nineteen hundred officers before events worked their way back to normal. The demonstrations resulted in numerous arrests and casualties—including a fire lieutenant shot through the wrist—and further increased the disconnect between the community, especially the youth, and the state.[22]

In the days that followed, residents questioned the actions taken by the police. A reporter for the *Globe* interviewed several young Roxbury men: "'Why did they have to start swinging the sticks Friday,' said several of the youth. 'They don't use the sticks over in Charlestown when people protest. That's because they're white over there. It was the police that started the riot.'"[23] People also questioned the massiveness of the police response. The *Globe* reported that only 1 percent of Roxbury's population had participated in the upheaval, but the city had sent in nearly two thousand officers. Many of the young people stated that the only way to quell the violence was for the police to leave Roxbury.[24] Not surprisingly, Mayor John Collins, a Democrat, defended the police action, saying that the police had demonstrated excellent restraint.[25] The mayor fully supported the police and the measures taken and placed the blame on "criminal elements." Roxbury residents argued that the upheaval resulted from political exclusion.[26]

In the aftermath, numerous Roxbury youths began to organize, in part to present grievances against the Boston Police Department. Many decried the community's lack of economic opportunities. One individual said, "The governor, the President, and all that, they say for us to stay in school. But then we get through school, and there's no job. They say you've got to be 21, or you've got to have a college degree."[27] Even with educational support and professional career opportunities, African Americans made on average less than three-quarters of the income of their white counterparts.[28] Then as now, institutional barriers hindered African American financial advancement and contributed to a sense of disenfranchisement.[29]

Government officials did acknowledge problems within the welfare system, and academics pointed to the inadequacy of its distribution of resources. Dean Robert F. Drinan of Boston College Law School, prior to the June upheaval, had conducted an in-depth analysis of the welfare system in Roxbury and the South End and concluded that the system was inherently invidious. He wrote to the Committee on State Administration of the Massachusetts legislature: "The most pertinent conclusion (of the panel) is that the system that has evolved for dispensing welfare funds and attempting to meet the needs of thousands appears to result in discrimination against the impoverished regardless of how well intentioned those who administer the system."[30] Following the initial

MAW protest at Grove Hall, Police Commissioner Edmund L. McNamara had met with leaders of the NAACP, as well as other civil rights leaders. "It is very helpful if any group aids the community," the June 3 *Globe* quoted him as saying. "We are soliciting the aid of any person or group willing to assist in maintaining peace in the community."[31] Government and civil rights representatives alike emphasized the necessity in maintaining law and order in the city.

Dean Drinan was not alone. A 1965 sociological study on ghetto rebellions argued that when segments of society are excluded from government practices, they were more likely to react with violence and protest than they would be if not excluded. Neighborhoods with adequate representation were less at risk for insurrection and seditious activity.[32] MAW mirrored this finding. Their attempts to promote change within the existing structure had been stonewalled, and thus they had turned to direct action. Immediately following the upheaval of June 2–4, 1967, Massachusetts U.S. senators Edward M. Kennedy (D) and Edward W. Brooke (R) publicly recognized a deficient welfare system in the state. The senators released similar statements deploring the violence but saying that the state needed to address and reform inadequacies within the system.[33] The *Globe* quoted Brooke as stating that the protesting mothers were demanding an "adequate voice in the allocation of funds. I think the mothers are entitled to a voice." Likewise in the *Globe*, Kennedy acknowledged the discontent within the young and how funding and programs addressing youth employment were lacking in the state due to budget cuts.[34] These statements acknowledge an underserved community and suggest the importance of truly including Roxbury citizens in policy making.

Clearly the black community saw an absence of opportunities and a lack of goods and services. The Roxbury riots of June 1967, while brief, demonstrate hostility against the state, especially the police and especially by young people. It was within this tense period that the Black Panthers emerged in Boston.

The Black Panther Party in Boston

Founded primarily by former members of the Student Nonviolent Coordinating Committee (SNCC) in the late spring and early summer of 1968, the Boston chapter of the BPP remained largely "hidden behind the heavy curtains of its storefront office at 375 Blue Hill [Avenue]," according to the *Boston Globe*.[35] In sync with the general mission of the BPP, the Boston Panthers aimed to foster community consciousness and provide basic needs as well as serve as a platform to voice grievances and demands. Doug Miranda, reared in Roxbury, states that the Panthers were "in the community to serve poor people" and were endeavoring to "create a situation where these little brothers and sisters [could] become revolutionaries."[36] The Panthers aimed to enlighten the Boston community regarding class struggle and promoted an ideology that focused on radical community development through what the party called survival programs (free breakfast for schoolchildren, among others). It was not until August 9, 1968, however, that the party made its first public appearance in Boston with a "Service for Oppressed Peoples" in support of its minister of defense, Huey P. Newton, who was on trial in California.[37] This event was held at the St. Philip Catholic Church in Roxbury in conjunction with other radical groups, such as the United Farm Workers (UFW) and the Massachusetts Catholic Peace Committee.[38] At the service, Panthers Jerry Verone and Chico Neblett (a former SNCC member and a reported BPP field marshal) spoke to the congregation about Newton and the "Free Huey" movement.[39]

As summer faded into fall, the Boston Panthers were organizing for the national boycott of non-union-grown California grapes, teaching political education classes for adults and youth, and forming connections to other leftist groups in the Boston area.[40] The Boston Panthers' participation in the grape boycott is not surprising, considering the California connection: the Panthers and the United Farm Workers had worked together in Oakland.[41] In California, scholar Lauren Ariza writes, the "willingness and ability to find class-based commonalities across racial lines ... enabled the [UFW] and the [BPP] to form a successful, mutually beneficial alliance."[42] In Boston, the *Globe* reported at the time, the Panthers were part of a boycott coalition made up of "white housewives, [Students for a Democratic Society groups], peace groups and hawks, Resisters [sic] and politicians, professors and dropouts, old and young."[43] Connections formed through the boycott likely strengthened ties between activist communities in Boston. This may have led to the Panthers' invitation to speak at a rally to end the Vietnam War, under the rubric Massachusetts Mobilization to End the War in Vietnam, on Saturday, November 9, 1968.[44]

As in Panther chapters across the country, political education classes were a mandatory part of being a full-fledged member of the party. The list of political readings varied. Among them were Fanon's *The Wretched of the Earth*, *The Autobiography of Malcolm X*, Kwame Nkrumah's *I Speak of Freedom*, LeRoi Jones's *Blues People*, E. D. Cronin's *Black Moses*, Lerone Bennett Jr.'s *Before the Mayflower*, and W. E. B. Du Bois's *Black Reconstruction in America* and *Souls of Black Folk*.[45] The Panthers also formed a "Junior Black Panther Party" for young boys, which Panther leader Delano Farrar explained to the *Bay State Banner* as "teach[ing] culture, economics and politics to youngsters as a means of providing a positive male image, especially for fatherless kids."[46] These classes were held in Northeastern University's Ell Center and at Operation Black at 366 Blue Hill Avenue a couple of days each week. They were taught by Wendell Bourne, the Boston deputy minister of education, and Frank Hughes, Boston deputy chairman.[47]

Political education classes were open to members of the community. The Panthers strove to assist African American residents in developing a political consciousness and understanding of their role in the community. Through achieving this, residents would learn how to change the status quo. To be sure, the Boston Panthers also used these classes to teach Panther ideology as well as the role of the party in the community, nation, and the world. Through these classes the Panthers tapped into a large young adult population that felt disengaged from the political process. As the 1967 disorders demonstrated, these residents felt that government agencies were not assisting in the betterment of their communities but rather perpetuating the inequalities that existed. The Panthers believed that through these political education classes they could foment a revolutionary consciousness among the people.

There are some notable omissions from the Boston Panther political education booklist. The absence of socialist and Marxist literature by Mao Zedong and Ernesto "Che" Guevara speaks to differences in the ideology of local Boston Panthers and the national leaders who had been heavily influenced by the likes of Mao. Some of this difference likely stemmed from the Boston Panthers' SNCC connections and influence. SNCC had become, through the leadership of Stokely Carmichael, a black nationalist group focused on identity and blackness as the most important hallmarks of radicalism and consciousness. The Panther leaders in Oakland, although influenced by black nationalism, were much more focused on a struggle founded on class consciousness. They identified the intersectionality of race and class through an emphasis on Third World revolutionary socialism, most strongly identified with Mao Zedong and his "Little Red Book." The Black Panthers and SNCC, after a brief merger, would split over this ideological difference. The Boston Panthers seem to have been in a similar position, adhering to SNCC ideology while calling themselves Black Panthers.

The year 1968 was one of changes for Boston and for the United States. The Black Panther Party grew nationally in the spring, summer, and fall, and the Boston Panthers were a part of this rapid growth. The deaths of Martin Luther King Jr. and Oakland Panther Bobby Hutton, the arrest of Panther minister of information Eldridge Cleaver, the political force of the "Free Huey" campaign, and the temporary alliance between the Panthers and SNCC created a national imperative for Panther chapters to form.[48] Boston's black activist community readily accepted the Black Panther Party as a new actor in the radical tradition of the city. But the ways the Boston chapter was founded—and the people who founded it—eventually caused tension in the ranks, sparking a revolt and a purge. More than one purge would transpire in the spring and summer of 1969, and these would change the shape and impetus of the party in Boston.[49]

1969

The New Year did not immediately bring change to the Panthers in Boston. They continued to support black student groups, backing, for example,

Brandeis students in their takeover of Ford and Sydeman Halls demanding "better minority representation on campus."[50] The *Globe* reported that, six days into the occupation, the Panthers had "made frequent trips to Ford Hall to help operate workshops on politics, political tactics, [and] black pride."[51] The first record of the Black Panther Party as an official part of the Boston Black United Front (BBUF) dates to notes of a February 17 meeting where Delano Farrar, the Panther representative on the BBUF steering committee, was selected as "Communication" chair for the committee.[52] The Panthers seem to have continued in this role in April, when they were delegated to be in charge of communications for Operation STOP.[53]

The first reported harassment of Panthers by the Boston Police Department was January 21, 1969, when Boston police arrested Farrar and another Panther, Michael Atkins, for allegedly stealing a woman's pocketbook.[54] In his write-up of the incident for the *Black Panther* newspaper, Wendell Bourne emphasized that the charges of "purse-snatching, possession of marijuana, and receiving stolen goods" were ridiculous for a variety of reasons.[55] Such falsified charges were a common police tactic to intimidate dissenters, like the Panthers, and attempt to get them off the streets. One tactic the FBI employed to target the BBP was to deny them access to the *Black Panther* newspaper. This was part of COINTELPRO's systematic attack on local chapters of the Black Panther Party over a number of years.[56] The Panthers in Boston would have a similar experience over a year later. In August 1970, of twenty-two boxes of the *Black Panther* sent to the Panthers in Boston, only seventeen would be received. Of these seventeen, three would be found to have been drenched with kerosene "to have the print run."[57]

Much of this repression may have come about due to how the Boston Panthers were perceived. The Panthers in Boston could match national BPP leaders with fiery rhetoric. In January 1969, T. D. Pauley, assistant field marshal of the Boston Panthers, told a group of Nasson College students in Springvale, Maine, to "leave us [the 'black ghetto areas'] alone and either do missionary work in your own community or commit suicide."[58] Pauley is an interesting study of members the Boston Panthers attracted. He was a graduate of both Harvard University and the Boston College Law School.[59] It is likely that Pauley's education allowed him to tailor his speeches to different communities and touch nerves and push boundaries in the ways that were most advantageous to the mission of the Boston Panthers. As Jane Rhodes explores in *Framing the Black Panthers*, the rhetoric and media presence of the Panthers were consciously used to catch the attention of, and anger, the established power structure of the United States while appealing to the militant fervor of radical communities in the country.[60]

But the Panthers in Boston were not just firebrands; they were politically conscious and interacted with much more moderate strains of the black liberation struggle. On April 4, 1969, the one-year anniversary of the assassination of Martin Luther King Jr., a Good Friday memorial march was held through Roxbury.[61] One of the stops on the march was in front of the Panther office on Blue Hill Avenue, where Delano Farrar read a eulogy for King as well as for several slain Panthers.[62] Ingratiating themselves with the community in Boston and connecting with the popular image of King allowed the Boston Panthers to attract more supporters than would have come to a rally focused on freeing Huey Newton. This adaptability and tailoring of message depending on the context were important for the Panthers as they gained supporters and members.

But the Panthers in Boston also continued to support their imprisoned leader. On May 1, 1969, the Black Panther Party organized rallies around the country to support Newton. Rallies were held at federal courthouses in San Francisco, Chicago, Los Angeles, Indianapolis, Des Moines, Kansas City, Denver, Detroit, and Boston.[63] The Boston Panthers seemingly worked in line with the national leaders of the party. But something was amiss. The *Black Panther* of July 19, 1969, declared of the Boston chapter, "As of May 24, 1969 these renegade, cultural nationalist opportunists are no longer members of the Black Panther Party." The paper stated that seventeen listed party members were purged for the following reasons:

1. Failure to follow the teachings of Minister of Defense, Huey P. Newton.
2. For complete disregard for the discipline of the Party.
3. Subjectivism.
4. Opportunism against the people.
5. Propagating cultural nationalist madness inside the Party instead of class struggle.
6. Racism.
7. Individualism.[64]

All of the Boston branch leaders were purged. Chico Neblett, field marshal; T. D. Pauley, assistant field marshal; Delano Farrar, area captain; Frank Hughes, lieutenant of information; Karen Flippen, lieutenant of finance; Kay Glaspy, communications secretary; Rene Neblett (wife of Chico), lieutenant of culture; Yazid Nzinga, section leader; and Mike Claytor, subsection leader, were all expelled from the party. The story, as told by the *Black Panther*, is one of internal rebellion and an attempted coup led by Chico Neblett, but this makes no sense, as Neblett was the seemingly top-ranked Boston branch member, hence it is more likely that those who "affirmed annew [sic] the discipline of the Party and [have] purged these fools from the Party ranks" were the usurpers.[65]

Doug Miranda remembers the sequence of events leading up to the purge as follows: "Me and others didn't feel that the leadership was doing what it was supposed to be doing . . . they simply weren't providing the kind of leadership we needed. Then there was the question of ideology. . . . They focused on race.... They were more cultural nationalists, while we believed both race and class were important." The "we" to whom Miranda refers includes himself, Audrea Jones, Gene Jones, Gregory Jones, and Floyd Hardwick. According to Miranda, a call was placed to central headquarters and concerns were expressed. Not long after that, Panther field marshal Donald Cox, aka DC, arrived in Boston along with Robert Webb. Says Miranda: "So DC comes.... Robert Webb is with him as his security.... We meet at the old Blue Hill office.... You could feel the tension. They're on one side, we're on the other.... DC listens to both sides.... DC is a very calm and deliberate Brother. Like I said, Robert Webb is there too.... Webb's a good comrade, Brother. Very helpful. He's relatable. He listens to folks. The meeting ends with DC purging the leadership of the chapter."[66]

With that, new leaders were installed. Miranda is quick to point out that the majority of the rank and file made it known that they wanted a change in leadership. Miranda was selected as the area captain, Audrea Jones took on the duties of communications secretary, Gene Jones was lieutenant of information, Gregory Jones was lieutenant of defense, and Floyd Hardwick was lieutenant of education.[67] The new cadre of Boston Panthers was not only more in tune with the goals and objectives of the national party leaders but with the community as well. According to Miranda, only a few members of the previous regime were native Bostonians, whereas everyone among the new leadership was a native. While this may seem a minor point, the new leaders apparently had an immediate advantage over the previous regime. They were in tune with the machinations of the Boston power structure, they knew the lay of the land, and they had contacts with groups and people that had been built over a lifetime (albeit not decades—members ranged from their teens to mid-twenties).

The new leaders took the opportunity to assert their authority and shape the Panthers in Boston as they saw fit. Greg Jones recalled that the split in Boston was between those Panthers who read and internalized Mao's "Little Red Book" and those in the party who carried the book around but did not read it. Jones remembered, "We were talking socialistic ideas," while "they [the purged members] were always cleaning their guns" and "thought it was a black struggle," not a class struggle.[68]

The expulsion of Chico Neblett specifically was also tied to the dynamics between the Black Panther Party and SNCC. The *Black Panther* stated, rather harshly, that Neblett had "joined the party with the other boot-licker Stokely Carmichael."[69] Carmichael officially resigned from his post as prime minister of the Black Panther Party on July 3, 1969, because of his disagreement with the Panthers' "willingness to ally with whites."[70] Not surprisingly, the marriage between the Panthers and SNCC ended just as abruptly as it began.

The placement of Doug Miranda, only twenty years old in 1969, into a leadership role proved to be a turning point for the chapter. Miranda had grown up in Boston, in a steady, working-class, two-parent, Cape Verdean household that included six children, three boys and three girls. Miranda's father, a World War II veteran of the U.S. Air Force, was a factory worker (a material cutter), and his mother was a homemaker who worked outside the home sporadically until her mid-thirties, at which point she earned her GED and started working for the Boston welfare department. The values that Miranda learned from his parents stood him in good stead as head of the chapter. "They impressed upon me a sense of fairness and justice.... I also learned the importance of treating people with respect and decency," recalls Miranda. A graduate of Thompson Academy, a prep school located on Boston's Thompson Island, Miranda had a familiarity with the city that one would expect of someone who had lived there all his life. While Miranda's father was by all accounts conservative politically, his mother supported progressive black politics, so it wasn't entirely surprising when Miranda elected to join the Black Panther Party.

Miranda became involved with the party at the urging of Kathleen Cleaver, Eldridge's wife, whom he met while vacationing in Hawaii. Says Miranda, "It was in the summer of 1968, and Eldridge was running for president.... The Peace and Freedom Party had invited Kathleen out there to speak.... After she spoke I walked up to her and introduced myself.... I shared with her that I liked what she had to say and that I was interested in joining the party. Then she asked me where I was from, and I told her Boston, at which point she told me that if I was interested in joining the party I should go back to Boston and join there." Miranda had flown to Honolulu from the Bay Area, where he had been living for a time. After a stint at North Shore Community College in Massachusetts and having lived in Massachusetts all his life, Miranda had wanted to get away and so had moved west. In Miranda's opinion, "The movement on the West Coast was much more politically developed." After moving west, Miranda supported the 1968 student and faculty strike at San Francisco State College although he was never a student there.

After meeting Kathleen Cleaver, Miranda eventually returned to Boston where he joined the Black Panther Party. Says Miranda, "There was a group of us who went by the Panther office to join up.... I don't remember who greeted me at the office, but not long after that I was doing the work that Panthers do... selling the newspaper and things like that." Later, after members of branches and chapters were summoned to the Bay Area, Miranda would help organize a strike at Merritt College in the early 1970s. Miranda remembers that there was a move by authorities to close down the Grove Street Campus of Merritt College. "Huey told me to mobilize support among the students and others in response to what many believed to be an impending closure of the campus... so I helped organize a strike.... That put an end to any ideas on the part of administrators and officials to shut down the campus."[71] It was not surprising that Newton chose Miranda for this task as he was seen as an extremely effective organizer. Miranda had shown an innate ability to inspire those around him while on the East Coast. He was able to deal with all kinds of people, even the privileged elite students at Harvard or Yale—by engaging with them or "trouncing a representative of [SNCC] in a public debate on Marxism"—while gaining the respect of elements of the party that required a firm hand.[72]

Following the purge of the "cultural nationalists" from the Boston chapter in May 1969, the new leaders of the Panthers in Boston took it upon themselves to reach out to the community more than the previous leadership had. They began a free breakfast program for schoolchildren, sold the *Black Panther*, taught political education classes, lent support to families in need (and at least one grieving mother), and organized meetings and outreach events, such as a rally to promote the image of the Panthers in Boston and raise community awareness. As the new leaders reached out to the community, Miranda recalls, "we also worked hard internally to strengthen the chapter ... developing the cadre in a holistic manner."[73]

The BPP had begun as a group dedicated to the protection of the African American community, and as the Boston Panthers reinvented themselves they followed this model of community outreach. On June 28, 1969, they worked with the community to support and lend protection to a black family that had moved into an all-white neighborhood in Dorchester.[74] Joseph Fontes, a father of three, was injured by a brick, and the family's apartment door had been kicked in and windows smashed by a "gang of [white] youths." After calling the police and getting no response for more than an hour, Fontes called the Black Panther Party, who sent members immediately. Gregory Jones was arrested by the police when the Panthers arrived on the scene, for carrying a rifle openly on the street.[75] On June 30, the Panthers pledged to continue to protect the Fontes family for as long as was required. However, their presence was not welcomed by all in the Dorchester community: the *Boston Globe* reported that a "[white] kid" had stated that "everyone is scared" because the Black Panther Party was coming to their neighborhood.[76] This focus on community protection continued into the summer. On Sunday, July 20, at one in the morning, Panther Bob Jackson received a phone call from the daughter of Marion Alston, who had been arrested. Though it does not seem that the Panthers intervened—Alston's husband was able to cover bail—the calling of the Black Panther Party itself was seen as a dangerous political act by the police, who were said to have threatened that "if any Panthers came over to protect her, they would shoot them."[77] In a similar act of community protection, the Boston Panthers were reportedly called to a riot-like situation brewing in the Maverick housing project in East Boston on September 6, 1969.[78]

The Panthers in Boston also stood up for the legal rights of the African American community there, with acts of community solidarity and support in addition to physical protection. Ruby Ransom was the mother of an eleven-year-old who drowned at a Metropolitan District Commission (MDC) pool in Dorchester on July 6, 1969. The Panthers held a press conference on July 12, in front of their office at 375 Blue Hill Avenue, to distribute pamphlets and place blame for Ransom's son's death on the MDC for their lack of upkeep of the pool. The Panthers claimed that the pool was "filthy at the time of the drowning... [and that] it was over-crowded, preventing proper supervision."[79] This led to an investigation of the pool that verified the accusations.[80]

By July, the Boston Panthers' breakfast program was feeding somewhere between thirty-five and fifty children every weekday morning at the Tremont Street Methodist Church in the South End, a meal of "orange juice, cereal and pancakes."[81] Breakfast programs, a mainstay of Black Panther chapters across the country, are essential to understanding the Panthers beyond the rhetoric and firearms. The idea was to fill a need in the African American community, to feed malnourished schoolchildren. The Boston Panthers served food to children who would "not otherwise be fed in the morning and have to settle for the inadequate lunches that are prepared at the public schools."[82] In an article titled "To Feed Our Children," the author writes that "this program was created because the Black Panther Party understands that our children need a nourishing breakfast every morning so that they can learn." Without this basic sustenance, black children could not cognitively perform in school, which affected their relationships with their teachers and fellow students. The article further states: "The Breakfast for Children is the first of many programs by the Black Panther Party to satisfy the pressing needs of our Black Community. In order that these programs are fully responsive to The needs of the people, we are organizing men and women From all areas of life and all economic backgrounds in our community To serve the people as a community Advisory Committee to the Black Panther Party." This demonstrates how the Panthers developed support. Gaining community buy-in and collaboration was essential in order for the Panthers to sustain credibility. Furthermore, the Boston Panthers acknowledged how economic disparities not only affected education but also physical and mental growth. Without proper nutrition, children would not be able to actualize their full potential, physically, spiritually, or intellectually.

Though the Panthers were successful with their breakfast program, they faced pushback from businesses from which they requested support, according to an article in the *Black Panther* from July 1969.[83] They also faced some pushback against their efforts to hold "liberation classes" following breakfast in the morning. The intent was for Panthers to help to create a situation where "little brothers and sisters [could] become revolutionaries," according to Miranda.[84] The church originally hosting the breakfast program pushed back against the establishment of liberation classes. Most members of the community—black or white, revolutionary or conservative—agreed that feeding hungry children was a good thing, but not all could agree with the propaganda it was implied that the Panthers would feed these children along with cereal and juice. J. Edgar Hoover, director of the FBI, was staunchly against the Panther breakfast programs, specifically because of the threat that he saw of indoctrination into revolutionary thought. Of course, this was part of the Panther model, and they desired to build community support, and the community included schoolchildren. But the breakfast program was also what it superficially seemed: a service that benefited those most in need, hungry children who had previously gone to school on empty stomachs.

To help reestablish themselves as a legitimate group after the purge by national Panther leaders, the Boston Panthers began a public outreach campaign. They received more national Panther promotional materials, put posters up all around Roxbury, and pushed sales of the *Black Panther* newspaper.[85] Gene Jones claimed that at the Newport Jazz Festival in July 1969, about seventy miles south of Boston, the Panthers were able to sell four thousand copies of the *Black Panther*.[86] In Boston, according to Miranda, three of the best places to sell the *Black Panther* were Dudley Station, Downtown Crossing, and Harvard Square.[87]

On July 18–20, Miranda and Floyd Hardwick attended the United Front Against Fascism conference in Oakland, organized by the party's central committee. They wanted to connect with other local chapters across the country, build interracial and intersectional coalitions, and keep the Boston branch in alignment with the national organization.[88] Through the Boston Black United Front, Miranda was able to secure $500 for the trip to California. While in the Bay Area, Miranda remembers, he went to a "revolutionary bookstore" in San Francisco and bought a truckload of books that he took back with him to Boston. "I had everything... books by Stalin, Lenin, Fidel, and Mao.... I brought these books for the comrades in the chapter.... I knew we had to develop politically.... We pored over this stuff... we discussed it... we analyzed it... we learned what we needed to learn." Also key to the chapter's political maturation was Floyd Hardwick, who, Miranda says, "was instrumental in teaching us politics.... Floyd was older than the rest of us.... He knew the players in Boston.... He helped us understand Marxism.... He taught us a lot.... He grounded us in the politics of the times."[89]

A native of Trenton, New Jersey, Hardwick had been in the military and the workforce before joining the party. "You have to understand, I was ten to fifteen years older than many of them," says Hardwick. He had come to Boston from New Hampshire, where he had served in the air force from 1956 to 1960. Hardwick was also married and had four kids. "I think I may have been married for ten years by the time I... joined the Black Panther Party," he recalls. Hardwick had attended the Wentworth Institute of Technology, where he had studied aeronautics and space engineering. Although he did not complete the program, what he learned there served him well in the two white-collar jobs that he secured in the following years. Hardwick worked as a research technician in the Department of Environmental and Health Sciences at the Harvard School of Public Health for approximately four years. His job was to study nuclear power plants and the best ways to clean up waste in the event a plant broke down or blew up in a densely populated area. After this job he worked as the director of a methadone clinic at Boston University. Hardwick decided to join the party after he read the ten-point platform in the Panther newspaper. "When I read the ten-point program/platform, I knew this was the organization for me," he says.[90]

When asked to comment on Miranda's recollections of him and the manner in which he conducted political education (P.E.) classes, Hardwick offers:

> I had been studying Left literature before the Black Panther Party ever arrived in Boston.... Plus I already had a background in left-wing circles. I helped deepen their understanding of the material they read. Most of what I talked about in P.E. class, if I remember correctly, was the 10 point program/platform. I encouraged discussion in P.E. class.... When I went to Oakland and San Francisco I was shocked at how P.E. classes were carried out. Let me just say that in Boston there was no intimidation, no bullying... the atmosphere was relaxed. What I wanted to do was interpret the party line in a way that the people in the room could relate to and understand in their own lived experience. I did not use terms like 'off the pig' in P.E. class.... I focused on helping people understand their culture, their history, and recognize the marginalization of black folk and what we needed to do about it.

Hardwick is quick to point out that when he went to Oakland for the United Front Against Fascism conference, he noticed some stark differences: "The Panthers in Boston, at least during my time as a Panther, were not lumpenproletariat.... We were people who were holding down jobs or going to school; we were leading normal lives.... Things were a bit different in Boston than they were in Oakland."[91]

The establishment of a branch of the National Committee to Combat Fascism (NCCF) in Cambridge, Massachusetts, by the Boston Panthers was one of the tangible outcomes of the United Front Against Fascism conference, further connecting Boston Panthers to the white left.[92] Headed by Kitty Harding, a graduate of Connecticut College, the NCCF was located on Western Avenue, and a free breakfast program was operated here. Harding was one of a number of progressive whites who supported what the Panthers were doing in a myriad of concrete ways. Throughout the summer of 1969 the Panthers organized a couple of public meetings that included participation from various groups, with the intention of increasing community response and activity with the Party. Boston Panthers were interviewed on the radio station WEZE in July, and at the Blue Hill Christian Center on Blue Hill Avenue they held a "people's meeting" on the night of July 1, to discuss ways in which they could bring people together.[93] On the evening of July 3, the Black Panther Party of Boston met at the Cambridge YWCA in Central Square to talk about the "goals and tactics... plus [explain the] new breakfast program for children."[94] The Boston Panthers were reaching out to a wide Boston audience to promote their programs and services.

On July 6, the Panthers organized a rally at Franklin Park for the African American community in Boston.[95] Three hundred people, adults and children, gathered for the picnic-like atmosphere of the rally, which demanded "community control of the police" and the renaming of Franklin Park to Malcolm X Memorial Park.[96] At the rally, the Panthers set out the platform and program of the Black Panther Party. In addition, Miranda called on the community: "Tell us what you want. Tell us what you need." The Panther speakers discussed the breakfast program, a desire for liberation classes, and the need for community control of the police. Gene Jones explained community control as "'a separate and autonomous' police force, to be controlled by 'the working class—not the bourgeoisie, not the ruling class, not the bootlickers they call community spokesmen.'" The audience also heard a speaker from the Black Student Federation and one from the Parents for Justice in Welfare Rights discussing their own programs and ideologies.[97]

The Boston Panthers worked in solidarity with other activist groups in the city to build support. At South End rally in support of Cuba, the Panthers spoke about the party's endorsement of "the 'people's struggle' against the [Boston Redevelopment Authority]," showing their alignment with leftist organizing already going on in the city.[98] On August 9, the Panthers took part in a march organized by a variety of radical organizations, walking the Freedom Trail, a two-and-a-half-mile path through downtown Boston, with three hundred people to protest the Vietnam War.[99] These appearances helped cement their involvement with radical politics in the city and to make their presence known.

While the Panthers in Boston were furthering their goals of community control of social services, the police and FBI were stepping up their efforts against the Panthers. That same week, Miranda, John Cheatham, William Jackson, David Quick, and Ida Walston were arrested while driving back from a rally in New Haven to support those accused of the murder there of Alex Rackley.[100] The five were all charged with "conspiracy and actual transportation of a stolen vehicle across state lines"—the car that the Panthers had rented to drive to New Haven had apparently been "taken from a Seattle [Washington] rental agency June 13th, by use of a stolen credit card."[101] The Panthers' lawyer said that the charges lacked certain seriousness and seemed to be more of a tactic to harass the Panthers than actually imprison them.[102] Miranda remembers the incident clearly and is able to provide details not found in the press: "We went to New Haven to speak at a rally... [and] we were arrested on the highway as we were returning to Boston.... Let me be clear when I tell you that we, meaning my comrades and I, didn't rent that car. In fact, we were led to believe that the vehicle belonged to Ida Walston.... We didn't know anything about the car being a rental or about any stolen credit card. We would have never gotten involved in anything like that. Ida gave us the impression that the car belonged to her... she had been driving the car the whole time I knew her." Who was Ida Walston? Miranda says, "This was a sister who came around the office one day and said she wanted to get involved in what we were doing... she said she was from the West Coast and that she had two kids." The story about the two kids turned out to be true. In fact the children, a boy and a girl, accompanied the Panthers on that trip to New Haven. Whether or not Walston participated in a set-up of the Boston Panthers is unclear. What is indisputable, however, is that at no time did Walston ever make an attempt to disclose to the Panthers the particulars regarding the vehicle, "nor did she ever mention that she was wanted for smuggling," says Miranda.[103] Walston's case is typical of other Panthers who were thought to be informants but were never proven to be. A Panther's actions or recklessness leads to the arrest of other Panthers. Said Panther is separated from his or her comrades upon being arrested and taken into custody, never to be seen or heard from again.

In response to this incident, and to raise bail money, the Boston Panthers were involved in a film festival during the weekend of August 15–17 in Boston.[104] Free on bail, Miranda was again targeted by the police, this time in Boston, on August 17, when, accompanied by Gene Jones, he was accused of a traffic violation. Miranda and Jones were on their way home on the final night of the film festival, when the Boston Police Department "brought 10–12 carloads of pigs with guns drawn, within two minutes" of the initial stop.[105] As in many cases of police harassment of the Black Panthers across the country, the actual charges were factual—in this case Miranda pled guilty to driving without a license—but the methods employed to carry out stops and arrests entailed overwhelming force in an attempt to intimidate and break the spirit of the Panthers.[106] The excessive show of force by the Boston police against two Panthers shows the threat that was felt by the Boston power structure.

One of the most important Panthers in Boston, both as an organizer and as a symbol of the party, was Robert "Big Bob" Heard. He was an imposing figure on the Boston streets. A report in the *Black Panther* said that Bob was six foot seven, weighed 390 pounds, and was willing "to lay down his life to achieve our goal of liberation."[107] However, this only conveys half of the story. Heard was imposing physically, but he was also an active organizer and valuable teacher, making him doubly dangerous for the Boston Police Department. For the Panthers, Heard was a symbol of the party's best, as showcased by his valorization in the *Black Panther* for his numerous arrests and police harassment. On August 20, 1969, Heard was arrested for "taking scraps of metal from an open field"—a seemingly ridiculous charge that, if true, could only have been a pretense to detain Heard for intimidation reasons.[108] On October 23, 1969, Heard was arrested, and taken to Boston Police Department's tenth station, where he was confronted by a woman named Marilyn Taart.[109] Taart, whom the *Black Panther* would later call a traitor to her race and an agent of the police, identified Heard as one of the two men who had stolen her pocketbook at gunpoint on October 21.[110] A rally was held on November 12 to protest the arrest of Heard and other "political prisoners" in the United States.[111] The Boston Panthers gathered supporters against the police brutality and harassment that was now evident nationwide in cases such as those of Bobby Seale in Chicago, Huey Newton in Oakland, Ericka Huggins in New Haven, and now Heard in Boston.[112] Gene Jones, in the immediate aftermath of the event, accused the police of executing a setup, showing meticulous planning to take Heard off the streets.[113] It wasn't simply an arrest: there was an outrageously high bail fee.[114] Jones's view that the case was a frame-up was confirmed by Heard's first trial—which resulted in a hung jury—and during his second trial, when the prosecution fell apart as various members of the plot were unable to keep their stories straight.[115]

On August 31, 1969, the Black Panther Party sponsored a "People's Rally to Combat the Construction of Dudley Police Station." This was a protest of the construction of a new "pig station"—as they called it—instead of "better schools, health centers and housing," which they cited as sorely lacking in Roxbury.[116] In a steering committee meeting of the Boston Black United Front, Hardwick, the Panther representative at the meeting, reiterated to the group that they desired "decentralization of the police station," meaning control by the community.[117] In October, the Panthers organized a committee made up of community members to collectively protest the construction of the Dudley Street station.[118] Six members of the party who were part of an ongoing picketing effort to stop the construction were arrested on September 3 when they were selling the *Black Panther* at the nearby Dudley Street MBTA station.[119] The Panthers claimed that the protesting group had been attempting to stop students "being pushed around" by the police, which escalated into a physical confrontation between the police and Panthers. Those arrested were Heard, Gene Jones, Winfield Chambers, Gregory Jackson, Russell Murchison, and Robert Rogers.[120] Chambers was injured in a scuffle with the police and had to be hospitalized.[121] On September 9, the Panthers were back in force at the construction site, where again they were harassed by police.[122] Heard was handing out leaflets when he was arrested for assault and battery, loitering, idle and disorderly conduct, and trespassing."[123] Fortunately for him, the findings were inconclusive, and charges were dropped.[124] At a September 15 meeting of the Boston Black United Front steering committee, Hardwick reported that the Panthers would continue to picket the new police station and were hoping to hold a rally to get more community people vocal about their opposition to it.[125]

During the winter of 1969–70, the Panthers continued to be involved in Boston area radical organizing, particularly with the November Action Coalition (NAC), an organization formed at the Massachusetts Institute of Technology. Along with the Panthers, the NAC was made up of "the Committee of Returned Volunteers [former Peace Corps volunteers] . . . several Students for a Democratic Society chapters, the Massachusetts Liberation Front . . . , the Old Mole [an underground paper] . . . , Bread and Roses . . . , and November Action Committees on 25 local campuses."[126] The Panthers were also organizing with black student groups at MIT and other schools to stage "separate militant protest . . . in conjunction with the main NAC action."[127] On November 4, the Panthers took part in the NAC demonstration at MIT that rallied between four hundred and eight hundred people and drew more than one hundred reporters.[128] As evidenced by its size, the event was successful in its ability to draw attention to the anti–Vietnam War movement.

In August 1969 Black Panther Party national leaders transferred Doug Miranda to New Haven to help organize the comrades there.[129] The Rackley murder case severely hurt the chapter in New Haven, and Miranda was tasked with getting the group back into shape. Boston became an important organizing center for the Panthers on the East Coast, and Miranda brought Boston Panthers to New Haven to rally activists, students, and the Panthers there. On November 22, 1969, over five thousand people gathered in New Haven to protest the charges against the New Haven Panthers.[130] Audrea Jones, who had become area captain of the Black Panther Party in Boston after Miranda left for Connecticut, was at the rally, and spoke on "the nature of fascism, its use of racism, and the necessity for proletarian internationalism."[131]

The promotion of Jones to lead the Boston Panthers seems to have been uncontroversial, with Miranda recounting that she was the most qualified person to assume leadership because of her impressive skill set.[132] "She also had the respect and support of the membership," Miranda says. She was "passionate and committed to the struggle . . . she possessed a command of the chapter; these qualities only brought her respect from her peers in the party."[133] However, the Boston chapter was pushing the envelope in terms of gender politics—whether they felt this or not. When Jones took command of the chapter she joined a small group of Panther women who were top party leaders.[134] Nevertheless, it appears that Jones did not see her leadership as particularly special. She did not believe that the political education classes held in Boston needed periods of reflection on the female experience within the organization. She recounted later that there was more focus on politics than the personal—something that could have prevented many women in the Boston group from voicing complaints about gender dynamics. Still, Jones recalled that the party developed over time, and they "engaged in this struggle because of internal contradictions as well as external."[135] Apparently a positive environment for women was encouraged in Boston: the absence of gender discrimination there was noticeable compared to other chapters. Jones was not blind to gender concerns within the wider organization. In 1972, in a paper to the national leaders, Jones argued that the party needed to encourage male and female Panthers to use birth control so that costs associated with children could be kept down.[136] Although the greater gender politics of the Boston branch of the Black Panther Party are unclear, it is apparent that Audrea Jones was a strong-willed, capable leader and a valuable Panther.[137]

In Chicago, at approximately 4:30 a.m. on December 4, 1969, Fred Hampton, deputy chairman of the Illinois state chapter of the Black Panther Party, and Mark Clark, defense captain of the Peoria, Illinois branch, were murdered by members of the Chicago Police Department, who were under the direction of the Cook County state's attorney, Edward V. Hanrahan. Hampton and Clark became instant martyrs for the party. To honor their memories, rallies denouncing the Chicago Police took place all over the country. Two days after the assassination, Panthers in Boston organized a rally at City Hall Plaza.[138] At the rally were hundreds of white students, including people from SDS, the Young Patriot Party, and any number of other groups. Audrea Jones was there to speak for the party and "unleashed a string of vulgar obscenities at the police" in understandable rage. A brilliant orator, she incorporated call and response into her speech. "I am a—" she would start. "Revolutionary!" the crowd would fill in. This had been a mainstay of Hampton's speeches. That day it not only involved the crowd but also fired them up in the cold December air.[139] According to the *Bay State Banner*, the crowd responded favorably to Jones's call to "pick up the gun and intensify the struggle" instead of mourning the deaths. The crowd had responded with cries of "right on" and "power to the people."[140]

The last year in the decade, 1969, brought enormous changes to the Black Panther Party of Boston, including the purge of the original leadership and the establishment of the free breakfast program. The chapter also reached out to it radical allies around issues such as Third World revolutionary solidarity, resistance to the construction of a new police station in Roxbury, the New Haven murder trial, and the assassination of Hampton and Clark. The Panthers in Boston became more involved with the greater community of Boston—including both white and African American radicals—through organizations like the November Action Committee and Students for a Democratic Society. The shift away from a pre-purge focus on cultural nationalism allowed the Panthers to broaden their base and seek aid from "mother country revolutionaries"—white allies—as well as refine their message to the grassroots: socialist revolution and community welfare. In the next year, the Panthers in Boston would further their involvement in community welfare with the establishment of their most important program: the Franklin Lynch People's Free Health Center.

1970

In January 1970, the Black Panther Party of Boston instituted new programs for the city's African American community. After more than two months of work, a free clothing program was opened in Mission Hill, at 81 Parker Street, on January 9.[141] The first day, about one hundred people came to a basement in the Mission Hill Extension Projects to receive free clothing provided by the Panthers.[142] This program developed out of a need, according to Robert Heard, that had been voiced by the "welfare mothers" of the Boston community.[143] The idea, similar to other survival programs, was to provide an alternative to government-provided aid. The clothes were donated by local businesses and individuals, and the Panthers hoped that eventually the program would be able to run once a week.[144] As James Young, one of the coordinators of the program, explained, "These programs have a twofold meaning: (1) meeting the basic material needs of our people and (2) raising the political consciousness of our people."[145] Tying the free clothing program to the other survival programs of the Panthers, Young clarified, "[The Panthers] believe people are entitled to the best [that] technology can produce" and that can be provided by "free breakfast programs, liberation schools, free medical clinics and other socialist programs to serve the people." "Food, shelter and clothing," he said, "are central things to people's needs; these three factors determine one's health. Black people in Roxbury suffer under [shortcomings in] all of these conditions."[146]

On February 11, the Panthers held a rally at Pemberton Square, in front of the Boston Federal Court Building, to support Huey Newton on his bail hearing that day in California. Although only attended by about fifty people, the rally was filled with "revolutionary songs and chants." Gene Jones spoke about the commonality of police repression in the United States and how it was something to which anyone could relate. The Panthers also announced another rally for March 1, at the Roxbury Boys Club, which would include Panther speakers Doug Miranda and Audrea Jones, as well as Virgil Wood, a Roxbury clergyman.[147]

Honoring the fifth anniversary of the assassination of Malcolm X, the Boston Panthers opened their new offices at 23 Winthrop Street on February 21, 1970. They moved into one part of the larger Malcolm X Community Information Center. This move was both a symbolic breaking from the past of the party—the pre-purge leaders had chosen the location on Blue Hill Avenue— and an attempt to integrate the party into the community in a more constructive manner. The Community Information Center was a "place where black people [could] meet and hold community meetings and other political and social functions," according to Gene Jones. The center was also to serve as a new, centralized location for Panther programs such as the breakfast program, the clothing program, and a liberation school. It also contained a library of books "relating to the conditions of black people and the struggle for liberation, especially in the Boston community." The library complemented the liberation school, which had as its goal to provide "an education unlike the present racist education." Not unlike political education classes, its organizers aimed to teach children the true history of black people and their contributions internationally. Based on his experiences in California, Huey Newton maintained that the educational structure made blacks ashamed of themselves, and he argued that the school system was a tool of the state used to oppress the African American community. The Panthers' liberation schools were put in place to counteract this. At any rate, Jones explained that the move from an office to a community center, where people were encouraged to use the resources "for whatever purpose they need," was important to create a more personal and intimate atmosphere for the Black Panther Party in the community.[148]

In 1970 the Panthers in Boston continued to aid community members who had suffered police brutality and other injustices. On the morning of March 24, Gregory Daniels called the party for assistance against the Development Corporation of America, which was planning on evicting Daniels's mother and other family members from their apartment. After a tense standoff, the Panthers were able to help Mrs. Daniels by lending her money to "pay off these pigs" and catch up on her rent.[149] Similar to how the Panthers viewed the free clothing program, aiding those unable to pay rent and working to stop evictions were not just ways of exercising community control. They also exposed what the Panthers saw as the corruption of capitalism and the exploitation of the black community by racist landlords. The Panthers proclaimed, "If Mrs. Daniels consistently had trouble paying her rent, [then] the landlord was charging her too much for the apartment."[150] This radical shift in the discourse was vital to the image of the Panthers. They were strong advocates for the African American community in Boston and for fundamental change in the system that oppressed African Americans and other people of color.

Although the Boston Panthers were unable to stop the brutal police beating of Flozell Johnson in his own apartment on June 14, 1970, they were the first called after the incident occurred.[151] The community saw the Panthers as a protective force that was there for them, as opposed to the Boston Police Department, which abused them. Another example of this trust occurred on September 7, 1970, when Ali Muhammed, a father and local resident, came into the Panther offices to discuss problems with the school system. Muhammed's son had been "ridiculed and even beaten" for not saluting the U.S. flag.[152] Community members as young as fifteen came to the party for assistance. Chip Fitzgerald ran away from his school in Dorchester and came to the Panthers complaining of the horribly racist climate of the institution and the abusive treatment he had received there.[153]

The Panthers were receiving aid from supporters in Boston, but the free breakfast program faced serious challenges. Attempts by the FBI to vilify the program seem to have seeped into the mind-set of the Boston Housing Authority (BHA). The BHA, the *Globe* reported, "changed the locks on the doors of the breakfast room at the Mission Hill project and refused to give the [party] new keys."[154] The *Black Panther* claimed that over 250 schoolchildren a week were being fed by the Mission Hill breakfast program when it was shut down.[155] The party attempted to move the program to the Orchard Park housing project but was similarly rebuffed there by the BHA.[156] At Orchard Park, the Panthers had received the approval of the residents and solicited wide support for a breakfast program to begin on June 1, but Sidney Holloway, director of the Orchard Park Day Care Center—where the Panthers wanted the breakfasts to take place—refused to allow the Panthers access until the BHA approved the setup.[157] Finally the Boston Panthers were able to find a location to reestablish the breakfast program—the Bromley-Heath housing project. The program there would start at the beginning of November 1970 and within a few weeks would serve close to seven hundred schoolchildren.[158]

In the category of Panther alliances, on April 14, 1970, the Panthers held a gathering at Boston's Kenmore Square as a prelude to a massive rally the next day that would encompass a large number of radical activists.[159] The April 14 rally involved a speech by Doug Miranda, visiting from New Haven, that called on white radical supporters to "pick up a gun to kill the pigs or you'll have to pick up a gun to defend yourselves."[160] However, similar words from Miranda the next day got him shouted down by chants of "Peace Now!"[161] Evidently Bostonians were leaning toward a more moderate peace activism and away from the fiery militancy of the Black Panther Party. The April 15 rally of somewhere between forty-five thousand and one hundred thousand people on the Boston Common involved peace advocates calling for an end to the war in Vietnam and Black Panthers demanding dropping the charges against the New Haven Eight (previously the New Haven Nine).[162] Audrea Jones spoke alongside Howard Zinn, then a Boston University professor, and Artie Seale, the wife of Panther cofounder Bobby Seale, one of the New Haven Eight.[163]

More massive rallies followed in 1970, mainly focused on the Vietnam War, allowing space for the Panthers to connect U.S. imperialism in Southeast Asia with racism at home. Identified as the "East Coast defense captain of the Black Panther Party," Miranda spoke at a rally at Soldiers Field in Cambridge on May 8 and declared that "the black people are the vanguard" of the U.S. antiwar movement. At this rally between thirty thousand and fifty thousand people gathered to hear Miranda and other radicals speak about Cambodia, Kent State (where the Ohio National Guard had four days earlier killed four students), and the Panthers.[164] The *Globe* the next day quoted a Boston University freshman who said that Miranda was "too radical for me, but I can appreciate how he feels because the government is trying to wipe out the Panthers who [are] the vanguard of this whole movement."[165] These words seem to echo the peace protesters who shouted down Miranda's rhetoric on April 15. Although Boston University students participated in rallies with the Panthers, their description of the Panthers as too radical indicates a change of mind among liberal white allies. The Boston Panthers would need to focus more on their popular survival programs and community support if they were to keep white student radicals engaged.

On the heels of the Cambridge rally, the Panthers organized a rally at Boston University's Nickerson Field on May 10. While not as large as the rally two days prior, seven thousand people came out to listen to music and speeches. The event was a fund-raiser for the legal defense fund of the New Haven Panthers. Panther Donna Howell kicked off the afternoon by defining what the Black Panther Party was fighting for: the right and ability for "each person to stand up for himself and fight for his rights as promised 'by this so-called democracy.'"[166] Although militant in style and approach, the speech by Howell, at least in what the *Globe* reports, is very different from Miranda's. Howell identified the problems as systemic and arising from a fault in American democracy, problems that could impact white students who felt dissatisfied with politics as well as communities of color that have been historically marginalized. Moving away from calls to pick up the gun and increasingly speaking of fixing democracy, the Boston Panthers angled their rhetoric toward their diverse audience and built alliances.

On May 31, 1970, the most important Panther service in Boston officially opened its doors, the Franklin Lynch People's Free Health Center, named after a black man shot and killed by Boston police officers in March 1970.[167] Located on Ruggles and Tremont Streets, the trailer that housed the health center was placed on land that was to be part of the proposed Southwest Expressway. Plans had the expressway cleaving Roxbury, damaging the community irrevocably. This radical occupation of land increased Panther solidarity with the people of Roxbury.[168] It also modeled productive use of overlooked resources. The Boston Panthers were providing a social service to the community that the city's government did not provide, while doing so on land that the city's government had bulldozed but did not use.[169] The center was at first open only four days a week because of a staffing shortage, but party members wanted to build a truly revolutionary medical clinic open to everyone in the community at any hour.[170]

The free health clinic was not a Boston invention, nor was the concept the brainchild of Panther leaders in Oakland, although by 1970 the central committee of the party had mandated that each local branch set up such a clinic.

The Panther headquarters did not provide supplies or funding to build or staff clinics, so Panthers had to rely on ingenuity, persuasive skills, and hard work to secure funding, supplies, and trained doctors and nurses. Health activism in response to health inequality was part of a long tradition among African American communities before the civil rights movement, and the free clinics tie the Panthers into the larger black liberation struggle. As author and scholar Alondra Nelson argues, the Panthers consciously and unconsciously drew on the tactics and language of the "medical civil rights movement" to argue for the necessity of health care for the African American community and to unite their own struggle with those of the past.[171]

This attempt to create a true alternative to other medical options suggests how the Boston Panthers saw the existing health-care options in Boston: as broken and in need of something different. The free medical center primarily focused on preventative medicine to improve the health and wellness of the Roxbury community. But it also provided "checkups, immunizations, blood tests," and other medical care.[172] The center also provided "people's advocates" and drivers for those who needed to go to a hospital and needed transportation there and an advocate for their medical rights upon arrival.[173]

The training of lay medical experts was critical to the Panthers' mission in Boston. Of the approximately one hundred thousand African Americans in the city, there were only nine black physicians, the *Globe* reported, and their median age was sixty-two. There were "only four health clinics providing average health services—nothing like comprehensive health services." And one of these clinics was the People's Free Health Center.[174] As a result, the Panthers had to "rely heavily on white doctors" for the clinic to function effectively.[175] The Boston Panthers attempted to work around this problem by encouraging community involvement. Donna Howell, the organizer of the center, commented, "This is a black community project... so we need black people working here. If you really identify with the struggle for black people this is one way you can help."[176] An example of lay medical experts in action was the coordination of the health center and "a group of welfare moms" in conducting "a series of lead-poisoning test[s] for approximately 300 kids."[177]

The health center also provided classes in first aid and using technical lab equipment to aid the community in becoming lay experts.[178] Community health-care shortcomings were not solvable by the Panthers alone, but the impact of a community health center focused on the needs of the people and working for the benefit of the African American community cannot be understated. Alondra Nelson notes how this radical approach to medical care aligned the Panthers with the writings of Mao Zedong and Ernesto "Che" Guevara in "conceptualizing how health and medicine fit with broad political aims."[179] Another in the Panthers' canon, Frantz Fanon, showed the potential dangers of medicine in the hands of an untrustworthy state. The writings of these three men were particularly important to the Panthers. They were read and taught at all political education classes and integral to Newton and Seale's original conception of the party. Guevara—a doctor by training before becoming a revolutionary—stressed the necessity of the revolutionary group taking up the institutions that supported the community—health and wellness centers, for example. Maoist thought on the importance of the people as a mass, not just those with specialized training, influenced the Panthers' insistence on the medical training of lay people and the expansion of health care to all, not just the elite who had the resources to pay for it. The direct impact of Maoist medical practices were seen by Panthers in two different trips to China in 1970 and 1971, where party members were exposed to the "deprofessionalization of medicine" in China through their "Barefoot Doctors" program.[180]

Ultimately the Panthers' free medical clinics were operations that were in some ways an extension of their policing-the-police programs. In a place like Boston, where policing the police directly was untenable, this service program was a revolutionary alternative. The Panthers "policed the medical sphere" for poor, black communities by providing an alternative to the often coercive, authoritarian, and racist treatment of African Americans by the medical establishment. Across the country the Panthers' free health clinics empowered people who were otherwise seen by the medical community as non-experts. The health centers were sites of social change that "attended to more than just narrowly defined health needs."[181]

In general, the Panthers encouraged community-based organizations and appear to have placed a premium on engagement and participation. The goals of the Boston Panthers—expressed through press statements and newsletters—were to unite and develop the community.

By the middle of the fall of 1970, the Franklin Lynch Center was much better staffed and available at nearly all times, meeting the desires of its organizers when it first opened. The Panthers who ran the center and the doctors, nurses, and lay helpers who staffed the clinic did not just wait in the center for people to come to them. On September 29, at six thirty in the evening, some Boston Panthers were walking home and came upon a man lying on the ground "motionless, and rigid." The man did not answer to his name. Finding his pulse weak, these Panthers took the man to the health center and the doctor on duty there. The *Black Panther* would report: "Panthers Save Brother near Death from Drugs."[182] On November 15, in the late afternoon, there was a car crash outside the health center. Doctors and nurses rushed outside to help and took a seventy-two-year-old man into the clinic to make sure he was unhurt. Soon after, police arrived and attempted to take the injured man out to question him, which the Panthers prevented. The Panthers acted as gatekeepers, leveling the power relationship between this man and the police and allowing him to make his own decisions regarding the interaction.[183] This inverse of the power dynamic normally observed, particularly in health care matters, modeled for the black community how the Panthers desired to equalize its relationship with the white power structure.

Though the Panthers ran the clinic competently, money for the center was often hard to come by. Large amounts of money for the Panthers nationally came from wealthy white allies, and this was no different in Boston. One of the best examples of this was Harvard Medical School professor Jonathon Beckwith donating $500 of a $1,000 research prize to the Panthers' medical center to help pay for its opening.[184] There was generally a positive opinion of the health center among both black and white Bostonians. People like Reginald Eaves (director of the Mayor's Office of Human Rights), Ellen Jackson of Operation Exodus, and Leon Nelson, president of the Boston chapter of the NAACP, all supported the social programs of the Panthers in Boston but particularly the health center because of its importance for the community.[185] The Boston Black United Front also helped to financially support the center and its services.[186]

The Boston Police Department was adamantly opposed to the health center and its revolutionary potential, and police seem to have taken out their anger by shooting up the empty trailer in the early morning hours of July 5, 1970. The Boston Panthers accused the police of the drive-by shooting, based on bullets recovered from the scene, the same type as used in BPD handguns. Despite damage to the trailer, the center was open as usual the following day. The Panthers promised to continue operating it and not back down.[187] Other than this possible intimidation effort by Boston police, the government of Boston did not attempt to remove the center in any other way, which would have been legally justified since the Boston Black United Front and the Panthers were squatting on the land. Donna Howell, before the official opening of the center, worried about this, saying, "They'll just try and take the clinic away."[188] Part of the stability of the center was likely due to its mass appeal and its positive impact on the community, which made it hard for the Boston government to condemn it publicly. While the police were not thrilled about the health center, they did not vow to destroy the Panthers like the police vowed in Detroit.[189] Although this difference has as much to do with the city as with their police forces, the Boston People's Free Health Center was able to galvanize support, white and black, in Boston, which prevented it becoming too much of a target for the Boston administration.

On July 31, 1970, in the aftermath of riots in New Bedford, Massachusetts, earlier in the month, about sixty miles south of Boston, New Bedford police raided a building repurposed to be an NCCF office and arrested twenty people. Three of them were members of the Black Panther Party of Boston. Boston Panthers had been in New Bedford since the middle of July, organizing the NCCF.[190] New Bedford natives had requested this help.[191] During the July

31 police raid, the New Bedford group was connected by telephone to Boston in the person of Audrea Jones, who in turn was on the line with David Hilliard in Oakland. The Panthers placed great importance on the New Bedford NCCF and saw the possibility of a firefight breaking out between Panthers and police that night, hence the phone chain to central headquarters. According to Johnny Viera, one of those in the NCCF office, Jones ordered the surrender—as relayed to her from Oakland—and told the Panthers defending the building to stand down.[192] The next day, Jones was in New Bedford denouncing the raid at a rally as "'a blatant conspiracy' against 'anyone working for the salvation of black people.'"[193] After the raid, the Boston Panthers became increasingly interested in New Bedford. They provided support and resources, and highlighted the importance of the raid for the Panthers.[194]

In the late fall and early winter of 1970, the Boston branch of the Black Panther Party saw a need to provide transportation for people from Boston to their loved ones in prison. The Panthers were able to get support from other community organizations and began the program by busing people to visit prisoners at the Norfolk State Prison thirty miles southwest of Boston. They also sought to expand the program to Walpole and Concord State Prisons and the women's reformatory in Framingham.[195] In addition to busing the relatives and friends of prisoners, the Boston Panthers set up a program to provide free Christmas food to the prisoners in Norfolk Prison. The program was a runaway success for both the prisoners and the community, and bringing the two together met the goal of linking "oppressed communities in the struggle to transform society."[196] The Panthers also had connections with at least one prisoner at Deer Island Prison, Robert Jackson, who was apparently a Panther before being imprisoned for carrying a concealed weapon.[197]

The revolutionary activism of the Franklin Lynch People's Free Health Center tapped into the medical civil rights movement identified by Alondra Nelson and modeled a world the Panthers wished to see created. The health center developed into a community cornerstone, transforming the way that the black community of Boston thought about their health care. The clinic was tangible evidence of the Black Panther survival programs in the city. During the first full year of the new leadership, Doug Miranda was moved to New Haven and Audrea Jones stepped into the top leadership role.[198] The trial in New Haven drew the attention of Boston Panthers from Massachusetts to Connecticut, and the raid on the NCCF office in New Bedford moved that attention to New Bedford. The black communities of Boston and New Bedford were drawn closer as Panthers traveled back and forth between the cities to support one another.

1971

By February 1971, the Boston Panthers' People's Free Medical Center was firmly entrenched in the community, and thanks to the clinic fourteen-month-old

Stacey Burston received a corrective operation on her eyes relating to a birth defect. When Burston was six months old, doctors at Boston Children's Hospital had simply told her parents to get her glasses, but this did nothing to correct the problem. Her parents were not informed that a series of simple operations could straighten out her eyes. After she was brought to the Franklin Lynch health center she received an appointment with an eye specialist who arranged the operations to allow Burston to have normal vision. The Panthers went to great effort on behalf of the community to make the health center a viable option for health care for the African American community in Boston. As the *Black Panther* explains, "Without the people, the Free Health Center would not be accomplished and would also lose the reason for its existence, that being to serve the people . . . hundreds upon hundreds of other community people will receive the fruits of life that they deserve. Only through survival programs such as this can we survive the racist oppression of American society."[199]

In the spring of 1971, the Boston branch of the Black Panther Party was still involved with housing concerns in the community. After their apartment was destroyed by a fire, the Parrigo family, whose children took part in the free breakfast program, sought help from the Boston Housing Authority, but the BHA refused to provide any temporary housing, which effectively left the family out in the cold. The Panthers were able to secure temporary and eventually permanent housing for the Parrigos, and the Panthers' clinic "treated [the family] for the effects of the fire and smoke."[200] The Boston Panthers also continued to be attuned to everyday police brutality. For example, on June 22, Philomena Brewer, sixteen years old, and her sister Andrea, fourteen, were accused of stealing in a department store and "Philomena [was dragged] toward the security office." A bystander called the Panthers, who then acted as advocates at the police station for Philomena Brewer and two women arrested for physically intervening on behalf of the girls.[201] The Boston Black United Front took part in a boycott of the specific store, in the Zayre chain, as did "the Urban League, Panther Party, Teen Center, Multi-Service center, and Black Student Federation." This coalition also worked to get the store to fire the security guard who was involved.[202]

At the end of July, the BBUF decided that a central hotline was needed for community members to be able to call if they needed assistance regarding police brutality and harassment. Because of the police brutality work the Boston Panthers had done in the community over the prior couple of years, their office phone at 23 Winthrop Street was chosen as the designated hotline.[203] With their designation as the go-to people regarding police brutality, the Boston Panthers in some ways returned their practice to the roots of the BPP in community control and defense.

On Sunday, May 30, 1971, the Boston Panthers celebrated the one-year anniversary of the opening of the Franklin Lynch People's Free Health Center. The celebration included dinner, political discussion, and a report on the party's other community survival programs. The *Black Panther* claimed, "Hundreds of people have received treatment, health counseling, and preventative medical education by the staff of our health center. The People's Free Health Center has also enabled many people of our community to be trained as technicians, medical secretaries, and nursing assistants."[204] The clinic also provided pregnancy tests, immunization, tuberculosis tests, and gynecological services.[205] This is all exactly in line with the Panthers' mission of radical health care, a way to "transform the society." The clinic was also a place where "all the power belongs to the people."[206]

The Panthers' health center also began an outreach program in 1971, taking health-care services directly to the community. The Panthers sent trained medical teams to visit community organizations and community functions, and they made house calls to provide free testing for sickle cell anemia.[207] Beginning June 12, the Panthers administered free sickle cell testing at the Franklin Lynch clinic as part of a nationally organized drive to test for the disease.[208] The *Boston Globe* and the *Bay State Banner* reported that between 1,300 and 2,000 people tested for sickle cell anemia at the Panthers' clinic in Boston, with about 120 found to carry the trait. The *Globe* noted that the clinic contained "background material on diseases, cabinets full of medical supplies and rooms for testing during the hours in which the trailer functions as a clinic."[209] In 1970 and 1971 many groups in Boston took part in sickle cell anemia testing, and the Panthers' program was one of seven supported by the Boston City Hospital.[210] Although the Panthers' initial health-care outreach program was designed around sickle cell anemia, the plan was to expand to tuberculosis and lead poisoning testing.[211] Providing this free health-care service entailed expenses for the Panthers, and they continued to seek donations and request money from groups like the BBUF to finance it.[212] The Panthers also requested material resources from the BBUF, like mimeograph paper to create leaflets about their sickle cell testing campaign.[213] In addition to their own outreach program, the Panthers took part in a Community Relations and Public Health Information Day in Roxbury, with participants including the Boston Police Department and McDonald's. The event, held on November 27, involved the Panthers at a table "where technicians did free blood tests for sickle cell anemia."[214] The Panther involvement with an event as broadly based as this shows their importance in the community and their ability to work alongside, and inside, the mainstream in matters such as health and wellness.

Sickle cell anemia was an important part of the Black Panther Party's health activism nationally, not just in Boston. According to Gene Jones, "There has been a lot of misinterpretation as to what the Sickle Cell trait is and the effect it has upon black people." He claimed that "most medical schools do not train their students in testing for the traits of sickle disease."[215] Alondra Nelson asserts that the Panthers used sickle cell anemia as a "vehicle for Party political ideology," seeing racism in the medical establishment's failure to devote resources to the predominantly African American disease.[216]

In 1971 Boston Panthers continued many of their community programs, and expanding their health center by adding sickle cell anemia testing was immensely important for the African American community. This was a case not only of identifying a need of the people and meeting it, but also promoting party ideology and keeping the Panthers relevant. But despite the health center becoming more and more important, the Panthers in Boston were increasingly less a part of political discourse and political action.[217] Their remaining importance as a community organization dedicated to serving the people shows the value of the Black Panther Party beyond the ideologies and rhetorical posturing.

1972

The Franklin Lynch People's Free Health Center continued its work in 1972. On the afternoon of May 24, eight-year-old Devon Pugh was shot by a police officer while he was outside playing. Boston police had arrived at the Orchard Park housing project after hearing of someone there with a gun. Police shot at a twenty-one-year old man, John Simms, who was walking away from them, but shots went wide, and one struck Pugh. Simms was arrested and the police left the scene—leaving Pugh to be taken to the hospital by his mother, where he required "surgery for extensive muscle and nerve damage." Pugh stayed at the Boston City Hospital until Friday, May 26, when his mother decided that he was being treated poorly, not getting "proper medication or food." She brought him to the Panther clinic, and after that a doctor there began house calls on Pugh to treat him until another hospital was found to treat the boy.[218]

Sickle cell anemia testing continued into 1972 as well. On January 4, the Panthers asked the Boston Black United Front to reach out to Boston Public Schools regarding sickle cell anemia, in an effort to test more schoolchildren for the trait.[219] On July 14, the Panthers again took part in a community health day in Roxbury where they conducted sickle cell anemia tests for members of the community. The health fair included such groups as the Red Cross, Tufts Dental School, and the Massachusetts Cancer Society.[220] This was likely one of the last events in which the Boston branch of the Black Panther Party participated.

The Panthers emphasized their role in providing for the community, but some in the community feared an ulterior motive in the Panthers' social programs. While many focused on the charitable aspect of the community survival programs, others worried that the programs indoctrinated young children with Black Panther propaganda. Numerous groups criticized the Panthers for employing what they saw as overly aggressive mobilization tactics within the black community, but this did not stop people from joining the local chapter to contribute to community development. In some sectors, the militant ideology of the Boston Panthers, even as toned down as it was, undercut public support. But the Panther survival programs maintained a more positive image. Even the director of the Mayor's Office of Human Rights, Reginald Eaves, believed that the survival programs were positive initiatives, but he questioned the transparency of the local Panther chapter, saying, "You only know what they want you to know." Another black community leader, Ellen Jackson, director of Operation Exodus (a desegregation project in Roxbury), said to the *Boston Globe*, "I generally support the social and political element of the party's program for black people, which is so vitally needed." But she noted that the image of the Panthers developed in the media had harmed the mission of the party. Panther leaders recognized the importance of projecting a positive image to gain and maintain support as well as the need to parry any negative publicity in the mainstream media. In the *Black Panther*, Ed Buryn wrote, "Panthers get too much public notice for hate and violence. But dig ... Panthers also mean love, and seek change through good works too. The kids at the breakfasts know it, and so should you."[221] The Panthers wanted to demonstrate that they were socially conscious and filling basic needs in the community. But despite the Panthers' efforts to put their best foot forward, they were still on the Boston Police Department's radar.

Government versus Panthers

Local government officials viewed the Boston Panther chapter in a different light than how they saw the party's national headquarters in California. The Boston Panthers did not have the run-ins with law enforcement, much less shoot-outs with the police, and they were not associated with serious criminal activity.[222] Boston Police Superintendent William Bradley said, "I don't know of any particular violent activity perpetrated by the Black Panthers in Boston," and he added, "I have no evidence that they have arsenals in the city."[223] Despite the peace, the Panthers and police maintained a cold war, and Panther arrests did sometimes transpire. In one incident, mentioned earlier, local Panthers were passing out literature at an MBTA station and were told by police to leave the premises. The Panthers did not vacate, six members were arrested, and another Panther was treated at a hospital for head contusions.[224] The BPP alleged that the arresting officers had abused the Panthers and caused the injuries of the wounded member. "While the brothers were held there for half an hour, the pigs kept saying that this is the reason why the Black community will not cooperate and also why they need more police to keep us 'niggers' down." In this article, Brother Cheatham, a Panther, referred to this incident as illustrating a way that the Black Panthers were repressed by the police. Following physical encounters with police officers, the Panthers demonstrated how those interactions represented the subjugation of the black community by the state.

In Boston and across the nation individual party members were targeted by police, but so were party programs. The popularity of the survival programs alarmed the FBI, which made them the target of counterintelligence operations. These programs helped promulgate Panther ideology among the masses, and it was this that threatened the FBI. In documents from the time, the FBI stated that it was not against feeding children, it was against the indoctrination of children. The FBI attempted to disrupt free breakfast programs by sending anonymous subversive letters to institutions—including churches—that served as venues for the programs and to markets who donated food. The government reportedly prevented the Panthers from using public buildings to accommodate the breakfast programs and liberation schools. As noted earlier, the Boston Housing Authority changed the locks of one building, at Mission Hill, and would not grant the Panthers access to the facility.[225] Other bureaucrats would not permit the Panthers access to various premises. "The FBI attempted to vilify our breakfast program, charging that we were feeding our children poison[,] and they also intimidated the mothers," the *Globe* quoted Gene Jones as saying. Jones said the party had attempted to start another breakfast program, at Orchard Park, "but we were refused the keys although the mothers there wanted one."[226]

Inhibiting the Panthers' ability to conduct political education classes was another tactic the FBI used against the party. By January 1969 the bureau had sent a letter to Northeastern University administrators, including excerpts from the *Black Panther*, in an attempt to dissuade them from allowing the Panthers on campus. Whether or not administrators responded is unknown.[227]

By working to isolate the Boston Panthers from other organizations, law enforcement officials attempted to hinder the community survival programs and thus the promotion of Panther ideology. In addition to these quietly disruptive measures, the FBI also used more visible efforts against the Panthers. This including breaking into breakfast program locations and destroying foodstuffs. As described earlier, the Panther health clinic was shot up one night, which Panthers attributed to police. The *Boston Globe* reported that the Franklin Lynch clinic had been fired at thirteen times with a .38 special. The Panthers noted that Boston's police were known to carry this weapon. The community, the Panthers said, "embraced the Free Health Center as their own and refuse[d] to cower beneath racist attacks by the Boston Pig Department."[228]

In 1972, the party's central committee ordered all branch offices around the country to close and Panthers to come to Oakland as part of a shift toward running the electoral campaigns for Panthers Bobby Seale and Elaine Brown. Seale would run for mayor of Oakland in 1973 and Brown would run for city council. Local branches of the party shut down all over the country, from Denver to Seattle to Los Angeles to Boston. Boston Panther leaders who moved to Oakland included Audrea Jones and Donna Howell.[229] Thus the Boston Panther chapter ended with a whisper rather than a bang, as might have seemed appropriate given the grandiose rhetoric of the Panthers in the late 1960s. The Boston Panthers fell off the radar of city officials and the press, and leaders did not return to the city after the electoral campaigns in Oakland. While Harvard professor Martin Kilson argued in the *Bay State Banner* in 1973 that the Panthers had to move toward electoral politics, otherwise face the guns of the state or eventual disbanding by entropy, the Boston Panthers themselves tell a different tale.[230] As Alondra Nelson so eloquently states, "The activists rejected capitalist liberalism and laid claim to democracy's radical potential as ... articulated in the 'WHAT WE WANT' and 'WHAT WE NEED' that was the Party's ten-point platform."[231] The Black Panther Party of Boston was efficient and functional, creating socialist programs designed to aid the city's African American community. They served as a model for what a different type of society could look like. Their greatest achievement, the Franklin Lynch People's Free Medical Center, is a testament to the importance of the Panthers beyond the rhetoric and police reports, beyond the Free Huey rallies and speeches. The Panthers in Boston are essential to remember for their survival programs that changed the communities for the better.

Conclusion

This examination of the Boston branch of the Black Panther Party is by no means exhaustive. It needs to be further expanded through more interviews with Boston Panthers, locals who were not in the party but interacted with it, and stakeholders like members of the Boston Police Department, the city government, and members of other black liberation organizations in Boston. It is our hope that this work serves as a starting point and inspiration for future scholars.

The Boston chapter of the Black Panther Party was a multifaceted and multitalented group of men and women working to better the conditions of the African American community in Boston. Through their activism they worked to make Boston a true "cradle of liberty" for African Americans, a dream that had long been deferred. The Boston Panthers are little remembered today because they engaged in no shoot-outs with police and kept safe from the assassin's bullets of the FBI. But these qualities are positive, not detrimental.

This essay, in uncovering the importance of the Black Panther Party of Boston, gives the chapter a key place in the historiography of the Black Panther Party. Up to this point the historiography of the BPP is too focused on branches where violent revolution was expected and clashes between police and Panthers mask the survival programs that prospered in the city. For example, "Urban guerrilla warfare" was central to the Detroit Panthers and emblematic of how it was "carried out and narrated by some Panther chapters across the country."[232] The black struggle with a repressive police force in Detroit existed before the Panthers and survived after they were gone, but African Americans in that city who joined the Black Panther Party had an ideological framework legitimating their struggle and empowering them as part of a national struggle. Many Detroit Panthers saw a need for an immediate and violent African American revolution. "Taking it to the pigs" was seen as the next step in revolution, and some of the Black Panthers in Detroit saw themselves as the ones to lead this assault.[233] The Boston Panthers, on the other hand, tapped into the same national struggle but used different methods to bring about the changes they wished to see.

The Boston Panthers' survival programs, most importantly the Franklin Lynch People's Free Medical Center, were central to the way the party functioned in the city. Panthers in Boston took their jobs as agents of revolutionary change seriously, but in a very different way than some Panthers in other cities. It is difficult to pinpoint exactly why this was so. However, it is clear that the social landscape of Boston and the physical segregation and racism inherent in the city played a part in making the Boston chapter what it was. The Boston Panthers focused on survival programs as the most effective way forward toward revolution in Boston without losing sight of the national struggle of the time. The Boston Panthers established an effective free breakfast program, a free clothing program, a program providing transportation to visit prisoners, and the People's Free Medical Center. Together these define the Panthers in Boston in ways that the rhetoric of violent revolution never will. Boston Panthers worked for revolutionary change by modeling a system they desired to see.

The dichotomy between the Detroit chapter and the Boston chapter illustrates part of why the BPP is such an important historical force in the Black Power movement and the black liberation struggle. The Panthers' ten-point program was broad enough to cover almost all aspects of African American life and spoke to various radical activists differently. Individual Panther chapters conceptualized and lived out the values of the party through divergent tactics. Boston is an important example of a chapter that did not embrace the gun but actively worked to improve the welfare of the community through socialistic programs.

The history of the Black Panther Party needs to include chapters like Boston where the rhetoric was only occasionally blazing and the guns were silent. The Boston Panther chapter demanded that the black community of Boston be treated as more than statistics. They claimed their rights as fully human. And unlike the Detroit and D.C. Panthers, the Boston branch did not emerge within a sea of other Black Power groups, jockeying for prominence and the vanguard role in a violent quest against the police. The Boston Panthers were both idealistic and practical. They modeled a society controlled by the community members, caring for each other and constantly striving to ameliorate suffering, most excellently modeled by the Franklin Lynch People's Free Medical Center. The Panthers called for community control but also community peace. Working to better the conditions of all those they could reach, the Boston Panthers served as the vanguard of a movement redefining the realities of life in the city's black community. They embodied the party's beliefs and carried high the banner of "intercommunalism" in their drive for land, bread, housing, education, clothing, justice, and peace.

NOTES

1. Stephen Kantrowitz, *More than Freedom: Fighting for Black Citizenship in a White Republic, 1829–1889* (New York: Penguin Press, 2012), i, 8, 45–46.

2. The Great Migration was an exodus of African Americans from the South during the twentieth century. The first wave was between approximately 1915 and 1930. The second wave was between approximately 1940 and 1970. For further information, see James Gregory, *The Southern Diaspora: How the Great Migrations of Black and White Southerners Transformed America* (Chapel Hill: University of North Carolina Press, 2005); Farah Jasmine Griffin's *"Who Set You Flowin'?": The African-American Migration Narrative* (New York: Oxford University Press, 1995); James Grossman, *Land of Hope: Chicago, Black Southerners, and the Great Migration* (Chicago: University of Chicago Press, 1989); Isabel Wilkerson, *The Warmth of Other Suns: The Epic Story of America's Great Migration* (New York: Random House, 2010).

3. With this black population increase came an increase in the number of whites in Boston leaving for the suburbs. From 1950 to 1970 the African American population in the city was not so much rapidly growing in number as in proportion. Richard Alan Ballou, "Even in 'Freedom's Birthplace': The Development of Boston's Black Ghetto, 1900–1940" (PhD diss., University of Michigan, 1984), 72; Stephan Thernstrom, *The Other Bostonians: Poverty and Progress in the American Metropolis, 1880–1970* (Cambridge, Mass.: Harvard University Press, 1973), 179.

4. James Jennings et al., *Perspectives on Poverty in Boston's Black Community* (Boston: Boston Foundation, 1992), 9.

5. Ballou, "Even in 'Freedom's Birthplace,'" 98.

6. Lance Carden, *Witness: An Oral History of Black Politics in Boston 1920–1960* (Boston: Boston College, 1989), 66.

7. Jack Tager, *Boston Riots: Three Centuries of Social Violence* (Boston: Northeastern University Press, 2001), 174.

8. Cappy Pinderhughes, telephone conversation with Judson L. Jeffries, November 22, 2016.

9. Robert O. Self, *American Babylon: Race and the Struggle for Postwar Oakland* (Princeton: Princeton University Press, 2003) explores the role of suburbanization and city development and their effect on community development in the Black Power era. Focusing on the years 1945–78, Self analyzes special elements in the economic and

political structure that shaped regional development and underdevelopment. Focusing on the tension between urban Black Power organizations and the suburban-based tax-reform movement, Self explores how economic and urban policy generated and consequently affected metropolitan development.

10. Tager, *Boston Riots*, 175. Tager provides an in-depth analysis of riots in Boston. In analyzing the 1967 disorders, he notes how the powerlessness of the African American community led to direct action, writing that "powerlessness was the reason blacks resorted to violence" (177).

11. Robert Rosenthal et al., *Different Strokes: Pathways to Maturity in the Boston Ghetto* (Boulder, Colo.: Westview Press, 1976), 15, 16, 19–20.

12. Lance Carden, *Witness: An Oral History of Black Politics in Boston 1920–1960* (Boston: Boston College, 1989), 20–22.

13. Jama Lazerow, "The Black Panthers at the Water's Edge: Oakland, Boston, and the New Bedford 'Riots' of 1970," in *Liberated Territory: Untold Local Perspectives on the Black Panther Party*, eds. Yohuru Williams and Jama Lazerow (Durham: Duke University Press, 2008), 87.

14. Michael Newton, *Bitter Grain: Huey Newton and the Black Panther Party* (Los Angeles: Holloway House, 1980), 156.

15. In "The Black Panthers on the Water's Edge," Lazerow argues that the New Bedford raid on July 31, 1970, constituted a raid on the Boston Panthers. We disagree. This ties the two branches too closely together, and melds the unique situation of each community. The Panthers in Boston tapped into the situation in New Bedford, committed themselves to aiding in the trials, and were deeply invested in the actual events of the raid. However, this was not like the New Haven trial or Chicago raid where the event became the defining characteristic of the branch.

16. Sociologist and activist Richard Flacks has written about the tensions between action involved in the "sustaining of everyday life" and action involved in the "making of history." In this conception, the Panthers in Boston gave up the former to take up the latter. The making of history, according to Flacks, is less about different actions and more about the decision to make history. The Panthers purposely redefined what it meant to hold power in the system, traditionally pertaining exclusively to the elite, to be more encompassing. They worked to build community services and structures that would allow the African American community of Boston to become history makers as opposed to sustainers of the everyday. Richard Flacks, *Making History: The American Left and the American Mind* (New York: Columbia University Press, 1988), 1.

17. Franklin Lynch was shot in the Boston City Hospital by a police officer guarding him in March 1970. The Panthers were involved in the community response to the shooting, a "People's Trial" held in Roxbury and organized through the Boston Black United Front. Floyd Hardwick, a Boston Panther, was one of the organizers. Lorraine Baber, "Panther Clinic Opening Delayed," *Bay State Banner*, May 21, 1970; "Police Trial Committee," March 11, 1970, Boston Black United Front records, box 13, folder 8, Special Collections, Roxbury Community College Library.

18. D. L. Chandler, "Little Known Black History Month: MAW and the Roxbury Riots," BlackAmericaWeb.com, https://blackamericaweb.com/2015/06/02/little-known-black-history-month-maw-and-the-roxbury-riots.

19. "Timetable of Events in Roxbury," *Boston Globe*, June 4, 1967.

20. "Sit-In Escalates into Riot," *Boston Globe*, June 3, 1967.

21. Robert L. Turner, "How the Tension Grew," *Boston Globe*, June 4, 1967.
22. Ibid.; Jonathan Fuerbringer and Marvin E. Milbauer, "Roxbury, Quiet in the Past, Finally Breaks into Riot," *Harvard Crimson*, June 15, 1967, http://www.thecrimson.com/article/1967/6/15/roxbury-quiet-in-past-finally-breaks.
23. Christopher Lydon, "Youths' View: Police at Fault," *Boston Globe*, June 6, 1967.
24. Ibid.
25. Elliot Friedman, "Collins Orders Probe of Welfare," *Boston Globe*, June 5, 1967.
26. Tager, *Boston Riots*, 183.
27. Lydon, "Youths' View."
28. Tager, *Boston Riots*, 173.
29. Institutional functioning is an important aspect in society. How government institutions develop improved workflow and outputs, how people participate within the system, and how government agencies respond to citizen complaints are essential in maintaining law and order in a community.
30. "Welfare Bill Would Help," *Boston Globe*, June 5, 1967.
31. Quoted in "Sit-in Escalates into Riot," *Boston Globe*, June 3, 1967.
32. Tager, *Boston Riots*, 177–78.
33. "Brooke, Ted Deplore Violence," *Boston Globe*, June 5, 1967. Brooke was the nation's first African American elected by voters to serve in the U.S. Senate since Blanche Bruce in the nineteenth century.
34. Elliot Friedman, "Collins Orders Probe of Welfare," *Boston Globe*, June 5, 1967.
35. Victor Chen, "Boston Panthers Stalk New Goal," *Boston Globe*, July 6, 1969; Queen, "Who Are The Black Panthers," *Bay State Banner*, December 5, 1968. The sources are split on the exact month of the founding of the Panthers, which likely reflects a difference in who news reporters talked with about this. The *Bay State Banner* in December 1968 put the founding in July 1968, while the *Boston Globe* in July 1969 put the founding in June 1968.
36. "Panthers Feed Kids," *Bay State Banner*, July 10, 1969; Doug Miranda, conversation with Judson L. Jeffries, November 23, 2016.
37. "Service Held for Oppressed People," *Bay State Banner*, August 22, 1968.
38. Ibid.
39. "Service Held for Oppressed People"; "Northern Racism," *Black Panther*, January 25, 1969.
40. Arthur Lyons, "The Grape-Pickers' Story: Behind the Boycott," *Boston Globe*, October 27, 1968; Queen, "Who Are the Black Panthers"; Dan Queen, "Panthers Try to Reach All Black People," *Bay State Banner*, December 12, 1968.
41. Lauren Araiza, "'In Common Struggle against a Common Oppression': The United Farm Workers and the Black Panther Party, 1968–1973," *Journal of African American History* 94, no. 2 (2009), 200–223.
42. Araiza, "In Common Struggle against a Common Oppression," 200.
43. Lyons, "The Grape-Picker's Story."
44. "Drizzle Dampens Viet Rally," *Boston Globe*, November 10, 1968.
45. Queen, "Who Are the Black Panthers."
46. Queen, "Panthers Try to Reach All Black People"; "Off the Pigs: More Panther Harassment," *Black Panther*, February 2, 1969.
47. Queen, "Panthers Try to Reach All Black People."
48. Bobby Hutton joined the Panthers as a fifteen-year-old in 1966 and was the par-

ty's first treasurer. He was killed by Oakland police on April 8, 1968, during a shootout with the police. Eldridge Cleaver, then thirty-two and the Panthers' minister of information, was the leader of what he later described as a "planned [Panther] 'ambush' against police officers that went awry." Joseph, *Midnight Hour*, 209, 228.

49. Bloom and Martin, *Black against Empire*, 345–46.

50. "The Student Occupation of Ford Hall, January 1969," in *Remembering Ford & Sydeman Halls, Brandeis University*, Brandeis University Library and Technical Services, http://lts.brandeis.edu/research/archives-speccoll/exhibits/ford/occupation/index.html; "City's Blacks Rally behind Students," *Boston Globe*, January 14, 1969.

51. "City's Blacks Rally Behind Students."

52. "United Front Steering Committee," February 17, 1969, Boston Black United Front records, box 2, folder 7, Special Collections, Roxbury Community College Library, Roxbury Crossing, Massachusetts.

53. Operation STOP was a BBUF initiative designed to stop construction of a proposed highway through Roxbury that would have devastated the community. The group forced the Boston Redevelopment Authority to undergo a two-year study of the effects of the proposed highway and eventually fully halted the construction. In the meantime, BBUF groups used the land for various community projects. "United Front Steering Committee Meeting," April 14, 1969, Boston Black United Front records, box 2, folder 7, Special Collections, Roxbury Community College Library; "Appendix 2: Comments from Elected Officials," Boston Planning and Development Agency, http://www.bostonplans.org/.

54. "Off the Pigs."

55. Ibid.; Dan Queen, "Panthers Charge Party Slandered," *Bay State Banner*, April 24, 1969.

56. "Repression of the Black Panther Newspaper," *Black Panther*, August 8, 1970.

57. Michael Fultz, "The Voice of the Panther Shall Be Heard throughout the Land," *Black Panther*, September 5, 1970.

58. Quoted in "Black Panther Warns Liberals: 'Leave Us Alone,'" *Boston Globe*, January 26, 1969.

59. Ibid.

60. Jane Rhodes, *Framing the Black Panthers: The Spectacular Rise of a Black Power Icon* (New York: New Press, 2007), 91.

61. Ann-Mary Currier, "Holy Thursday Begins Passion," *Boston Globe*, April 3, 1969.

62. Robert A. Jordan, "Parade, Rally in Roxbury Honors King," *Boston Globe*, April 5, 1969; Dan Queen, "Roxbury Honors Slain Black Leaders," *Bay State Banner*, April 10, 1969.

63. "Nationwide Rallies to Free Huey," *Black Panther*, May 5, 1969.

64. "Boston Purge," *Black Panther*, July 19, 1969.

65. Ibid. Others who were expelled were Paula Firmin, Les Wood, Monica Miller, Mike Grattan, Roger Freeman, Bernadette Mount, Pamela Hayes, and Maurice Kalhman.

66. Miranda conversation.

67. Ibid.

68. Lazerow, "The Black Panthers at the Water's Edge," 100.

69. "Boston Purge."

70. Chen, "Boston Panthers Stalk New Goal."

71. Miranda conversation.

72. Bloom and Martin, *Black against Empire*, 253.

73. Miranda conversation.

74. Chen, "Boston Panthers Stalk New Goal"; "Youth Attack Black Family in Dorchester," *Boston Globe*, June 29, 1969.

75. "Youth Attack Black Family in Dorchester."

76. Alan Lupo, "Dorchester Area Quiet after Attack," *Boston Globe*, June 30, 1969.

77. Bob Jackson, "Boston Pigs Mace and Brutalize Mother," *Black Panther*, August 2, 1969.

78. Lupo, "Dorchester Area Quiet after Attack."

79. "Boy's Drowning in MDC Pool Raises Dispute," *Boston Globe*, July 12, 1969; Robert A. Jordan, "Mother's Battle Resulted in Pool Study," *Boston Globe*, August 13, 1969.

80. Jordan, "Mother's Battle Resulted in Pool Study."

81. Chen, "Boston Panthers Stalk New Goal"; Eugene W. Jones, "From Boston Chapter," *Black Panther*, July 19, 1969; "Panthers Feed Kids," *Bay State Banner*, July 10, 1969.

82. "Panthers Feed Kids."

83. "Boston Breakfast," *Black Panther*, July 19, 1969.

84. "Panthers Feed Kids."

85. Chen, "Boston Panthers Stalk New Goals."

86. Jones, "From Boston Chapter."

87. Miranda conversation.

88. "United Front Steering Committee Meeting," July 14, August 11, and September 8, 1969, Boston Black United Front records, box 2, folder 7, Special Collections, Roxbury Community College Library.

89. Miranda conversation.

90. Floyd Hardwick, telephone conversation with Judson L. Jeffries, January 3, 2017.

91. Ibid.

92. The Cambridge NCCF even had a breakfast program.

93. "TV Changes, Radio Notes," *Boston Globe*, July 20, 1969; "Panthers to Meet," *Bay State Banner*, July 1, 1969.

94. "Metropolitan Calendar," *Boston Globe*, June 29, 1969.

95. Chen, "Boston Panthers Stalk New Goal."

96. Victor Chen, "300 Hear Panthers' Speakers," *Boston Globe*, July 7, 1969; Jones, "From Boston Chapter"; "Panthers Feed Kids."

97. Chen, "300 Hear Panthers' Speakers."

98. Viola Osgood and Robert Jordan, "Balloting Is Heavy in So. End Election," *Boston Globe*, July 27, 1969.

99. "300 Trek Hub's Freedom Trail to Protest War," *Boston Globe*, August 10, 1969.

100. Alex Rackley was a twenty-four-year-old Panther from the Harlem (New York City) chapter who was in New Haven with George Sams, in retrospect a likely police informant in the party. In New Haven, Sams denounced *Rackley* as a police informant and held him hostage in the basement of the Panther offices. On May 20 Sams took Rackley and two other New Haven Panthers, Lonnie McLucas and Warren Kimbro, to a swampy area up the interstate from the city. There Sams convinced Kimbro and McLucas to shoot the defenseless Rackley on "orders from national." The murder swirled into a national controversy that implicated Bobby Seale and entailed a massive manhunt, nine arrests, and eventually two trials. The arrests and

trials severely depleted the New Haven Panthers, hence the heavy involvement from Boston and the transfer of Miranda to New Haven as an organizer. Zayd, "Conn. Fascist Pigs Vamp On Panthers," *Black Panther*, August 23, 1969; "5 of Hub Area Arrested in Ct.," *Boston Globe*, August 10, 1969; "Boston Panthers Arrested in Conn.," *Bay State Banner*, August 14, 1969; Yohuru Williams, *Black Politics/White Power: Civil Rights, Black Power, and the Black Panthers in New Haven* (St. James, N.Y.: Brandywine Press, 2000), 139–40, 141, 142.

101. "5 of Hub Area Arrested in Ct."; "Boston Panthers Arrested in Conn."
102. "Boston Panthers Arrested in Conn."
103. Miranda conversation.
104. Ibid.
105. Eugene Jones, "Boston Pigs Rampage," *Black Panther*, September 13, 1969; "Panthers Arrested in Roxbury," *Bay State Banner*, August 21, 1969.
106. "Panthers Arrested in Roxbury."
107. "Continued Harassment," *Black Panther*, January 31, 1970.
108. Ibid.; "Repression Ad—Preliminary Draft: Section #2: Case of Robert Herd [sic]," March 25, 1970, Boston Black United Front records, box 13, folder 9, Special Collections, Roxbury Community College Library.
109. Or possibly Tartt, as spelled in Lorraine Baber, "Panther Acquitted on Robbery Charge," *Bay State Banner*, May 21, 1970.
110. Floyd, "Another Pig Plot to Frame Panther 'Big Bob,'" *Black Panther*, June 13, 1970.
111. "Panther Rally for Prisoners," *Bay State Banner*, November 20, 1969.
112. Ibid.
113. Eugene W. Jones, "Frame Up," *Black Panther*, November 8, 1969; Floyd, "Another Pig Plot To Frame Panther 'Big Bob.'"
114. Eugene W. Jones, "Frame Up," *Black Panther*, November 8, 1969; Floyd, "Another Pig Plot To Frame Panther 'Big Bob.'"
115. Floyd, "Another Pig Plot To Frame Panther 'Big Bob'"; "Panther Rally for Prisoners"; Lorraine Baber, "Panther Acquitted on Robbery Charge," *Bay State Banner*, May 21, 1970.
116. "Black Panthers Arrested at Dudley; Protest against Police Continues," *Bay State Banner*, September 11, 1969.
117. "United Front Steering Committee Meeting," September 15, 1969, Boston Black United Front records, box 2, folder 7, Special Collections, Roxbury Community College Library.
118. "Panthers form Committee," *Bay State Banner*, October 16, 1969.
119. "6 Panthers Arrested," *Boston Globe*, September 4, 1969; "Rally against Police Station," *Bay State Banner*, August 28, 1969.
120. "6 Panthers Arrested"; "Rally against Police Station"; "Black Panthers Arrested at Dudley."
121. "Black Panthers Arrested at Dudley."
122. "Continued Harassment"; "Repression Ad—Preliminary Draft."
123. "Continued Harassment"; "Repression Ad—Preliminary Draft."
124. "Continued Harassment."
125. "United Front Steering Committee Meeting," September 15, 1969, Boston Black United Front records, box 2, folder 7, Special Collections, Roxbury Community College Library.

126. Parker Donham, "MIT Sides Square for Takeover," *Boston Globe*, October 30, 1969.

127. Ibid.

128. Crocker Snow Jr., "800 in Antiwar March at MIT," *Boston Globe*, November 5, 1969.

129. Bloom and Martin, *Black against Empire*, 253.

130. Cappy Pinderhughes, "Free Our Sisters," *Black Panther*, December 6, 1969; Bloom and Martin, *Black against Empire*, 254–55.

131. Cappy Pinderhughes, "Free Our Sisters," *Black Panther*, December 6, 1969; Bloom and Martin, *Black against Empire*, 254–55.

132. Angela D. LeBlanc-Ernest, "Black Panther Party Women," in *The Black Panther Party Reconsidered*, ed. Charles E. Jones (Baltimore: Black Classic Press, 1998), 311.

133. Miranda conversation.

134. LeBlanc-Ernest, "Black Panther Party Women," 310–11; Charles Jones and Judson L. Jeffries, "Don't Believe the Hype: Debunking the Panther Mythology," in Jones, *The Black Panther Party Reconsidered*, 34–35.

135. Robert S. Oden and Thomas A. Casey, "Power to the People: Service Learning and Social Justice," *Electronic Magazine of Multicultural Education* 8, no. 2 (2006): 11, 12.

136. LeBlanc-Ernest, "Black Panther Party Women," 312, 319–20.

137. Though this study does have the resources to effectively study the gender dynamics of the Boston branch in depth, it should be noted that many women appear in the various newspaper sources on the Panthers in Boston. Women such as Donna Howell were essential to the functioning of the party in Boston, and further study is needed to more deeply explore the gender politics in the Boston branch.

138. Gordon D. Hall, "Blazing Rhetoric or Cold Week-end," *Boston Globe*, December 12, 1969; Parker Donham, "BU Denies Student Demands, SDS Votes Monday Takeover," *Boston Globe*, December 5, 1969; "Panther Rally for Slain Leader," *Bay State Banner*, December 11, 1969.

139. Hall, "Blazing Rhetoric or Cold Week-end."

140. "Panther Rally for Slain Leader."

141. James Young, "Boston Free Clothing Program," *Black Panther*, January 31, 1970; "Panthers Begin Free Clothing Program," *Bay State Banner*, January 15, 1970.

142. "Panthers Begin Free Clothing Program."

143. Big Bob, "On the Necks of the Greedy Businessmen," *Black Panther*, May 19, 1970.

144. "Panthers Begin Free Clothing Program."

145. Young, "Boston Free Clothing Program."

146. "Panthers Begin Free Clothing Program."

147. "Panthers Rally for Huey Newton," *Bay State Banner*, February 19, 1970.

148. Lorraine Baber, "Panthers Open New Headquarters," *Bay State Banner*, March 12, 1970.

149. "Landlordism," *Black Panther*, April 18, 1970.

150. Ibid.

151. Bob, "Boston . . . Pigs Beat Mr. Johnson in His Home," *Black Panther*, July 18, 1970.

152. Roland Chambers, "11 Year Old Brother Beaten for Not Saluting 'The Symbol of Fascism, the American Flag,'" *Black Panther*, September 26, 1970.

153. Mike Ellis, "15 Year Old Brother Escapes Racist School," *Black Panther*, October 24, 1970.

154. Robert A. Jordan, "'You Can Jail a Revolutionary but Not a Revolution'—Black Panther," *Boston Globe*, July 26, 1970.

155. "Life in Concentration Camps—Boston," *Black Panther*, March 27, 1971.

156. Jordan, "You Can Jail a Revolutionary"; Diana Roberson, "Determining Our Destiny," *Black Panther*, July 3, 1970.

157. Roberson, "Determining Our Destiny."

158. Michael Fultz, "Pigs Attempt to Sabotage Free Breakfast Program," *Black Panther*, November 21, 1970.

159. "Hub Probe of Police Brutality Charge Delayed," *Boston Globe*, May 2, 1970; Parker Donham, "Panther Posture at New Haven," *Boston Globe*, April 26, 1970.

160. Quoted in Donham, "Panther Posture at New Haven."

161. Michael Kenney, "Thousands Pack Common for Vietnam Moratorium," *Boston Globe*, April 16, 1970.

162. Parker Donham, "War Protest Week Begins in Boston," *Boston Globe*, April 14, 1970; Kenney, "Thousands Pack Common for Vietnam Moratorium."

163. Donham, "War Protest Week Begins in Boston"; Parker Donham, "War Protest Due Today On Common," *Boston Globe*, April 15, 1970.

164. Michael Kenney, "30,000 Gather in Quiet Demonstration," *Boston Globe*, May 9, 1970.

165. Quoted in Ken O. Botwright, "Pre-med Student Marches, Vows to Work for Changes," *Boston Globe*, May 9, 1970.

166. Arthur Jones, "7000 Rock in Sun for Panthers' Defense Fund," *Boston Globe*, May 11, 1970.

167. "The Black Panther Party Peoples' Free Health Center," *Black Panther*, June 13, 1970; Lorraine Baber, "Panther Clinic Opening Delayed," *Bay State Banner*, May 21, 1970. Franklin Lynch was a black singer who was shot, while in the Boston City Hospital, by a Boston policeman who was guarding him in March 1970. The People's Free Medical Center was dedicated to Lynch "to show that even though they murder one of us, the people are going to keep on fighting," according to Donna Howell. The Panthers were involved in the community response to the shooting—a "People's Trial" held in Roxbury and organized by the Boston Black United Front. Panther Floyd Hardwick was one of the organizers of the trial. "Police Trial Committee," March 11, 1970, Boston Black United Front records, box 13, folder 8, Special Collections, Roxbury Community College Library.

168. "Black Panther Party Peoples' Free Health Center"; Baber, "Panther Clinic Opening Delayed."

169. "Roxbury Intern Plan Provides 'Black Adult Examples,'" *Boston Globe*, August 23, 1970.

170. "The Black Panther Party Peoples' Free Health Center."

171. Alondra Nelson, *Body and Soul: The Black Panther Party and the Fight Against Medical Discrimination* (Minneapolis: University of Minnesota Press, 2011), 18, 6, 8–9. Nelson says, "On the medical civil rights movement, see Herbert Morais, *The History of the Negro in Medicine* (New York: Publishers Company, 1967), chap. 9."

172. Lorraine Baber, "Black Panther Health Clinic Opens in Roxbury," *Bay State Banner*, June 4, 1970.

173. "The Black Panther Party Peoples' Free Health Center."

174. "Roxbury Intern Plan Provides 'Black Adult Examples.'"

175. "Community Health Care Centers—a Two-Page Report: Dim Prognosis for New Health Care Efforts," *Boston Globe*, October 11, 1970.

176. Baber, "Panther Clinic Opening Delayed."

177. Diana, "People Unite to Deal with the Slumlords," *Black Panther*, September 26, 1970.

178. "The Black Panther Party Peoples' Free Health Center."

179. Nelson, *Body and Soul*, 73.

180. Ibid., 65, 70–71.

181. Ibid., 187, 15, 114.

182. Lydia, "People Save Brother near Death from Drugs," *Black Panther*, October 24, 1970.

183. "Pig Harasses Brother at People's Free Health Center," *Black Panther*, December 26, 1970.

184. Richard Knox, "Scientist Donates Award to Panthers," *Boston Globe*, April 28, 1970.

185. Robert A. Jordan, "Reaction to Panthers Varied," *Boston Globe*, September 27, 1970.

186. "Leonard A. Durant to Sister Donna Howell," September 15, 1971, Boston Black United Front records, box 5, folder 4, Special Collections, Roxbury Community College Library.

187. "Racist Bandits Attack Peoples Free Health Center," *Black Panther*, July 18, 1970.

188. Quoted in Baber, "Panther Clinic Opening Delayed."

189. Ahmad A. Rahman, "Marching Blind: The Rise and Fall of the Black Panther Party in Detroit," in *Liberated Territory: Untold Local Perspectives on the Black Panther Party*, eds. Yohuru Williams and Jama Lazerow (Durham: Duke University Press, 2008),189–91.

190. Lazerow, "Black Panthers at the Water's Edge," 92.

191. Roland Chambers, "Concerning the New Bedford N.C.C.F.," *Black Panther*, September 5, 1970; Joseph Harvey, "Wouldn't Tell Bristol County Jury about Night with Panthers: Supreme Court Hears Case of Reporter Who Refused to Testify," *Boston Globe*, January 6, 1971; "The New Bedford 20," *Black Panther*, September 5, 1970.

192. Lazerow, "Black Panthers at the Water's Edge," 110–11. At this time, Hilliard was the highest ranking Panther on the central committee because Newton and Seale were both involved in trials.

193. Robert A. Jordan, "New Bedford Blacks Object to Police 'Occupying Us,'" *Boston Globe*, August 2, 1970.

194. Lazerow, "Black Panthers at the Water's Edge," 111.

195. "Free Prison Busing Program in Boston," *Black Panther*, November 21, 1970.

196. "An Open Letter of Thanks to the Black Community of Boston," *Black Panther*, January 16, 1971.

197. "United Front Meeting," August 12, 1970, Boston Black United Front records, box 6, folder 2, Special Collections, Roxbury Community College Library.

198. Jones was essential to the Boston Panthers and took over the leadership after Miranda was transferred to New Haven because of her "impressive skills, which made her the most qualified person to assume the captain's position." In her chapter in *The Black Panther Party Reconsidered*, Angela D. LeBlanc-Ernest continually praises Jones for her leadership capacity and skill and heavily implies that she was critically import-

ant to the strength and functioning of the Boston branch of the Black Panther Party. Jama Lazerow, in his chapter in *Liberated Territory* also emphasizes Jones's importance to the Boston Panthers and that she was a very strong leader. LeBlanc-Ernest, "Black Panther Party Women," 305–34; Lazerow, "Black Panthers at the Water's Edge," 94, 100.

199. "People's Free Health Center Aids in Correcting Child's Eyesight," *Black Panther*, March 20, 1971.

200. "Another Family Evicted," *Black Panther*, May 22, 1971.

201. "Black Shoppers Beaten and Robbed," *Black Panther*, July 10, 1971.

202. "General Body Meeting," July 14, 1971, Boston Black United Front records, box 6, folder 2, Special Collections, Roxbury Community College Library.

203. "General Body Meeting," July 28, 1971, Boston Black United Front records, box 6, folder 2, Special Collections, Roxbury Community College Library.

204. "Boston Celebrates First Anniversery [sic] of People's Free Health Center," *Black Panther*, June 12, 1971.

205. "The Boston People's Free Health Center Will Come to You," *Black Panther*, October 4, 1971.

206. "Boston Celebrates First Anniversery [sic] of People's Free Health Center."

207. "Boston People's Free Health Center Will Come to You"; Walter Haynes, "Panthers Conduct Sickle Cell Testing," *Bay State Banner*, October 21, 1971.

208. "The Black Panther Party Is Giving Free Sickle Cell Anemia Tests in These Areas," *Black Panther*, June 12, 1971. Sickle cell anemia is a genetic disease that predominantly appears in people of African descent. Alondra Nelson describes it as "an incurable and ultimately fatal genetic disease that causes typically round red blood cells to take a sickle shape, depleting their ability to circulate oxygen through the body." The sickle cell anemia testing campaign not only screened members of the community for a disease that was relatively unknown—and not tested for—but was also a way to educate the community, to provide them with information that they otherwise would not have had. The Panthers saw the medical community in the United States as ignoring African American citizens on purpose, and the problem entailed a "history of racial slavery, contemporary racism, and the inadequacies of profit-driven healthcare." Nelson, *Body and Soul*, 4, 19, 115, 123.

209. Ann Marie Currier, "2000 of Boston's Blacks Get Sickle Cell Test by Panthers," *Boston Globe*, October 25, 1971; Walter Haynes, "Panthers Conduct Sickle Cell Testing," *Bay State Banner*, October 21, 1971.

210. Currier, "2000 of Boston's Blacks Get Sickle Cell Test by Panthers."

211. "Boston People's Free Health Center Will Come to You."

212. "Steering Committee Meeting," September 13, 1971, Boston Black United Front records, box 3, folder 4, Special Collections, Roxbury Community College Library; "Leonard A. Durant to Sister Donna Howell," September 15, 1971, Boston Black United Front records, box 5, folder 4, Special Collections, Roxbury Community College Library.

213. "Use of Resources Form," November 5, 1971, Boston Black United Front records, box 1, folder 7, Special Collections, Roxbury Community College Library.

214. Viola Osgood, "Health Day Held in Roxbury," *Boston Globe*, November 28, 1971; "Youth Have Their Day in Roxbury," *Bay State Banner*, December 23, 1971.

215. Haynes, "Panthers Conduct Sickle Cell Testing."

216. Nelson, *Body and Soul*, 116.

217. "Panthers in Boston were increasingly less a part of political discourse": this

is likely because sympathy for the party nationally was falling during the early 1970s. After Huey Newton was released from prison, the party lost clout with many leftists for its claim that an African American could not receive a fair trial in the United States. In addition, the Newton-Cleaver split, which resulted in internal warfare, along with a series of high-profile trials, affected the perception of the party. Some white Leftists came to see the Panthers as thugs.

218. "So It's Backyards and Bullets for Black Youth," *Black Panther*, June 17, 1972.

219. "Mail Log," January 4–5, 1972, Boston Black United Front records, box 1, folder 2, Special Collections, Roxbury Community College Library.

220. "Blood Test," *Boston Globe*, July 15, 1972.

221. Ed Buryn, "Suffer Not, Little Children," *Black Panther*, April 27, 169.

222. Robert A. Jordan, "Reaction to Panthers Varied," *Boston Globe*, September 27, 1970.

223. Jordan, "You Can Jail a Revolutionary."

224. "Black Panthers Arrested at Dudley."

225. Jordan, "You Can Jail a Revolutionary."

226. "Welfare Bill Would Help," *Boston Globe*, June 5, 1967.

227. Federal Bureau of Investigation, Letter to SAC, Boston, December 17, 1968, document in possession of authors.

228. "Police Attacking Free Health Center," Freedom House Archives, 1941–2004, box 57/84, Northeastern University.

229. Cynthia Bellamy, "Black Panthers Shift from 'Guns to Butter,'" *Bay State Banner*, August 2, 1973. After a trip to China in 1972, Audrea Jones would remain in Oakland, and she eventually became a director of Bobby Seale's mayoral campaign and the George Jackson Free Health Clinic. Jones would also be elected to the Berkley Community Development Council in 1973. After Donna Howell moved to Oakland, she became one of the directors of the Black Panther Party's Oakland Community School. Former Boston chapter leader Doug Miranda also moved to Oakland. He had been working with the New Haven chapter. LeBlanc-Ernest, "Black Panther Party Women," 317, 318, 319; Lazerow, "Black Panthers at the Water's Edge," 101.

230. Bellamy, "Black Panthers Shift from 'Guns to Butter.'"

231. Nelson, *Body and Soul*, 184.

232. Joel Rhodes and Judson L. Jeffries, "Motor City Panthers," *On the Ground: The Black Panther Party in Communities across America*, ed. in Judson L. Jeffries (Jackson: University Press of Mississippi, 2010), 127.

233. Ibid., 127, 173.

From Civil Rights to Black Power in Texas

Dallas to Denton and Back to Dallas

AVA TIYE KINSEY AND JUDSON L. JEFFRIES

When people, scholars included, think of the Black Panther Party, few, if any, associate the group with the Lone Star State. Until Charles E. Jones's 2010 work on the People's Party II in Houston, virtually nothing of a scholarly nature existed on the Black Panthers in Texas. Indeed the footnote that is the Black Panther Party in Texas is a microcosm of the way the black liberation struggle in Texas appears in the literature generally. Historian Stefanie Decker posits one reason, albeit a debatable one, for the noticeable gap in research on the civil rights movement in Dallas: that city "appeared to lack the deep segregation of other Southern cities."[1] This could not have been further from the truth. In his work, *An Empire for Slavery: The Peculiar Institution in Texas, 1821–1865*, Randolph B. Campbell posits that "so long as Texas is not seen as a southern state, its [white] people do not have to face the great moral evil of slavery and the bitter heritage of black-white relations that followed the defeat of the Confederacy in 1865. [White] Texans are thus permitted to escape a major part of what C. Vann Woodward called 'the burden of Southern History.'"[2]

Like elsewhere, many Dallas residents (especially younger ones) are barely knowledgeable of struggles for social justice that have occurred in their own city. Historian Michael Phillips reasons that "academic neglect of Dallas... represents amnesia by design. In this obsessively image-conscious city, elites feared that a conflict-marred past filled with class and racial strife represented a dangerous model for the future. City leaders transformed the community into a laboratory of forgetfulness."[3] The essay that follows, while providing a glimpse into black people's struggle for racial equality, focuses on the period from 1965 to the mid-1970s. Still, an appraisal of Dallas's earlier history is required to understand the "amnesia by design" that government officials strategically implemented even at the city's beginning.[4]

Although founded by John Neely Bryan in 1841—the origin of the name is still a matter of controversy—Dallas took much of its spirit from La Reunion, a community established in 1855 a few miles west of Bryan's site.[5] The founders of La Reunion, Victor Considérant and a group of French, Swiss, and Belgian socialists, sought to create an earthly heaven on the Texas prairie, where physical and intellectual needs would be fully satisfied through a system of cooperation. For a variety of reasons, the experiment failed, but the ideal of a perfect city would remain, despite considerable alteration by time and circumstances.[6]

Dallas as a proverbial city upon a hill, to be emulated, was part of an intentional "process of myth-making [that] marks the key moments of Dallas history from its founding," Harvey Graff writes.[7] Graff quotes medieval historian Gervase Rosser, who asserts that such urban myths do well to give "people a shared urban identity, located on common ground." According to Rosser, "The effect of these urban myths was not merely to reflect the cultural and social *status quo*, but to transform it."[8] This origin myth is detailed in several texts about Dallas. Jim Schutze's *The Accommodation: The Politics of Race in an American City* illuminates the inner workings of cosmopolitan Dallas: "Dallas clings stubbornly to a particular myth of the city's origin that has been soundly disproved by historians but whose persistent retelling tells volumes about the city's psyche. The contention is that Dallas was founded in the middle of nowhere, with no great navigable river or port or other feature of the planet on which to fix its purpose. The end of the story, as it is told in Dallas, is that Dallas became a great city anyway, in spite of its purposelessness, because of the zeal and grit and determination of its people." Schutze maintains that Dallas was an anomaly "until after the Civil War, when the arrival of the railroads made it a terminal town."[9]

The Dallas origin myth would extend throughout the twentieth century to the civil rights movement era. Decker affirms this and details how the myth was strategically implemented. "After violence erupted in Little Rock, Arkansas, Birmingham and Selma, Alabama, and Jackson, Mississippi, Dallas' elites decided to begin the process of integration and control before others launched the civil rights movement on a path they did not wish to trod.... Known as the 'Dallas Way,' these men governed the social, economic, and political structure of the city."[10] After the *Brown v. Board of Education* decision in 1954, the Dallas news media "warned this was the first step in the NAACP's effort to promote social intercourse between blacks and unwilling whites, something the [city officials] did not like," historian Robert B. Fairbanks writes. "When school officials refused to allow twenty-eight African American students into white schools in 1955, the Dallas NAACP sued [with the help of Thurgood Marshall].... Fearful of the violence that occurred in some southern cities such as Little Rock and New Orleans, the [Dallas Chamber of Commerce] worked out a plan to promote peaceful integration ... [and to] sell integration to the city."[11] In many ways, city leaders attempted to anticipate the tactics of civil rights activists in Dallas in order to prevent the upheaval that occurred in other cities.

In the words of Mark Herbener, white pastor of the African American parish of Mount Olive Lutheran Church in South Dallas, "Dallas had the problem in that it never had the meanness of Birmingham.... When black folks walked down the street... they were greeted with 'Good morning.' They weren't treated uncivilly.... [The city government] learned that you don't fight. You just use a pillow.... It was a strategy. It was a great strategy.... 'We'll give. You can come in. You can today, but you can't tomorrow,' and people think it's integrated."[12]

City leaders perceiving a need to act preemptively against African American movements often referred to "Dallas as a whole," which was, Schutze writes, "the emblematic phrasing the Citizens Council always used in its heyday to signal its own authority, wisdom, and concern for the greater good of the city."[13] In 1961 city officials commissioned filmmaker and advertising executive Sam R. Bloom to create *Dallas at the Crossroads*.[14] This twenty-one-minute film, narrated by Walter Cronkite, showed eager white Dallasites successfully participating in integration.[15] The film was not shown throughout the South so as not to undermine the city's economic and business interests. In that same year the Dallas Chamber of Commerce was in action. Fairbanks writes,

> Fearful that black-initiated efforts to integrate downtown Dallas might thwart efforts by the chamber to recruit more business, civic leaders formulated a program of managed integration, although not before certain blacks started picketing downtown stores that would not serve them. Under this growing pressure, the [chamber] arranged for blacks to walk into forty-nine downtown restaurants and be served on July 26, 1961, without incident. The action brought the city good national publicity. For instance, the *New York Times* observed that "there seems to be today a dominant spirit of moderation and goodwill [in Dallas]."[16]

To do their bidding, Dallas's white ruling class handpicked several African Americans—businessmen plus clergy who presided over large congregations—to serve on an integrated council of fourteen members, seven blacks and seven whites, to facilitate a desegregation plan that was palatable to white city planners.[17] This was confirmed by the election of Dr. Emmett Conrad, the first African American appointed to the Board of Trustees of the Dallas Independent School District. Conrad held that "the majority of Negro people in Dallas want to bring about change in the same way we have always done it in the past—through discussions with the white leadership, and, if necessary, through the courts."[18] Albert Lipscomb, an African American community leader prior to the civil rights movement and a black nationalism advocate during the 1960s, also confirmed the existence of accommodating black leaders appointed by Dallas's white elite: "We'd go downtown with our hats in hands and talk to the establishment. The establishment would appoint some super spook leader. You'd see the same names on all the boards and commissions—the more responsible Negroes, as [Mayor] Erik Jonsson used to call them."[19]

In August 1960, the Dallas Community Committee (DCC), another racially mixed group, was assembled to "carry out the activities for improving race relations and desegregating public life that resulted from the negotiations of the Committee of 14."[20] The DCC was headed by the Reverend E. C. Estell whose St. John Missionary Baptist Church had one of the largest congregations in Dallas. He and S. M. Wright, pastor of People's Baptist Church, gravely disapproved of duplicating civil rights tactics that occurred elsewhere such as publicly boycotting racist systems and institutions.[21] The committee of fourteen and the DCC were both supported by the Interdenominational Ministerial Alliance (IMA), which was influential in swaying the minds and deeds of their African American congregants. The actions taken by Rev. Estell and his colleagues—especially his contemporary S. M. Wright—against the civil rights and Black Power movements were duplicitous to say the least.

Meanwhile, a local black newspaper, the *Dallas Express*, censored itself at the urging of city officials and did not cover stories that dealt with the mid-1960s demonstrations.[22] Not until 1977 would the *Dallas Morning News* suggest that a similar tactic was forced upon white media as well: "The Dallas [FBI] office's major suggestion was to encourage 'trusted and reliable' news media representatives to withhold coverage of the New Left events."[23] Phillips, Decker, and Graff concur that President John F. Kennedy's assassination, the October 1963 assault in Dallas on UN ambassador Adlai Stevenson, and the 1960 mobbing of then–U.S. senator Lyndon B. Johnson and his wife all tarnished Dallas's image and prompted local officials to tactically quarantine what they deemed to be negative press, which might slow down a growing local economy.[24]

To put things in context, a history of Texas follows, with special attention paid to black people's struggle for equality and the efforts on the part of state as well as non-state actors to keep blacks submissive.

Back-Mapping the Movement

Known sometimes as the "peculiar institution," southern states slavery was even more peculiar in Texas than elsewhere because of the territory's history of rule by different governing bodies. The boundary lines that now demarcate Texas were not fashioned as such early on. After Spaniards wrested much of Texas's land from the Comanche, Lipa, and Caddo peoples, among thousands of others who had lived in that region for centuries, the land mass known as Texas came under sometimes concurrent Spanish rule (1527–1821) and French rule (1687–1803). After Mexican independence, Texas was under Mexican rule (1821–36), then became its own country—the Republic of Texas (1836–46), a state in the Union (1846–61), a part of the Confederacy (1861–65), and was readmitted into the Union in 1870.[25] Because of its changing status—territory, nation, or lawless land—Texas offered a myriad of opportunities for enslaved

Africans to negotiate their freedom. Contrary to the common knowledge of escaped slaves all traveling north by following the North Star, some traveled south—or at least southwest—on the Underground Railroad, typically during the first Mexican Revolution (1810–21) and the years of Mexican rule, but even up until 1850, when the acting Mexican president, General Santa Anna, abolished slavery.[26]

Texas's tenuous status made it, more often than not, a lawless space. The so-called neutral zone, an ill-defined and ungovernable area in East Texas, became known as the Badlands. Its boundaries were vague, due to its various owners, and constantly subjected to renegotiation. The area attracted criminals on the run, land speculators, and pirates such as Jean Lafitte, who smuggled African slaves into Louisiana through Galveston. "To say that you had 'gone to Texas' meant that you had gone beyond the law, to a foreign country where the laws of the United States did not apply."[27]

Anna Irene Sandbo's 1915 article "The First Session of the Secession Convention of Texas" notes the marred Texas past: "Turbulence and violence were greater in 1860 than at any time during the last few preceding years. The newspapers were full of stories of crimes committed within its [borders]."[28] On July 8, 1860, a fire, thought to be the work of abolitionist-arsonists, spread throughout North, East, and West Dallas, causing between $300,000 and $400,000 worth of damage. Reports were circulated, often unfounded, of black uprisings and wholesale poisonings. Arson occurred in many parts of the state. Arrests led to the detection of a plot to perpetuate such acts on a larger scale. The Dallas fire was found to have been conceived by abolitionist preachers who hoped to demoralize by fire and assassination the whole of North Texas. When the country was reduced to a helpless condition, a general revolt of the slaves would follow, it was hoped.[29]

An elderly African man known as Old Cato or Uncle Cato Miller was said to have mentioned setting the city aflame and to have "implicated two other Negroes, [Rev. Samuel] Smith and Patrick Jennings as his accomplices."[30] The men maintained that they had been coerced into giving their testimony and that they had been under the influence of white northern abolitionists.[31] The preachers were allegedly whipped and told to leave Dallas. Historian Julia Garrett wrote in her 1972 history of Forth Worth, "A mass meeting of Dallas citizens held on Monday following Sunday's fire ... [agreed] to hang the three Negroes and appoint a committee to whip every Negro in the county."[32]

Although President Lincoln's 1863 Emancipation Proclamation freed enslaved Africans in the Union, the stronghold of the Confederacy and the vestiges of the Republic of Texas did not abolish slavery until June 19, 1865, subsequently a holiday known as Juneteenth. The Reconstruction era (1865–77) proved to be no less volatile for persons of African descent in Texas than previous years. When the newly freed men and women learned of their status, their response to the news was strangely mixed. Some stayed on the plantations on which they had been forced to live. Others left in search of their families. Some moved to cities to secure employment, while others sought to make lives for themselves by developing settlements and living directly off the land. Many who traveled to cities would not gain employment because urban whites believed that the freedmen would otherwise undercut their wages. The Ku Klux Klan began a large campaign against blacks statewide. Blacks who had been involved in the Civil War were somewhat able to defend themselves against those who wished to do them harm.[33] Others weren't so fortunate. History professor Marvin Dulaney writes, "Nearly two thousand African Americans were murdered between 1865 and 1868 through random violence, vigilantism, and attempts by former Texas slaveholders to keep them in slavery."[34]

Reconstruction led to the establishment of black schools, churches, and businesses. The *Dallas Express*, a black newspaper, emerged in 1892.[35] According to Merline Pitre in "The Evolution of Black Political Participation in Reconstruction Texas," black Texans did not begin to involve themselves in the political arena "until the passage of the Reconstruction Acts of 1867." Although Texas had the smallest black population of any formerly Confederate state, its freed people went to the polls on February 10, 1868, cast 35,952 votes in favor of a constitutional convention, and elected nine blacks to serve as constitutional delegates. From 1868 to 1898, forty-one men of African descent served in the Texas legislature.[36]

Roots of the Civil Rights Movement

At the turn of the century, black Texans sought to procure rights for themselves through political means. In 1907 "Dallas revised its charter to establish segregation of the races in all aspects of city life."[37] In 1918 George F. Porter, a Dallas educator, and attorney Ammon S. Wells chartered the Dallas chapter of the National Association for the Advancement of Colored People (NAACP). The success of D. W. Griffith's epic film *Birth of a Nation*, based on Thomas Dixon's novel *The Clansman* (1905), with its portrayals of Radical Republicans as villains, had helped foment racial animosity that had been simmering since Reconstruction. This resulted in the resurgence of the KKK in Texas, so much so that by the early 1920s state membership had swelled into the thousands. At about the same time, the Klan-dominated Dallas Police Department intimidated the NAACP virtually out of existence by mandating that a Dallas police officer attend all NAACP meetings to observe.[38] This intrusion halted the NAACP's productivity until its eventual resurgence in the 1930s. Nevertheless, African Americans continued to build autonomous and thriving communities and institutions in Dallas in spite of the city's efforts to undermine them.

The black church was undoubtedly the institution that anchored black lives and community initiatives. In the twentieth century's first two decades, the Pentecostal Church and its leaders and congregants endeavored to enhance the lives of Dallas's black citizens. The first bishop of the Church of God in Christ in Texas, Bishop E. M. Page, prided himself on instilling the value of education. Black Pentecostals were seen by the black Dallas Protestant elites as too "otherworldly," but in Texas they showed a dual commitment to spiritual and intellectual growth. In their view, holiness was the spiritual foundation for success. By becoming upstanding members of the community, students of the Page Normal and Industrial Bible Institute, a Church of God in Christ Educational facility, were better positioned to address social problems.[39]

The Pentecostal movement attracted the masses of blacks in a way that the older Protestant denominations did not. Through the incorporation of "come-as-you-are" worship fused with social uplift, the Pentecostal Church gave those who otherwise would not have had educational opportunities a venue for formal learning.[40] They encountered tremendous backlash from Dallas's black middle class, but the Pentecostal Church's popularity continued to rise into the 1930s.[41] Due to lack of government intervention, African American leaders and businessmen sought to fix community problems themselves, as had been the pattern historically. One such leader was the Reverend Maynard Jackson Sr., who was most well known for his 1936 campaign to put an end to the Democratic "white primary" (enacted by the state legislature in 1923) and the poll tax, both of which precluded black Texans from exercising their constitutional right to vote.[42]

Indeed it was Jackson, who, along with A. Maceo Smith and Ammon S. Wells, helped to establish the Progressive Voters League (PVL), an organization that would play an integral role in making black electoral power a reality in Texas. Established in 1934 as the Progressive Citizens League, the PVL was intended, much like the NAACP, "to encourage [blacks'] involvement in the political process and the positive use of the ballot to secure the needs of their community."[43] In fact, many PVL members had been actively involved in the NAACP's formation. Grassroots organizer Eva "Mama Mack" McMillan credits the PVL with spurring her involvement in the civil rights movement. McMillan became a sort of surrogate mother of the movement, particularly to young people in the Student Nonviolent Coordinating Committee (SNCC). McMillan recounts her involvement in the PVL: "My brother, Clifton Partee accepted a job with the prestigious Progressive Voters League to be the executive secretary of the organization.... He enrolled his siblings into the same ventures.... He immediately gave us a list of numbers and people to call... and we became phone bank callers to the voters in our precinct. We also walked the street distributing literature.... It was really an effort to define what we felt was important in those times and encourage blacks to vote."[44] It is worth noting that after the U.S. Supreme Court's *Smith v. Allwright* ruling ended the white Democratic primary in Texas, Maynard Jackson Sr. (PVL's first president) helped the Progressive Voters League spread statewide and nationwide.

The significance of the Texas NAACP, especially in Dallas, is apparent. One integral player in the early civil rights movement locally was the unrivaled organizer and field-worker Juanita Jewel Craft. Craft was recruited by Minnie Flanagan in 1935. Flanagan would become president of the Dallas NAACP in 1959 and begin to involve the organization in sit-ins a few years later.[45] When Craft joined the organization in 1935, it had three principal objectives: ending the racist and classist Texas Democratic primary election, providing more educational opportunities for blacks, and impelling courts statewide to include blacks on juries, especially on cases trying African Americans, for the specific purpose of safeguarding African American men from lynching.[46]

In 1937, Craft, then a field-worker, suggested that the Texas branches of the NAACP standardize organizing methods, a daunting task considering the size of the state. Reading about the executive secretary and acting president of the Houston branch Lulu B. White, Craft traveled to Houston to strategize ways to consolidate the Texas movement. Fusing what she learned from White with her own experience as a field-worker, Craft's procedure for organizing was to write to individuals interested in establishing an NAACP chapter in their community. She instructed them to organize a nucleus of prospective members and discuss the association's objectives. When fifty people agreed to join, the group applied for a charter. They launched the organization with a well-publicized mass meeting, at which Craft was the main speaker. Her visit was (according to member Donald Jones) "like a blood transfusion to a very weak patient."[47]

Between 1943 and 1945, the NAACP's membership increased by a whopping seven thousand due to a massive membership drive spearheaded by Craft. In late 1946, White was appointed director of branches, and Craft was elected state organizer, responsible for Texas. White and Craft would work in these unpaid positions for more than a decade. By 1958 Craft had established 182 branches statewide.[48] Craft also established the youth wing of the Dallas NAACP Branch, referred to as "Craft's Kids." In 1955, Craft organized a protest of the Texas State Fair with the help of the NAACP's youth wing. Her aims were to have African Americans boycott the fair's "Negro Achievement Day," the only day that Black people were allowed by law to attend the fair. The protest garnered substantial support. In total, approximately thirteen people boycotted the Negro Achievement Day, calling it "Negro Appeasement Day." The City of Dallas, responsible for the fair, refused to integrate it, and the following year, in 1956, students circulated a petition to ban segregation at the fair and launched an even larger protest. However, "The Dallas NAACP ... called off the protest when the state's attorney general and a group of East Texas legislators set out to destroy the [NAACP] in Texas."[49] Dulaney writes, "It took the NAACP more than three years to recover."[50]

After World War II and the Korean War, many African American veterans returned to Dallas looking to purchase homes for their families. Because the black neighborhoods were overcrowded, veterans began to move into predominantly white neighborhoods like South Dallas, which had a large Jewish population.[51] Located near the African American communities of Deep Elm and Freedman's Town, South Dallas provided veterans and their families with more appealing livable conditions than the shanties and condemned housing in West Dallas and Queen City that were sanctioned by the Dallas government. Veterans could now own their own property and not have to rent rooms in the homes of more well-off African Americans in Freedman's Town.

Despite resistance from Jewish residents as well as whites from other parts of the city, more African Americans began to move into South Dallas. From the mid to late 1940s through the 1950s, nightly bombings of black residents' homes were not uncommon. Some African American veterans responded with individual force, shooting back, and through the founding of the Fair Park Homeowners' Organization.[52] After several city-supported investigations of the bombings and an all-out manhunt for the perpetrators, a paper trail led to the door of the Dallas Citizens Council. It was discovered that the president of the South Dallas Bank and Trust Company, a member of the council, had paid members of two white South Dallas community organizations to bomb black residents' homes. To squelch the incessant violence against the growing black neighborhood in South Dallas, the city chartered a special neighborhood called Hamilton Park toward the northern border of Dallas near the Richardson city limits. This all–African American development offered housing for Dallas's growing black middle class without encroaching on white neighborhoods.[53]

1960 through 1964

During the early 1960s, African Americans on the DCC committee of fourteen and the board of the DCC and in the IMA sought to halt the direct action tactics of the civil rights movement. Dulaney writes that these clergyman and businessmen wished to "go along with the established way of doing things in the city's political culture ... [for they had] realized some benefits ... for themselves ... for years."[54] However, not all members of the IMA and DCC were so entrenched. New Hope Baptist Church pastor Rhett James was dissatisfied with the way prominent African American preachers complied with white city leaders' wishes.

In October 1960, James led the first organized picket of segregated downtown stores, using various members of the community—from beauticians to business owners—to staff picket lines each day for two months. Unfortunately, the backlash that James received from the DCC led to his resignation one year later. At the time, the DCC was under the strict order of S. M. Wright to stop all protests, boycotts, and picketing. After James's resignation, he continued, undaunted, to pressure the seven African American members of the committee of fourteen to begin desegregating the city. On January 1, 1961, according to Dulaney, "he sent the DCC a telegram . . . with the ultimatum that downtown lunch counters be desegregated by January 14, or he would begin immediate direct-action tactics." When the DCC did not adhere to James's wishes, he began sit-in demonstrations at downtown lunch counters. James led several other demonstrations throughout the year. His actions prompted the biracial committee to begin the desegregation process, and in July 1961 several businesses in the downtown area removed "white-only" signs and began serving African American customers. Dulaney writes, "To dramatize this achievement, the Committee arranged for 159 African Americans to waltz into 49 downtown lunch counters and restaurants and be served without incident."[55] This staged act of desegregation was seen as a triumph for Dallas's blacks while improving its image in the national media.[56]

In 1963, Rev. James invited Dr. Martin Luther King Jr. to speak at a rally for the United Political Organization. Members of the IMA, the committee of fourteen, and the DCC sought to bar King from speaking but were unsuccessful.[57] In 1964 ministers on both the biracial committee of fourteen and the IMA silently boycotted King, who was this time in Dallas to speak to students at Southern Methodist University and hold a special meeting with civil rights leaders at Fair Park in South Dallas. Rev. Mark Herbener, an active participant in the civil rights movement, stated that less than fifty people turned out to hear Dr. King speak at the Fair Park. Herbener holds that when he notified Rev. Wright about the King visit, Wright had agreed wholeheartedly to inform his parishioners as well as other ministers. However, none showed up. Herbener recalls that this upset King, who had never experienced such a large-scale boycott from his peers. "I remember a time when Rhett asked me to be on stage at the State Fair Music Hall when Dr. King was coming to town. And I will tell you that I got phone calls from some well-meaning friends saying, 'Do not go. It is far too dangerous.' . . . So I came. [And] as I remember it . . . the black ministers boycotted Martin Luther King."[58] Herbener's involvement in the movement was extensive. He gave members of the civil rights and black power movements the support of his church and the use of its facilities. His involvement was in grave contrast to the elite ministerial black "leaders" of the day.[59]

Moving toward the mid to late 1960s, the youth and college student movement played a key role in Dallas's civil rights movement, although protests and sit-ins continued to be facilitated by the city's older movement veterans. In 1964 the Reverend Earl Allen, pastor of the small Highland Hills United Methodist Church parish in Oak Cliff, chairman of Dallas's Congress of Racial Equality (CORE) and Dallas's Coordinating Committee on Civil Rights (DCCCR), led several peaceful protests in the city. One of two very prominent events that Allen organized was the twenty-eight-day picketing of Piccadilly Cafeteria, a business in downtown Dallas that served only whites. Allen's rationale for such a move was the city's unwillingness to legally enforce the Civil Rights Act of 1964. The picketing lasted from May 30 to July 2, 1964. On the last day of the protest, the business capitulated with protesters and desegregated the restaurant.

Another event Allen organized was the protest and picketing of the Dallas Independent School District after being barred from a hearing with the superintendent and nine-member school board. Allen and DCCCR were calling for an accelerated timeline for desegregating the city's public schools. When district officials continued to drag their feet, Allen and DCCCR staged a seventy-person protest outside the school district's administration building and rallied the participants behind exhausting "every legal method—including additional demonstrations—to achieve our goal." Allen afterward "challenged the city council to enforce the Civil Rights Act of 1964 or face the possibility of racial unrest and violence."[60] "He also boldly stated that if the city attempted to treat civil rights demonstrations as 'criminal acts' ... 'blood would flow in the streets.'"[61] No such blood was ever spilled, but it would take five years to begin an attempt to desegregate the city's public schools.

Black Power Comes to Dallas: 1965 through 1969

During the mid to late sixties, changes in the national movement for civil rights trickled down to Dallas. The student movement was greatly energized by the return of Marion Ernest McMillan Jr., a Dallas native who had gone to Morehouse College in 1963 and returned to the city to attend Arlington State College after much turmoil in Georgia.[62] In 1965, McMillan and some twenty-five students entered into a standoff with administrators at Arlington State College to have the Confederate flag and Rebel mascot removed from the institution.[63] This incident sparked Dallas's student movement.

Prior to enrolling at Atlanta's Morehouse College in 1963, McMillan traveled from his native Dallas to Noonan, Georgia, to live with his father, a United Methodist preacher. McMillan maintains, "Plans were to hang out with him until it was time to enroll in college. Those plans were cut short ... the police threatened my father [by saying] that I was 'stirring up trouble' trying to get people there to support the [March on Washington]. I was sent back to Dallas by my Dad and told to return in September for school only."[64]

Upon entering college, McMillan continued to be involved in the movement by organizing a companion demonstration for the 1963 March on Washington, in Noonan, Georgia, with SNCC, an organization whose history is intertwined with that of the Dallas Black Panthers. In the spring of 1964 McMillan left Morehouse to devote all his time to the movement. After securing his father's permission to work as a full-time staff member for SNCC, McMillan began working in voter registration programs and demonstrations in Fort Valley and Lee County, Georgia, with Willie Ricks (later known as Mukasa Dada). McMillan was later appointed field officer in Thomasville, Georgia, where, he says, "We registered voters, ran blacks for local offices, and supported the meat workers at the Sunny Side plant, among others."[65]

Shortly after the 1964 Democratic National Convention in Atlantic City, New Jersey, where McMillan participated in debates and protests, he returned to Dallas. He recalls, "After almost two years of fighting racism in the Deep South, it was a shock to come back to Dallas and realize that things were just like I had left them. Nothing had changed. Nobody in the Black community was doing anything." McMillan enrolled at Arlington State, now the University of Texas at Arlington. There he formed the Student Congress on Racial Equality (SCORE) but was soon kicked out of school for poor grades. McMillan left Dallas, hitchhiking to Houston, which was "more of an international city, [a] blue collar town with a lot of labor organizing with a greater respect or tradition for that [struggle]." In Houston, McMillan stayed with, learned from, and organized alongside Lee Otis Johnson, who possessed, according to McMillan, a greater talent for organizing and had led several successful organizing efforts in Houston. McMillan continues: "I never really read, in-depth, the rich history of Africa or even began to connect it in the way he had with the history of Black people in this country . . . just the whole perspective he [Johnson] used, which was down-to-earth, lively, grass roots talking. Not just high, pie-in-the-sky intellectualism, but really something you could grasp and put your hands on. [This] really helped me to return home feeling I was better armed and better prepared to immerse myself in the struggle for Black Power."[66]

SNCC: A Bunch of Outside Agitators

McMillan again returned to Dallas, this time to form a SNCC branch in 1966. Upon the formation of SNCC, the corporate media began a campaign of misinformation against McMillan, calling the Dallas native an outside agitator sent to stir up trouble. McMillan's mother, Eva, remembers: "The news media immediately jumped in and said that he was not a citizen of Dallas . . . that he was from Alabama and that he was here only to cause trouble."[67] Eva, like her son, became an integral organizer, leader, and community fixture. Although she credits her brothers with encouraging her involvement in the Progressive Voters League, she credits her son for involving her in the discourse for power and liberation in Dallas. She also states that when her son got involved in the movement she was at first reluctant, but once her son began to get arrested she became a champion of the movement. Young people called her Mama Mack. Her home was a safe space for movement people to congregate and find refuge from law enforcement and people opposed to the movement who intended to do them harm. It was also home for those ostracized by their families because of their involvement in the Black Power movement.

By 1968 SNCC had made a name for itself. An event that brought both SNCC and Ernest McMillan to the fore of a more radical phase of the movement was a televised panel on race relations in Dallas entitled "One Nation Indivisible." The panel included Mayor J. Erik Jonsson and other wealthy members of the Citizens Council affirming that Dallas was a premiere city on the road to change.[68] While business elites were describing a one-sided view of race relations in Dallas, the SNCC field secretary stood up and started debating the mayor about what he perceived as falsehoods being espoused by the panel.

McMillan's mother, Mama Mack, also recalled the televised event being a watershed moment, saying that it resulted in daily harassment from local police from that point on.[69] Through this television exposure, several young people became aware of the Dallas SNCC and signed up. The Harris brothers (Edward and Eddie) were intrigued by the sentiments Ernest McMillan had conveyed during the "One Nation Indivisible" broadcast. Edward Harris remembers his feelings: "I was at my girlfriend's house looking at TV, and a program came on.... There was a young man on a panel that was kind of giving the local law enforcement, you know, hell about how they were treating our African Americans. That's when ... I first got introduced to Ernest, on TV. So I told some of my family members, 'I need to meet this guy.' I said, 'Black Power is coming to Dallas and I want to see what this is all about.'" Edward Harris became a voter education and registration specialist in South and West Dallas. He also became a draft counselor at the height of the Vietnam War.[70]

SNCC members continued to be active on different fronts. On June 17, 1968, Matthew Johnson, Ernest McMillan, Mike Dodd, and other SNCC representatives handed out leaflets announcing a black community meeting. The purpose of the meeting was to make the community aware of SNCC and about the possible organizing of rent strikes in order to improve housing for people in the community. Upon entering the Good Luck Restaurant Drive-Thru, SNCC representatives were approached by Willie Linthicum, the owner of Linthicum Security Service, and told to vacate the premises. Because Linthicum did not identify himself when asked, the SNCC cadre remained on site. After being forcefully told to get out, co-leader Matthew Johnson said to Linthicum before leaving, "Okay, we know how to handle people like you." Feeling threatened by Johnson's remark, Linthicum pressed charges against SNCC members, and on June 26, 1969, "Fred Bell and Ernest McMillan were arrested on charges of threatening the life of Willie Linthicum.... They were held on bonds totaling $40,000." Bail was later reduced to a total of $2,500.[71]

SNCC opposition in Dallas was similar to that faced by SNCC chapters around the country. Fortunately they also received similar support. With the unofficial help of local black police officers, SNCC was able to anticipate attempts to squelch their rallies and demonstrations. Although it is not commonly known, SNCC organized Vietnam veterans into a military and security wing of their organization, which was given the duty of patrolling the police. These patrols protected citizens who were being harassed and unjustly detained or questioned by police. SNCC activists patrolled with thirty-eight caliber guns, M1s, and twelve-gauge shotguns.[72]

While many cities erupted in mass violence during the late 1960s, Dallas did not. In fact, police at least once attempted to incite upheaval after a SNCC meeting in West Dallas, Eva McMillan recalls. SNCC leaders, surrounded and outnumbered by police brandishing weapons, called Mama Mack, seeking her counsel. After telling them to stay put, she frantically began calling Dallas police headquarters and FBI offices, ordering them to make the officers retreat from the West Dallas SNCC site.[73] She reminded them that the Kerner Report had revealed that police, not the people, instigated most disorders.[74] Her phone then rang incessantly as she received calls from SNCC members' families. They all called their local representatives, who in turn called police officials. Finally the police dispersed, leaving the SNCC members unharmed. Mama Mack and others felt that the police would have surely killed all of the SNCC organizers had the families not been vigilant.[75]

OK Supermarket Protest and Boycott

The community-based activities that SNCC was instrumental in organizing reached a peak with the boycotting of OK Supermarket, a ten-grocery-store chain in the city's southern sector. OK Supermarket had a reputation for selling rotten fruit and vegetables and charging exorbitant prices.[76] Using their civil rights movement training McMillan and his comrades surveyed South Dallas residents, asking them about the community's most pertinent problems. Many residents complained of being economically exploited by stores owned by people alien to their neighborhood. McMillan recounts: "After we mounted a boycott (that was reported 85% effective by the racist *Dallas Morning News*) we organized a campaign to purchase that chain."[77] Rev. Herbener remembers an experience he had at an OK Supermarket: "After shopping there one day, we came home and Donna [his wife] said, 'These hot dogs are bad.' So I said, 'Okay, I'll take them back.' So I went back to the store and said, 'These hot dogs are bad. We just bought them this afternoon and they're no good. They stink.'

And someone said, 'Shhh, shhh. Don't say anything.' Why? Because they would wash them off and put them back on the shelf."[78]

Earlier that year, 1968, the Black United Front was formed as an umbrella organization for the heads of the smaller black organizations in Dallas to meet and brainstorm best practices and ways of supporting the black community. Out of that came the OK Supermarket boycott and protest. Mama Mack attended those meetings during the summer of 1968: "On the days when the women would receive their welfare checks and the elderly would receive their checks, prices would go up. They were treated so poorly that the people in the community decided they would do something about it. So they held a meeting, called SNCC, and asked them to support the picket of the store."[79]

Black United Front officials adopted a twofold protest. One component was an "internal boycott" that consisted of "filling shopping carts with large amounts of foodstuffs, carrying these goods to the checkout counter, unloading them at the counter and then being unable to pay for them." "This tactic was intended to negatively affect the store's revenue. On the request of any store employee that payment... be made, such payments were... given." This was done because SNCC members did not want store officials to initiate legal action against them. They merely wanted to inconvenience the store management. The second aspect of the twofold plan was an external boycott with pickets by the black community, "with the organizational advice and counsel of the Dallas Chapter of SNCC."[80]

Mama Mack describes how the first tactic was employed:

The young men and women went in... they each filled a cart to the level with a lot of small items... and they let the store authorities there know that they were protesting the sale of goods [and] the way they treated the community, especially their customers. They would fill their carts and, for instance, one woman would drive up to the counter and she would say, "Oh, look at that clock! It says five o'clock. I promised my babysitter I'd be back," and she just walked out of the store and leave the cart there. The next person would stand there, then he would say, "I'm late to work," and he would run off and leave his cart. The next person might get his food tallied and then reach for his checkbook and said, "Oh, I left my checkbook at home! I'll have to go get it," and he'd depart. So, as a result, the store was full of carts of food that the employees at the store would have to replace back, like frozen foods. And some people in the community got really excited... somebody dropped a watermelon and broke it. Somebody dropped a bottle of prune juice and broke it. About three items were broken... the people at OK Supermarket did not complain.[81]

The *Dallas Morning News* reported in July 1968, "Witnesses at the grocery told police that 30–40 men and women entered the store about 10:40 p.m. and, at a signal, began breaking merchandise."[82] They ordered meat from the butcher but changed their minds upon receiving it, left perishable food items like milk and eggs out to spoil, and stocked grocery carts full of groceries that they did not intend on buying. Ernest McMillan and SNCC co-leader Matthew Johnson were charged with the malicious destruction of private property, a felony that was "punishable by a prison term of from 2 to 10 years."[83] McMillan believes that the total damages were no more than $300.[84] The two were released on bond and given a trial date of Monday, August 19, 1968.[85] On day two of the trial, the *Morning News* would report, "Mark Elston, 15-year-old son of a co-owner of OK Supermarkets testified... that he saw Marion Ernest McMillan and Matthew Johnson destroy store merchandise." The store manager, E. D. Tallas, would give a similar testimony. An African American attendant at the store would testify that "he witnessed the smashing but did not see McMillan or Johnson break anything."[86]

By the end of July the boycotts and pickets had succeeded, and the store owners gave in. On July 26 the *Morning News* reported, "OK Supermarkets...agreed...to sell all of [sic] part of its 10-store chain to an all-Negro group represented by black militant McMillan." According to the paper, "The supermarket owners gave McMillan's group 60 days to raise the money to complete the transaction. In exchange, McMillan agreed to halt the boycott and call off the pickets."[87] Before this compromise between SNCC and the OK Supermarket chain, the district attorney's office had considered issuing criminal charges against several picketers. The *Morning News* reported, "Dallas police furnished the district attorney's office affidavits saying one picket threatened to kill a store manager and burn down the store if the employe[e] didn't join SNCC. Other allegations included harassment of customers not observing the boycott and prevention of employe[e]s from engaging in their lawful vocation." But no criminal charges could be drafted against the people who allegedly threatened the store employees as their identities were not known to the police.[88]

SNCC members petitioned the Small Business Administration to finance a loan to aid them in purchasing the OK Supermarket stores, but SBA officials refused. SNCC then turned to black business owners to provide the loan to buy the stores.[89]

Unfortunately, in August 1968, before his trial with Johnson on charges of damaging private property during the OK Supermarket boycott, Ernest McMillan was charged with draft evasion after having reported to the draft board but not swearing the oath to serve in a branch of the military to actively fight in the Vietnam War.[90] Concurrently, McMillan and Johnson were awaiting trial and sentencing for damaging private property during the OK Supermarket boycott and protests. On August 24 McMillan and Johnson were found guilty and sentenced to serve ten years in prison for the destruction of OK Supermarket property. The judge ruled that McMillan's passport be confiscated, then reduced his and Johnson's bail from $10,000 to $5,000.[91]

While Johnson and McMillan were awaiting sentencing, SNCC members Fahim Minkah (Fred Bell) and Charles Lavern Beasley inexplicably robbed the Farmers and Merchants State Bank in Ladonia, Texas.[92] Bell, Beasley, and an unidentified third person made off with approximately $14,000.[93] A few days later, Beasley fled the United States, hijacking a plane midflight, at gunpoint, over New Brunswick, Canada. Beasley, referring to himself as "Mr. Garvey," told the flight crew to fly the plane to Cuba. His reason for hijacking the plane: the CIA was after him. He was not imagining this.[94]

Beasley reportedly allowed the plane to refuel in Montreal, at which point he permitted two flight attendants and seventeen passengers to exit the plane. While the plane was being refueled, a Royal Canadian Mounted Police assistant commissioner talked with Beasley by radio for twenty minutes and convinced him to surrender. Beasley gave himself up to the Mounties only after being informed by the Cuban consul that that country would not give him political asylum.[95] Canada, however, agreed to grant him asylum—or so he thought.[96] But Beasley was not granted asylum in Canada and was instead arraigned in the Canadian courts on September 20, 1968.[97]

Over the next several months SNCC remained in the news. In April 1969, police raided the homes of Ernest McMillan, Edward "Black Ed" Harris, Matthew Johnson, Donald "Kwesi" Williams, Ruth Jefferson, and other members of SNCC. A warrant was issued by the court for the arrest of these and other SNCC members due to "violating federal firearms laws ... [and] falsifying federal firearms registration records" based on rifles seized during the raids.[98]

Meanwhile McMillan remained free on bond and would not be arraigned on draft evasion charges until the next spring.[99] On June 20, 1969, McMillan was sentenced to five years in prison for his draft board infraction—the maximum possible—as well as ten years for his prior conviction for property damage, again the maximum sentence. McMillan continued to organize while waiting for his prison sentence to commence. Plagued by legal problems and convinced that the U.S. government was out to get him, McMillan decided that "it was in the best interests of my survival to completely withdraw from these direct attacks."[100] McMillan and Williams fled to Canada, and from there the two went to Africa, first Mali and then Ghana. Unsuccessful in gaining asylum in Mali and Ghana, the two lived in Liberia for a year and a half.[101] In 1969 the Federal Bureau of Investigation recorded in its files: "The SNCC group in Dallas has been discontinued."[102]

The Dallas NCCF Is Founded

As many of Dallas SNCC's leaders were imprisoned, on the run, or in exile, others began to shift their focus to the larger call for Black Power and sought to form a branch of the Black Panther Party (BPP) in Dallas. The SNCC-BPP connection in Dallas was not unique: numerous former SNCC members joined Black Panther Party branches around the country. It is widely documented that the two national organizations attempted a merger in the late 1960s that ultimately failed. The Dallas chapter of the Black Panther Party went through four different but significant iterations, all of which involved former SNCC activists at one level or another.

The cadre that comprised the Dallas branch of the National Committee to Combat Fascism (NCCF) was young—in their late teens and early twenties—and initially overwhelmingly male. Most of the members had been reared in working-class to middle-class families. Three of them were children of ministers. Several of the parents worked in the homes of middle- to upper-class whites as day workers. Almost all of the activists were high school graduates, and many were enrolled in college or had some college experience. Many were political novices although some obviously had experience in the civil rights movement. As with most other NCCFs, some members had military experience.

College students and grassroots organizing made for a dynamic combination. Not surprisingly, many parents cautioned about involvement in the Black Panther Party, but some were supportive. Akin Tunde Fonso remembers his father counseling him during his time as a Party member. Says Fonso, "My dad was militant so he understood what I was trying to do.... Hell, one time he took his congregation down to protest in front of the Dallas Independent School [District] headquarters to draw attention to the fact that conditions in the schools needed to be improved... for example, the Lisbon Colored School had no indoor plumbing."[103]

Rev. Dr. Leroy Haynes, pastor of Allen Temple Christian Methodist Episcopal Church in Portland, Oregon, is a former SNCC member who helped set up the Dallas NCCF that would eventually become the Dallas chapter of the BPP in 1969. Haynes says that SNCC members in the late 1960s were in consultation with members of El Centro College's Student Organization for United Liberation (SOUL), the Dallas junior college's black student union. Both groups were ready to take their struggle to the next level, and for some that meant starting a chapter of the Black Panther Party. As president of SOUL from 1969 to 1971, the resourceful and well-respected Haynes was uniquely positioned to mobilize support for a Black Panther chapter in Dallas. Haynes had joined SNCC while a student at historically black Huston-Tillotson University in Austin, where he enrolled in the fall of 1967.[104] Haynes joined the civil rights movement, however, at the age of thirteen, recruited by his pastor, who was leading the movement for desegregation in Beaumont, Texas. According to Haynes, some memorable road signs could be found in Beaumont. One along Interstate 90 from Beaumont to Lake Charles, he recalls, read, "Nigger, read and run; if you can't read, run anyway." Haynes says, "Pastor William B. Oliver III recruited me and my brothers into the movement.... I remember Rev. Hosea Williams came to town and trained us."[105] As a college student and SNCC member under the leadership of Larry Jackson, SNCC's Austin coordinator, Haynes learned a thing or two about organizing, managing people, and strategic thinking. Unfortunately, due to financial considerations, Haynes was forced to leave Huston-Tillotson and the Austin area and transfer to El Centro College in 1968.

Housed in the old Sanger Brothers department store building in busy downtown Dallas, El Centro College opened in 1966, catering to adult learners and students from working-class families. The school was so new that there were areas of the building that were still under construction two years after the school opened. According to Joyce Halton, a longtime Dallas resident and alum of the college, "El Centro gave students who never thought they could attend college the opportunity to earn a college degree."[106] As a junior college it also served as a stepping-stone to a four-year institution. Glenn Currier, a professor at the school for more than thirty years, remembers El Centro as "a place that was very open.... It had a reputation for being open to people who were different... it was a student-centered environment.... We had some of the best educators in the state there.... It was a place where students, especially minority students could go, be treated with respect, and get a good education."[107] Ironically, when the building housing the school was still a department store, African Americans had only been allowed to shop in the basement.[108]

Haynes says the school had two curricula, "one being the basic liberal arts track and the other being the career track for those who were interested in business and trade fields."[109] Former student and BPP member Skip Shockley says, "Although a sizeable number of the students were black, relatively few of the instructors were.... There [were] some Latino students but very few Latino professors that I remember... so it shouldn't be a surprise that the school didn't [teach] black history or anything like that."[110] Halton, who later enrolled at Dallas Baptist College after attending El Centro, recalls "a tension in the air between black students and the white professors.... We weren't exactly welcomed with open arms... Not all the white professors were like that, but some were."[111]

By 1969 Haynes was ready to move on from SNCC: "I had been having informal types of conversations and exploratory meetings about starting a Black Panther branch in Dallas as early as 1968.... Also, by that time SNCC was on the decline and the Black Panther Party had taken the mantle of the Black Power movement.... I thought the party embodied the direction that Malcolm X was headed before he was assassinated."[112] Donald "Red Dog" Lister, then a young and committed student, remembers his involvement in SOUL and subsequently the BPP: "We were attempting to get black studies at the school. We did succeed in getting a black history class—this was '69 and '70. Afterwards, the Black Panther Party came to town. I always said if an organization such as that came to town, I was going to join it."[113] Haynes was one of several former SNCC members who reached out to the Panthers' headquarters in hopes of starting a Panther branch in Dallas. The SNCC cadre was instructed by BPP central committee members to meet them in Los Angeles where a rally was to be held for George Jackson and Angela Davis. Says Haynes: "In the summer of 1969, we drove two carloads of people to Los Angeles, California—Watts, to be exact. After the rally we all headed to the Compton office, where we met with Chief of Staff David Hilliard and Raymond 'Masai' Hewitt."[114] The Dallas SNCC contingent was told that the party was not authorizing the formation of new chapters at that time. That matter would be addressed in July in conjunction with the United Committee to Combat Fascism conference, a three-day affair held in the Bay Area to rally those seeking to become affiliated with the BPP.[115] At the conference, it was resolved that anyone wishing to align themselves with the BPP were welcome to do so as members of the National Committee to Combat Fascism (NCCF).[116] Shockley remembers that "the NCCF was one of Eldridge's ideas. [Cleaver] organized the National Committee to Combat Fascism in order to build a coalition with white radicals."[117]

Odinga Kambui, a former Dallas Panther, recalls: "Because of the infiltration and repression that was going on in the party... they were not allowing any new chapters to be established. People who wanted to work in that vein were being allowed to set up National Committees to Combat Fascism." Kambui's initial foray into Black Panther politics was not in Dallas but rather Chicago, where he served as a community worker during the summer of 1970. Says Kambui:

> At the end of my first year at El Centro College I boarded a Trailways bus in downtown Dallas, headed for Chicago. I had relatives there so I went there looking for summer work. That was a long bus ride—it took about thirty hours to get there. On June 8 there was a rally on behalf of Bobby Seale. I went to the rally.... Deputy Minister of Information Chaka Walls was one of the featured speakers that day. Afterwards I walked up to him, introduced myself, and asked him where the Panther office was. Within the next day or two I go around to the office and attend my first political education class, which was conducted by Che Brooks. The next thing I know I'm a community worker... out there on the street selling Panther papers and doing whatever else needed done. At the end of the summer, sometime in September, I caught a flight back to Dallas.... I couldn't handle another thirty-hour bus ride.... When I got back to Dallas I hooked up with Skip and the comrades, who by that time had gotten an NCCF.[118]

The NCCF was placed under the supervision of Geronimo Pratt (later known as Geronimo ji Jaga), who at the time was deputy minister of defense of the Southern California chapter of the Black Panther Party. The murder of Bunchy Carter, Pratt's predecessor, on the campus of UCLA in 1969, had necessitated Pratt's ascension to that position.[119] Although Pratt had not been a Panther long, he was considered a legend, having come to the party with an impressive service record. Pratt had enlisted in the army in 1965 (at a time when the U.S. troops were occupying the Dominican Republic). As a member of the famed 82nd Airborne, he made more than fifty combat jumps and was awarded the Purple Heart and the Air Medal before the age of nineteen. An artillery expert, Pratt went on many long-range reconnaissance missions, some of which were in Da Nang, smack dab in the middle of the Tet Offensive. After Pratt's second tour of duty he returned home to Morgan City, Louisiana, having added a Silver Star, Bronze Star, Soldier's Medal, and Vietnamese Cross of Gallantry to his previous decorations.[120] Shortly thereafter, an elder informed Pratt that there were some people out west who could use his expertise. The exchange appears in Jack Olsen's *Last Man Standing*: "Those Panthers got some good ideas," the elder told Pratt, "but they need help organizing and defending themselves against the cops. You could do 'em a lot of good."[121] A few weeks later Pratt and his sister, whom he offered to drive to college at UCLA, put his 1967 GTO convertible on the road and headed to Los Angeles.

The SNCC cadre was approved as an NCCF branch, and the group operated out of an old house in Fair Park, not far from the famed Cotton Bowl. Curtis Gaines, a former SNCC activist, served as deputy chairman. According to Haynes, "Gaines was a little older than the rest of us ... probably in his mid to late twenties.... He was a cab driver but [a] very articulate and charismatic brother.... He was sophisticated in his political analysis ... very personable ... a big brother in stature, kind of on the heavy side."[122] Charlie Paul Henderson (later known as Khalif Hasan) was second in command. "Charlie Paul was a pretty sharp brother ... he had some military experience," says Haynes.[123] Rounding out the leadership were Haynes, who served as a section leader in West Dallas; James "Do Do" Woods, deputy minister of culture; and Phoebe Allen, who acted as the group's secretary and communications person. "Allen, the short, light-complexioned sister with the big natural, may have been small in stature and very quiet ... but her presence was huge.... She was a very sharp sister. She had organizing skills ... [and] was a thinker," says Haynes.[124] Another woman who played an integral part in the group's development was Beverly Gaines, the wife of Curtis Gaines. According to Haynes, "Beverly was very outgoing, a people person, one might say.... She was always upbeat ... encouraging the comrades to press on."[125]

Members of the newly formed Dallas NCCF hurried back to Texas after being placed under Pratt's supervision and began developing the survival programs, with mixed success. Their first order of business, however, was to sell the lode of Panther papers given them by Pratt before they left Los Angeles. Although the Dallas contingent was not a full-fledged party chapter, NCCF members were still expected to sell the *Black Panther*. Shockley says, "Weekly shipments of the paper would arrive at Love Field Airport in Dallas, while other times the papers would be picked up at the Continental Trailways or Greyhound bus stations. Sometimes we had to switch up in order to keep the authorities off-balance. If we kept the same location and schedule that would have made it easy for the FBI and the police to vandalize the papers."[126] Shockley's concerns were not far-fetched: both federal and local law enforcement officials had a history of drenching Panther newspapers with water or defacing them in some way, rendering them illegible. On one or two occasions the Dallas cadre fell victim to this, but for the most part they were able to pick up their shipment it without incident. Typically Odinga Kambui took it upon himself to retrieve the papers from the airport. Kambui describes the process: "I would catch the number 15 Ramona bus by my house to downtown. Then I would board the number 39 Love Field bus to the airport. I would then go to the Braniff Airlines terminal, show my ID, and pick up the papers. It took an hour to get there and an hour to get back, sometimes longer depending on whether or not the busses were running on schedule."[127] Haynes remembers a hot spot for unloading the newspaper. "We could sell a lot of papers downtown.... About a half block from H. L. Green's department store on Main Street and Elm was what one might call a square where people would eat their lunch, stop to catch their breath, or simply congregate."[128] As far as Kambui was concerned, the best place to sell the Panther newspaper was at the Lancaster-Kiest Shopping Center not far from where he lived.[129]

Like other Panther branches or affiliates around the country, the NCCF set up a free breakfast program. "The breakfast program, which operated out of a Lutheran church on Forest Avenue [Rev. Herbener's church, Mount Olive], didn't last too long... we were unable to sustain that," says Haynes.[130] According to Shockley, a second breakfast program was offered in the West Dallas Housing Projects "that lasted a little more than a year."[131] What the NCCF members did offer consistently was free pest control. Says Haynes, "We would buy Raid and other items at wholesale stores, then leaflet low-income communities about our pest control program. Interested parties would contact us by phone. We would inform them that it was important that they empty all cabinets... prior to us spraying and allow ample time for airing out before putting everything back.... Residents really appreciated this."[132]

Initially the NCCF operated out of Curtis Gaines's apartment in Oak Cliff, located in Southwest Dallas. Not surprisingly, the SNCC cadre was not enthusiastic about its new moniker. According to Shockley, he and his comrades disassociated themselves from the name:

The NCCF didn't wash well with us because we felt that most of the white so-called revolutionaries didn't seem serious. They seemed like they wanted to dance out in the streets and do antics, and Huey always said, "Look, this is for real. We're stepping out here and we're saying we're anti-government and that we want to change the system. Don't you think the system takes that seriously?" So you've got a group of people over here who are white [and] pulling all kind of antics. You know, flower children, which is fine ... but, hey, you're going to get killed because you want to act like a clown? You know, if we are true revolutionaries and are going to get killed, then we got to stand up for what we believe in, we can't be no clowns.[133]

Little did Shockley and the others know at the time is that, as far as the Federal Bureau of Investigation was concerned, they were Panthers. Proof of this can be found in an FBI document that states: "Curtis Gaines, Eddie Harris and Charles Paul Henderson have recently become active in a group calling themselves the Black Panther Party (BPP) in Dallas."[134] And not unexpectedly the young NCCF found itself confronted with many of the same challenges that other Panther chapters faced: infiltration, government surveillance, and police harassment.

Finally, We're Panthers

The NCCF was infiltrated at an early stage, and this is what perhaps prevented the group from maximizing its potential. By 1970, however, members of the group received a letter from the central committee of the BPP informing them that they were now a full-fledged branch of the Black Panther Party. By this time the cadre had become fairly well known in Dallas for offering a myriad of community survival programs, the most well known of which was the breakfast program. In 1970 the Dallas Panthers set up a free breakfast program in two locations, one in South Dallas and one in a housing project in West Dallas. The breakfast program was also accompanied by a free food giveaway, but Haynes admits it was not offered consistently.[135] The Dallas cadre graduated from operating out of Curtis Gaines's apartment and was now conducting business from an office on Second Avenue near Fair Park. Haynes remembers that "J. B. Jackson, a black realtor and civil rights activist, allowed the party free use of a suite of offices."[136]

From 1969 to 1970 members of the Dallas NCCF and Panther branch engaged in a vigilant campaign of political education within their ranks and throughout low-income Dallas neighborhoods. Understanding the forces that worked to keep them powerless was critical to figuring out the best ways to counteract these forces. Some of the Panthers' most receptive listeners were college students. In addition to El Centro the Panthers' recruitment efforts extended to Texas Women's College (now Texas Women's University), North

Texas State University (now the University of North Texas), and Lamar University. Among the high schools where Panther recruitment efforts proved successful were South Oak Cliff in Dallas, Lincoln High School and Jefferson High School in Port Arthur, and high schools in Beaumont and Tyler, Texas.[137]

Meanwhile, at El Centro, members of the BSU (SOUL) were urging other students to be active participants in their education. As at many colleges across the country, El Centro then lacked diverse course offerings to which many students have become accustomed today. Additionally, the dearth of faculty of color and black staff members was enough to prompt a 1970 student boycott, led by the BSU. "We blocked this large lobby area, blocked the elevators and the stairwells too," said Haynes.[138] Some administrators claimed that they felt threatened by the noisy and impassioned crowd. The boycotters initiated their protest during the lunch hour to ensure that the action would not go unnoticed. The crowd of protesters grew to more than one hundred students. The students sent El Centro's president a list of what they believed to be reasonable grievances. In a nutshell, they wanted an education that more accurately reflected the mosaic that was America. In response, the protesters received notice that they were being charged with disruptive conduct and that they would have an opportunity to defend themselves against this charge in a hearing to be held before a disciplinary committee.

But rather than hearing the students out and perhaps negotiating with them with the intention of reaching some common ground, the administration acted heavy-handedly. Leaders of the protest, who included Haynes, Clark Johnson, and Nathaniel Halton, were called into the office of the dean, Donald G. Creamer, told they were being expelled, and informed of their right to appeal. The protesters were given a hearing date, but in the meantime filed a lawsuit against El Centro. After a protracted court battle, the students would ultimately lose their case in district court in 1974.[139] Although the students were under no illusions and did not expect that all of their grievances would be addressed, they were surprised by such intolerance on the part of school officials.

Haynes's expulsion from El Centro did not temper his militancy. Although he was no longer a student at El Centro, he did not halt his Panther organizing efforts on the campus.

Party Cleavage

By 1971 the Black Panther Party nationally was in a state of flux, as leaders Huey Newton and Eldridge Cleaver squared off against each other publicly in a battle for control of the organization. The effects reverberated throughout the party nationwide. In Dallas, morale proved to be a problem. Shockley says, "For some reason we didn't have that great bond. Our leadership with

Curtis Gaines was kind of like a hierarchy. He was up here and we were down here, and we always wondered why there's a difference between... what we saw here and what we saw in other cities. There was also a rumor that Curtis was an agent who was feeding information to authorities—the FBI.... Half our chapter was saying 'Curtis is working with the police.'" An article in the *Black Panther*, which caught the Dallas cadre totally off guard, exposed cleavage within the Dallas branch.[140] Lister recalls: "A schism came down between those who followed the line of Huey P. Newton and those who followed the line of Eldridge Cleaver. You had some that were saying, 'Yeah, Huey is doing the right thing.' And you had some that said, 'Nah, Huey's not doing the right thing,' and Geronimo, who was really responsible for our being [chartered and developed], had been purged. This schism really was initiated by agents provocateurs who were working for the government's COINTELPRO.... At the time we didn't know it, but these were people whose job was to foment dissent and distrust by any means."[141] Haynes's view of the Newton-Cleaver split focuses on its local impact: "When the split happened in the party, we [B. L. Smith, Shockley, and myself] pulled back. Some of the brothers went with Curtis, but some of us went in another direction. We followed the philosophy of Huey. Curtis and his loyalists followed the philosophy of Eldridge. To me, they were mostly trying to act like gangsters. A year later, a couple of guys... we called them the Renegades... got busted, sent to prison, and, come to find out, Curtis [had] testified against them."[142]

Geronimo Pratt Arrest

In late 1970, one of the party's most accomplished and valuable members was taken off the streets, and not long after that the entire Dallas branch was expelled from the party. Geronimo Pratt had been arrested in connection with the December 1969 police raid of a Panther office in Los Angeles and following firefight, was released from jail in August 1970, and then, on orders from Newton, went underground for the purpose of training and fortifying an underground military wing of the Black Panther Party.[143] Several other Panthers who had been involved in the Los Angeles firefight also made the decision to go underground, some for different reasons. As can be gathered from information gleaned from several sources, Dallas was one of several cities in which Pratt went to work clandestinely. Others included New Orleans, Winston-Salem, Birmingham, and Atlanta. On December 8, 1970, Pratt, who had been given the responsibility of supervising the Dallas branch of the Black Panther Party (hardly a role for someone ostensibly working underground), was apprehended by Dallas police at one of the party's safe houses in South Oak Cliff. Among a host of charges, Pratt was accused of the 1968 murder of Caroline Olsen, a white elementary school teacher, in Santa Monica, California.[144] Other

Panthers arrested were Will Stafford, Wilfred "Crutch" Holiday, George Lloyd, Roland Freeman, and Melvin "Cotton" Smith. Officially Pratt was arrested on federal UFTAP (unlawful flight to avoid prosecution) warrants. He had failed to appear in court to face charges of conspiracy to assault with intent to commit murder and assault with a deadly weapon.

The exact details of the arrest are sketchy. Shockley recalls:

> One day, out of the blue, Curtis Gaines walked up to me and Norris Batts and instructed us to go to a Panther safe house and spend the night. Norris and I had been selling Panther newspapers all day. We were tired so we headed back to the office before Curtis and his entourage walked in. We barely had time to catch our breath before he walked in with this order. We didn't question it, despite the fact that Curtis never explained why he wanted us to do this. When we arrived at this apartment in a place called Big D Apartments there was a large cache of weapons... AK-47s, M16s, pump shotguns, .30-06s, and other weapons... just lined up along the wall out in the open. Naturally this caught our attention, but we rationalized it by convincing ourselves that this was the place where our arms were stored... an armory of sorts. There was no furniture in this apartment, nothing but some blankets and stuff on the floor. Norris and I passed the time by talking. We had a bite to eat. We didn't dare go to sleep, however, because we knew there was some weird stuff going on. We stayed up all night, and when the sun came up we walked out the front door.... A while later we ran into a comrade who told us that Geronimo had been arrested. Curtis never explained to us why he wanted us to spend the night at that apartment, but you can't tell me that the two incidents weren't connected.[145]

In Pratt's biography *Last Man Standing*, Jack Olsen offers a rather generic explanation for Pratt's presence in Dallas:

> Pratt was contacted by his fellow Panther, Melvin "Cotton" Smith, and advised that Huey Newton had ordered both of them to a meeting in Marshall, Texas, 150 miles east of Dallas. The theme would be unity.... When Newton failed to appear at the Texas rendezvous, Geronimo was puzzled.... But Cotton Smith urged him to stay put.... Three more days passed before Cotton Smith said he'd finally reached Newton and had been ordered to deliver Geronimo to a BPP safe house in Dallas. As soon as they arrived, Dallas police arrested them on federal UFTAP (unlawful flight to avoid prosecution) warrants.[146]

Melvin Carl "Cotton" Smith was highly regarded within Panther circles. Ex-Panther Flores Forbes paints a colorful portrait of Smith, calling him "a mean muthafucka, legendary in the BPP for his stealth and guile under extreme pressure."[147] He had been present on that eventful morning when eighteen Panthers had engaged in a five-hour firefight with Los Angeles Police Department (LAPD) officers, including members of their SWAT team, in early December 1969. In fact, according to Aaron Dixon's account of that morning, when the

SWAT team charged through the door, it was Smith who "let loose with a volley from his Thom[p]son submachine gun."[148] The manner in which Smith handled himself that morning only added to his stature. Pratt considered Smith a loyal soldier. Indeed, Smith had spent much of his time traipsing the country with Pratt, going from chapter to chapter, helping fortify offices and dig tunnels.[149] Smith was so well thought of that when he later turned state's evidence against those Panthers who fought it out with the LAPD in December 1969, it sent shockwaves throughout the party. For many, watching Smith testify against them was a hard pill to swallow. Johnny Cochran, Pratt's attorney, offered an interesting take on Smith in his autobiography. While history has depicted Smith as a former Panther who turned state's evidence, Cochran believed Smith to be an informer who had joined the Party, a distinction worth considering. Wayne Pharr, a former Los Angeles party member, disagrees with Cochran: "Cotton turned on us in the end, but I don't believe that he was a snitch while we worked together.... He thought G [Geronimo Pratt] was going to kill him because he led G, Roland, and the other brothers in Dallas to the area where they were arrested.... Knowing that he had been set up by Huey and then was under suspicion of G, Cotton probably thought the safest route was to work with the cops. He wanted to stay alive."[150]

At any rate, even before Smith testified against Pratt and his fellow Panthers, many believed, understandably, that Pratt had been set up. Hasan asserts clearly, "Gaines played a role in G's arrest."[151] Unfortunately for the other Dallas Panthers, they were caught in the middle and suffered a consequence. Because the Dallas branch of the BPP had aided Pratt in the past, providing him refuge, the branch was officially purged from the party by the central committee.[152] It wasn't just that members of the Dallas branch had assisted Pratt but that Newton loyalists believed (perhaps presumptuously) that the Dallas Panthers had *allied* themselves with Pratt. Moreover, Newton's dislike for Pratt is evident early on. David Hilliard relates that Newton, not long after being introduced to Pratt, told Hilliard he believed Pratt to be an agent, a charge with which Hilliard vehemently disagreed.[153] After his arrest in Dallas, anyone who was believed to be an ally of Pratt was sure to be purged, especially if the purge was on orders from Newton himself. Newton may have felt threatened by Pratt, whom he believed sided with Eldridge Cleaver, who kept imploring the party to elevate the struggle or take the fight to the "avaricious pigs" of capitalism.

While Pratt had been underground, the differences between Newton and Cleaver had widened, prompting the opportunist FBI to go to work spreading rumors that Pratt endeavored to eliminate certain national BPP leaders. Apparently the FBI's disinformation campaign was so successful that even some of the party's more intellectually sophisticated members—Masai Hewitt, for one—fell for it. In his memoir, *Will You Die with Me*, Flores Forbes recalls an exchange he had with Hewitt. According to Forbes, one day Masai informed him that "combat handgun training would be instituted for the officers of the day so we could properly defend the office against G and his band, who ... had made a direct threat to move on us."[154] Within a relatively short time Pratt had gone from being one of the party's heralded figures to an enemy of the people.

On January 23, 1971, Newton issued a statement in the *Black Panther* accusing Pratt of "counter-revolutionary" behavior, including threatening the lives of Newton and Hilliard. Newton warned, "Any Party member or community worker who attempts to aid them or communicate with them in any form or manner shall be considered part of their conspiracy to undermine and destroy the Black Panther Party."[155] By "them" Newton was referring to Geronimo Pratt, Saundra Lee (his significant other), Will Stafford, Crutch Holiday, and George Lloyd. When Pratt was handed a copy of the *Black Panther*, he could hardly believe the headline he saw: "On the Purge of Geronimo from the Black Panther Party." Flabbergasted, Pratt read the list of forty-four party violations of which he was supposedly guilty. Perhaps the most vicious passage was one that questioned Pratt's commitment to the black liberation struggle and suggested that he was a cold-blooded killer: "His devotion and allegiance [is] still to the ways and rules of the Pig Power Structure.... He is as dedicated to that Pig Agency as he was when he was in Vietnam, killing innocent Vietnamese women and children on various 'search and destroy' missions."[156]

A year later, Pratt was convicted of the murder of Caroline Olsen and would spend the next twenty-seven years behind bars. Even though numerous Panthers could attest to the fact that on the night of the murder Pratt had been attending meetings in the Bay Area (six hours away), none of them came forward on Pratt's behalf for fear of reprisal, with the exception of Kathleen Cleaver. Stuart Hanlon, one of Pratt's attorneys, says, "I'm sure many of those Panthers who saw G in the Bay Area that night didn't come forward for years because they feared for their lives."[157] Newton's actions affected Pratt's case in a myriad of ways including hindering access to political and financial resources that would have served Pratt and his legal team well.

The Black Intercommunal Party

Despite the expulsion of the Dallas branch of the BPP, Shockley remembers, he, Kambui, Haynes, B. L. Smith, and other members of the party reasoned that they would nevertheless continue on with their activism in one form or another. Shockley enrolled at El Centro College and was elected president of the Black Student Union.[158] In his capacity as president, Shockley attempted to mold the BSU in the party's image. One way he and the others did this was by creating two programs that resembled the Panthers' community survival initiatives. Initially they raised funds by selling Black Panther Party paraphernalia such as buttons and T-shirts. The free clothing program was one of the more practical programs. "We would set up oil drums on certain floors of the building... the arts students were kind enough to decorate the drums for us... then we would tell people what type of clothing we were looking for them to donate.... We would also place ads in the college newspaper.... All articles of clothing were welcome, but we would encourage them to donate certain items," says Shockley. The program proved very popular, but there were bumps in the road early on. For a while, when members of the BSU would retrieve donated clothes they would find that someone had poured a soda into the barrel or spit on the clothes. "That kind of behavior didn't last long, however," says Shockley.[159] Once the clothes were collected at the end of each week, the BSU turned them over to entities that served people in need, such as the Dallas Bethlehem Center.

Undoubtedly the BSU's most ambitious project entailed sickle cell anemia testing. Shockley recalls:

> There was a black doctor named Dr. Marion Brooks, and he was considered a rather progressive guy. One day in the spring of 1972 we drove over to his house in Fort Worth to meet him. When we got there I mentioned to him that I had sickle cell, and I thought it would be a good idea to test people for the disease. Dr. Brooks told us that we could test people... that there were these testing kits. He encouraged us to contact Southwest[ern] Medical School and make them aware of our intentions.... He said the folk there would do the testing for us. So we reached out to health care professionals at Southwest[ern], and we raised the money for the kits. Donations came in from such places as [a] Coca-Cola [bottler], a few supermarkets, and Henderson's Chicken, from what I can remember. We also asked students from Skyline High School to help out, which they did. To get people to participate we turned the thing into an event... in Glendale Park. Of course we got a permit from the city. A local band performed [and] students read poetry and did skits on black history.[160]

By that time Haynes had moved to Denton, where he was admitted to North Texas State University. Before long he embarked on a statewide organizing effort, establishing cadres in different locales. Within a year Haynes had convinced Shockley to move to Denton to help with the grassroots movement that was unfolding there. Shockley remembers:

> After the purge we tried to transform ourselves. Leroy [Haynes], B. L. [Smith], and myself, we said, "Let's try to take the party a little bit further," and we started recruiting statewide.... We were trying to figure out what we were going to do. I went to El Centro full-time, and I recruited new people: Paula Ransom, Malik, Anice and Janice Lewis, Carl Austin, Odinga... [Marvin Walton].... Me and Odinga kind of organized that together. We just took over the whole Black Student Union. That's where we ran Panther programs. We had a free clothing program, and we did some free breakfast

programs in the community, and we did voter's registration.... We got good support from some of the professors there. At the same time Leroy went to the North Texas State University in Denton... [and] there was a strong pan-Africanist organization there. So he said, "Man, I need some help up here." I said, "No, we're going to stay down here in Dallas to kind of feel it out." People like Al Lipscomb was getting strong.... Eddie Bernice [Johnson] was getting strong in politics. But what Leroy managed to do was organize a small group of people with Bernie Smith. So, the summer of '72, we left [Dallas] and went to Denton with Leroy. We stayed in Denton approximately two years.[161]

Again, the faction of the Dallas branch of the BPP that supported the philosophies of Newton continued to maintain several programs that were widely considered to be Black Panther Party initiatives. The faction renamed itself the Black Intercommunal Party (BIP). Its members set up shop in Dreamland Apartments in Denton, where the owner had given them the use of four units. During this period the BIP enjoyed an infusion of new blood, including U. S. Williams, who, like Haynes, was a Beaumont native. Williams had just graduated in May 1972 from Charlton-Pollard High School, where he had been a student activist. Williams had been one of the student leaders of a March 1972 protest that called attention to the school's inferior facilities. Students cited outdated equipment and supplies as well as unsanitary conditions. The students called themselves the Committee of Concerned Students for Improvements to Charlton-Pollard. Nearly seven hundred students walked out of their classrooms mid-morning on March 23, 1972. The school was a mere twenty years old, but its cafeteria, restrooms, and locker rooms were "a mess and unsanitary," they said, and many classrooms, the library, and school laboratories were not as well equipped as other city schools.[162] Williams says, "Our activism that year was noticed by Black Student Unions across the state.... We were being invited to visit colleges in the state as if we were All-American athletes, and we believed we really had a contribution to make wherever we went."[163] Student protests at Charlton-Pollard High School weren't uncommon. Two years earlier some of the same students had protested the principal's failure to recommend renewal of contracts for two teachers at the school. The result: the school board voted unanimously to renew the contracts.[164]

On graduation day Williams was elated to be moving on. While his schoolmates celebrated on graduation night, he packed his bags and the few checks he had received as graduation gifts and "rode to Denton where brother Leroy Haynes met me in front of City Hall."[165] Several young men and women, also from the Beaumont scene, joined the rank and file that summer. Williams had grown up with many of them: Don Batiste, Wilbert Franklin, Bob Shaw, and Charlotte La Pointe. There was also Ernest Foster, a cousin of Williams, who left high school in Denton to join the BIP. Foster was young and intense. He also paid attention and followed instructions well. Eventually he was assigned the role of second minister of defense, a job he took very seriously. Other Denton residents to join included Irene Mays and Gwen Pointer, who had graduated from Denton High School. Patricia Rayburn, from Tyler, also proved to be a valuable asset.[166]

It wasn't too long after Williams arrived in Denton that he was made minister of education of the Black Intercommunal Party. By this time the BIP's core leaders were Haynes (chief coordinator), B. L. Smith (field marshal), Shockley (chief of staff—"Chief," for short), Malik Anderson (deputy minister of culture), Charles Simeon (head of security), and Odinga Kambui (distribution manager for the Panther newspaper). Of the women recruits, Haynes recalls such "sharp sisters" as "Sunny Messiah, who coordinated the breakfast programs and the liberation school; Paula Ransom, the group's secretary; and Antoinette Simeon, who served as the public relations person."[167] "Messiah had a way with children... she just had that type of personality... she could relate to people," says Shockley.[168] Haynes remembers Ransom being "a hard worker and strong organizer [who] knew how to get things done." She had joined the BIP during her freshman year at North Texas State and was a dynamo when it came to selling the Panther newspaper. Ransom remembers, "Every weekend I would leave Denton and go [to] downtown Dallas... on the corner of Elm and Harwood, where H. L. Green's department [store] was located... and I would sell paper after paper.... I would sell about two hundred papers by myself.... Comrades would try to compete with me... there was a little friendly competition between me and a few of the guys, but I was just too good, I mean I was really good at selling papers."[169] Haynes remembers Simeon as "an intellectual, a deep thinker [who] was also good at promoting events and activities." Haynes admits that these capable and impressive women represented a gender minority: the cadre was overwhelmingly male.[170] Ransom confirms this but submits that "the Dallas Panthers didn't have the kind of male-female problems that existed out west or in other places.... Yes, there was a little male chauvinism, but there were no serious conflicts of any kind that I knew of."[171]

Shockley provides details about some of the programs they provided Denton residents: "We had the free breakfast program. It was very popular.... We went into a [housing] project called Dreamland and fed the kids before they went to school every morning. We would also organize different fraternities [and] especially sororities from TWU and North Texas... [who] helped us feed the kids. We began to develop good... coalitions with organizations [like the local chapter of] The Links."[172] Diane Ragsdale, a community worker and former member of the NAACP Youth Council in Dallas, recalls the free breakfast program fondly: "I got involved with the Panthers while I was in high school at James Madison High in Dallas, but it was in Denton where I really threw myself in[to] the party's community survival programs.... I really loved serving the kids their breakfast.... I could see the joy in their eyes... receiving a good wholesome meal.... There was also an appreciation on the part of the parents."[173] U. S. Williams also has vivid memories of his days as a Panther and his work in the community of Dreamland. About Dreamland he says: "The more than 600 unit complex was divided into sections. The front section was reserved for small families that required three bedrooms or less. The middle section was designated for students because Denton was a college town and the back section was mostly for single mothers with five or more kids, hence the need for four bedrooms. Air conditioning was optional. Management would install a unit for extra monthly rent. Of course we could not afford a unit so we spent many a day holding political education classes and other activities sweating in front of fans."[174]

Paula Ransom also has fond memories of the group's community survival programs, especially the free breakfast program, saying, "the breakfast program was very active; we had a lot of participation from the parents and their kids.... We fed the kids a hearty breakfast... we didn't just give them a doughnut and some juice. Sometimes we would give them cereal while other times we would give them bacon and eggs.... They ate good."[175] For a time, kids were also fed breakfast and lunch during the summer months.

About Denton, B. L. Smith points out that "in addition to our community survival programs we also cut down on crime in Dreamland.... We didn't allow drugs to be sold there."[176] Shockley says, "We point-blank told the drug dealers and thugs, 'Look, this is our territory, so if you want to be a bad guy, you join us. If you don't want to join us, you move out.' So we moved them out. In fact, during that time we had firepower, so most of the guys would say, 'Hey, man, I don't want to mess with y'all guys, 'cause you crazy anyway.' So we didn't have any problems."[177] Smith is also extremely proud of the liberation school that the BIP ran on weekday evenings. Although adults were welcome, kids were the biggest beneficiaries. At the liberation school kids got help with their homework, and sometimes there was someone there who would instruct them in martial arts and other activities. Says Smith, "We tried to instill in people, especially the youth, a sense of self-respect; we hammered home the notion that blacks needed to learn to love one another. As part of that we gave people heavy doses of black history, because that was something that most blacks did not get in school or anywhere else, for that matter. We really worked with the kids.... We took them on field trips.... The kids had gotten so sharp that they could explain dialectical materialism, and they were only in elementary school."[178] "It was also not uncommon for us to babysit some of the children who lived in the complex," says Ransom.[179]

Although kids benefited immensely from the BIP's programs, there was also something for senior citizens. A geriatric program run by Antoinette Simeon offered a range of assistance including arranging doctor visits, taking seniors shopping, or transporting them to a drugstore to get prescriptions filled. "We also sometimes helped with repairs around the house... things like that," says Shockley.[180] According to Haynes, the group's efforts extended beyond Denton to other parts of Texas, developing cadres as far away as Abilene, Tyler, and Beaumont.[181]

Smith had been the first president of the Black Student Union at Arlington State College (later the University of Texas at Arlington) in 1968. "He was a great recruiter and did a good job of establishing and maintaining a strong BSU–Black Panther bond," says Haynes. "He brought many BSU members from Denton into the fold." Some also remember Smitty "as an effective enforcer," Haynes notes.[182] Not too long after being expelled from the party and reinventing themselves as the BIP, the group decided to go to California again, this time to Oakland. Smitty recalls the trip like it was yesterday: "The excitement was high.... We drove a cargo van all the way to Oakland—about fifteen of us.... We took turns driving.... I think we had three flat tires on the way. We had one spare tire, but we ended up having to buy two tires.... Still, it was a fun trip.... For me, going to Oakland was like going to the holy city of Mecca."[183] Why did the group go to Oakland after having been expelled by the BPP leaders there? Haynes says, "Despite everything that had gone down, we still wanted to maintain a relationship with the party."[184] Also, by that time Khalif Hasan, one of the original Dallas NCCF members, had moved to Oakland, where he worked alongside David Hilliard. "I arrived in Oakland on the Fourth of July, 1971," says Hasan. Hasan's duties included running central headquarters and presiding over the East Oakland branch of the BPP. Hasan's transfer to Oakland was precipitated by the pressure he had constantly found himself under in Texas. He had continually been getting arrested. Hasan says, "I was busted for everything except murder.... One of my arrests even resulted in a forty-day jail term." His move to Oakland turned out to be beneficial to his Dallas comrades. Says Shockley, "Charlie Paul had a good relationship with Hilliard, and he helped smooth things over for us. Even though we were no longer allowed to officially use the Panther name, Hasan met with members of the central committee, including Bobby Seale, who ultimately supported our efforts as the Black Intercommunal Party... so much so that he placed us under the supervision of the Houston branch of the BPP."[185]

Although the Party's central committee supported the BIP's efforts, the party's brass did not, for whatever reason, broach the subject of reinstatement. The decision to keep the former Panthers at arm's length may have been politically motivated. The central committee enjoyed the best of both worlds. If the BIP continued to do the kind of community work for which the Panthers were known, it would undoubtedly have the consequence of reflecting well on the Panther organization. However, if members of the BIP engaged in any activity that was embarrassing, resulting in unfavorable media coverage, Panthers at central headquarters could maintain that members of the BIP were not Panthers.

Again, as the Black Intercommunal Party, the former Panthers continued to promote the party's survival programs. According to Haynes, "We were feeding several hundred kids in the free breakfast program. There were some very strong survival programs that were taking place. We were able to have an impact in the various communities throughout Texas and set stuff in motion, especially on police community control."[186]

In 1973, the Black Intercommunal Party followed Bobby Seale's and Elaine Brown's lead into electoral politics as Haynes, a student at the North Texas State University at the time, tossed his hat into the ring for the Denton city council. Nearly a dozen candidates ran for three seats. Haynes was one of three candidates recruited to run by some of Denton's progressive elements. The other two were Richard Yahr, an attorney, and Trish Pagan, a welfare caseworker, both of whom were white. It was a nonpartisan election, and there were no districts: candidates were elected at large, with the top three vote-earners elected to the council. Shockley believes that Haynes was the best candidate. "Leroy was well-spoken, and he was known in Denton because he was going to school there," says Shockley.[187] Although Haynes, Yahr, and Pagan were promoted as a slate by those who had recruited them, the three did not campaign together, nor did they pool their resources or strategize together. According to Yahr, "none of [us] had ever met one another before we were identified to run for city council."[188]

Haynes's candidacy may have been more symbolic than realistic as the Denton City Council had been dominated historically by white males. Until 1973 no woman had ever been elected to the city council, much less a black person. Haynes's campaign was both underfunded and understaffed, making it unlikely that he would be the first, although, "one didn't need a lot of money to run for the city council in those days," Yahr says.[189] Haynes's effort did not lack verve and ambition. U. S. Williams remembers: "We began a campaign with [the] youthful vigor of Spartans. We gave rallies in the community, gave away groceries with a chicken in every bag... we gave political speeches on campus."[190] Campaign donations came in from professors at local universities, nearby churches, Links chapters, and residents who were excited that there was a black candidate. Haynes stumped in barbershops, beauty salons, and cafes. Yahr remembers "appearing on radio shows and doing a lot of door-to-door campaigning."[191] Although Haynes and the Black Intercommunal Party succeeded in getting out their message, Haynes failed to be elected, but few can deny that he put up a good showing. Haynes received 1,028 votes, while Yahr and Pagan garnered 1,163 and 907 respectively. Although victory eluded all three, they may have started something. Denton elected its first woman council member that year, Lillian Miller, who collected 1,455 votes.[192] And the following year Denton residents elected Welton Stoker the city's first black school board member and first student ever elected to the board. Haynes notes with pride the role that the Black Intercommunal Party played in Stoker's election, saying that they registered voters and stumped on Stoker's behalf, canvassing neighborhoods and handing out campaign literature.[193] More than twenty years would pass, however, before Denton would elect its first black city council member in 1995, a Vietnam War veteran, Carl Young.

While the faction of the Dallas Panthers that followed the political views of Huey Newton continued their progress in Denton, the remaining purged members, at the behest of Curtis Gaines, renamed themselves the Vanguard. The name Grassroots Incorporated was also in association with this group of former Panthers. It is unclear as to whether these names were used interchangeably or if these were two separate groups established by Gaines himself. At any rate, Gaines and his followers attempted to continue the Dallas free breakfast program, free clothing program, the prisoner program, and pest control program. Donald Lister was put in charge of these programs.[194] Gaines was able to ingratiate himself with a rather mysterious and wealthy white woman from the well-to-do Highland Park section of Dallas who gave Gaines substantial funds for the survival programs. According to Odinga Kambui, "They had moved and set up shop in the fancy house they had built with the money that a donor had given them that was to go to community uplift... the rich white woman, I understand, who lived in Highland Park."[195] Once in the house, several members allegedly began to engage in illegal activity that Lister mentions without going into detail. Despite the support that Gaines received from donors, trouble always seemed to find him. In October 1972 he was arrested and charged with extortion in what police called "Mafia-type" demands for protection money from prominent businessmen. He was taken into custody after he was seen leaving the office of the owner of a chain of city apartment complexes with extortion money that was allegedly earmarked for his organization, the Vanguard.

Lister recalls the day in April 1973 that caused Grassroots Incorporated to be terminated:

> I think some of the guys had robbed a drug dealer and had some bricks of marijuana. We were going to start selling grass, selling dope, because you couldn't smoke all that grass, and I saw it. It was about three bricks. John Woods had run into the house saying, "The pigs! They vamping! They vamping!" "Vamping" means they're running down on you. And I don't think we had a phone or something. He had gone up the hill to a store and was using the pay phone, and, coming home, I think they followed him, and they kept on following him. They didn't turn off like they would usually do. Sometimes they would follow you, and then they would turn on off and go. But he ran in screaming, "They vamping! They vamping!"[196]

Rushing downstairs from his room with his gun in hand, Lister thought the police were shooting. He says that a woman and child were in the house and that he wanted to protect them at all costs, so he began firing on the officers. He shot and wounded one of them before he was subdued and beaten. Eventually he would be tried, found guilty, and sentenced to a minimum of fifty years in prison.[197] An independent newspaper, the *Ghetto Eye*, recounted the events of the Grassroots Incorporated bust:

> First, I shall deal with the initial contradiction, and that is, the purpose for the search warrant. It was stated in the white folks press that a search warrant was granted so that the officers might check for narcotics. Having been a member of the Grassroots Org., I can readily recall that narcotics were a no-no for all members of the organization.... Secondly, I shall deal with the problems of eight officers being sent to serve one search warrant from the rear of the house [in civilian clothes]. "Red Dog" [Lister] is being held under $150,000 bond for shooting a person who was not identifiable as an officer.... In conclusion, I see two basic possibilities: One, Republic Bank really issued the warrant... due to past dealings based on a substantial donation made to [Grassroots].... Two, some conniving individual, either within or closely attached to the Org. set the whole thing up and planted the dope—if the cops didn't bring it.[198]

While awaiting trial, Lister happened to thumb through his files and those of other members arrested in the police raid. It was then, he says, that he "learned that [Gaines's] goal was... to... either turn us in to informants or to get us busted."[199] Kambui says that Lister was a victim and didn't learn until later on that Curtis Gaines was an agent provocateur and had been on the government payroll: "I talked to him about this over the years and got more details on it. Of course, [Lister] ended up doing a considerable amount of time in the Texas Department of Corrections."[200] This evidence pointed to Gaines as the chief informant or agent provocateur of this phase of the movement. While in prison, Lister recalls, he thought back to a telling incident involving Gaines:

> I remember Curtis and I went up to D.C. They had another revolutionary tribunal, where Geronimo had sent Curtis up there to tell Huey to either do what the instructions were, [to follow through with] the plan... when they went underground, or just leave it alone because he wasn't getting any of the support that he was supposed to be getting. It was me, Curtis, Beverly... about five of us went. But when we got [there],... they left me in the room with the bodyguards.... Huey was in the next room. I remember Jane Fonda was there, and when [Curtis] got a chance to talk with Huey... I don't know who to believe, but some of it falls into place, some of it doesn't.... Curtis said Huey told him to poison Geronimo and the others. According to Curtis, Huey said, 'Buy them a lot of food and put poison in it.' Curtis told Geron-

imo, 'You know I was given the mission to assassinate y'all. They told me to buy y'all a bunch of food and lace it with poison.' And Geronimo said, 'That sounds about like what them cowards would do.' Now, I don't know if this was true... but again, Curtis being an agent provocateur, this is what they do."[201]

Because of the 1973 raid of Grassroots Incorporated, several members ended their involvement with the group; however, those in Denton continued to organize. In the summer of 1973, Fred Bell, the former SNCC member who allegedly robbed a bank in Ladonia, was absolved by a U.S. Court of Appeals after appealing his case several times.[202] Returning to Dallas, he changed his name to Fahim Minkah and formed the Angela Davis Liberation Committee. Later, Kambui says, he was given permission to relaunch the Black Panther Party in Dallas.[203] Minkah traveled to Oakland to obtain an official party charter from the BPP's central committee. Since no one at party headquarters knew of Minkah, Deputy Chief of Staff June Hilliard relied somewhat on the judgment of Khalif Hasan, who had been one of the original Dallas Panthers. Since it was believed that Hasan was familiar with the lay of the land and well versed in Dallas politics, he was dispatched to Dallas, reportedly along with Bunchy Crear from the People's Party II in Houston, and asked to evaluate the situation and report back. Hasan remembers:

> I left Dallas a little more than a year after the NCCF was founded. I went to Oakland and worked under David Hilliard. At some point in 1972, Minkah reaches out to Oakland seeking to start another chapter of the BPP in Dallas. No one on the central committee knew Minkah so I was asked to go to Dallas and check things out. When I got there I saw that there were two brothers looking to start a chapter, independent of one another. They were Akintunde Funso and Fahim Minkah. Although I had some misgivings about Minkah I wanted to approach this thing as objectively as possible. I knew that Minkah had a lot of contacts in the community and had a reputation for getting things done. I didn't know the other brother well enough to vouch for him. When I returned to Oakland I gave them my assessment. I was then asked could I think of a good reason not to grant Minkah permission to start a chapter, and I replied no. That's how Minkah got the chapter.[204]

Funso, a Dallas native, had attended Franklin D. Roosevelt High School before leaving school his senior year. After a short stint behind bars, Funso joined the party in 1971. Funso was enraged with the state of the political climate when he was released from prison, and he was ready to join a revolutionary organization. He expounds on his introduction to the party: "One day I was downtown Dallas, and up walks this sister name Antoinette Simeon with a bunch of *Black Panther* newspapers in her hand. Then Skip Shockley walks up... [and] we started talking.... I knew right then I was going to be a Panther... that is how I was formally introduced to the party."[205] Funso worked closely with Shockley and others in Denton before being sent to Houston. It was in Houston that he met Charlie Freeman.

As far as starting another Panther chapter in Dallas, Funso's story differs sharply from Hasan's. He admits to helping to relaunch the BPP in Dallas but only at the request of Houston's Charlie Freeman. He denies any notion that he was vying to head the chapter once it was established. In Funso's words: "In late 1972 Charlie Freeman of the Houston Black Panthers and I spoke by phone. In the course of that conversation Charlie says that he wants me to organize a chapter of the Black Panther Party in Dallas, so I was doing what he asked me to do, but I wasn't making any play to be the leader. And, like I said, I was surprised, like many others were when word came down that Oakland had given Fahim permission to restart the chapter and pegged him as the coordinator or whatever title they gave him."[206] Why Hasan elected not to vouch for those who headed Dallas's first BPP chapter is unclear, especially since Hasan was more familiar with them than he was with Minkah. Indeed, at one time, Hasan had developed a strong working relationship with the previous regime. Nevertheless, after Minkah and his small cadre got Oakland's blessing to start the new chapter, Funso continued organizing but within a different venue. In 1973, he enrolled in El Centro College, and while there, he got involved with the Black Student Union. Says Funso, "I enrolled at El Centro because that was where the young, energetic students were."[207] Like Shockley before him, Funso endeavored, with some success, to make the BSU into the image of the Black Panther Party by emulating some of the party's outreach initiatives as well as instilling in students a heightened political consciousness. Funso attended El Centro off and on from 1973 to 1978.

Minkah had a solid reputation within movement circles. "Minkah was also a standout track star at Arlington State College, so he was well known," says B. L. Smith.[208] This would stand him in good stead as he went about the business of trying to build the chapter. SCLC organizer Peter Johnson remembers how Minkah and his comrades secured picket lines, rallies, and marches with guards to ensure the safety of nonviolent leaders: "I had a good relationship with them.... They didn't like the nonviolence, but they knew that we knew best how to mobilize our people and to organize the masses of our people into large demonstrations in the street... and we didn't feel that we was in competition with them... and we had a good relationship with them."[209]

SNCC Revisited

After unsuccessfully attempting to achieve political asylum in Ghana, Mali, Liberia, and the Ivory Coast, former SNCC members Ernest McMillan and Kwesi Williams reentered the United States and settled in Cincinnati, where both were kept under surveillance by the FBI. McMillan remembers, "I was arrested in Cincinnati, Ohio, because there was a paid agent who gave me a plan and the directions and address to go find one of these War on Poverty jobs, but the whole route I was taking was known by the police, so they knew exactly the best point to ambush us. They had our pictures in their hands and ... said, 'that's Ernie McMillan, that's Kwesi,' you know, that kind of thing."[210]

The *Dallas Morning News* reported that a man with McMillan's birth certificate had been captured in Mount Gilead, Ohio, but released when the match for fingerprints rendered inconclusive results.[211] Meanwhile, SNCC co-leader Matthew Johnson, after appealing his case for three years, began serving his ten-year sentence in August 1971.[212] In December 1971, authorities caught McMillan in Cincinnati.[213] His lawyer, Ed Polk, made several attempts to transfer his charges of draft evasion to Cincinnati because "so great a prejudice exists against him [in Dallas]."[214] The judge denied this request, however, and McMillan was returned to Dallas by court order to face trial on the draft evasion, property damage, and illegal gun charges.[215] He was found guilty on all charges and sentenced to ten years in prison, which he began to fulfill later that year.

Because of his mother's activity with SNCC students and her early role as surrogate mother to several young people in the movement, and because she already worked closely with Black Citizens for Justice, Law, and Order, she worked with family members of political prisoners and other concerned citizens to form People United for Justice for Prisoners. Mama Mack comments: "I think our main thrust was against the prison system, the Texas prison system.... Families' loved ones were in prison, and we formed steps [with] which to help people get out of prison.... The first was to write a letter to Judge William Justice, who was a regional, district judge in Tyler, Texas, and let him know why your loved one was in prison and how he was in prison unjustly. We helped many people to get out of prison. And that was a wonderful feeling because we accomplished much doing that." She recalls,

> We could only visit [the prisoners] every other weekend, Saturday or Sunday, and we never failed because what we had learned and what we tried to preach to the people who have family members in prison was "never miss a visit because once they think you don't care, they treat [the prisoners] any [kind of] way." So we were there every other week to support Ernie, and we would pass out literature while we were there. We would go into the yard and say, "People United for Justice for Prisoners have ten points. Call us. This is our number," and people began to call us and wait for us, and when people would come to visit their loved ones they would say, "Would you help me?"

Then Texas state representatives Eddie Bernice Johnson and Mickey Leland formed a joint committee that partnered with the People United for Justice for Prisoners and held hearings regarding illegal practices in Texas state penitentiaries. Eva McMillan remembers, "About once a month we'd go to some town where a prison was to have a hearing on [a] wrong thing that the authorities would be doing to the inmates, and it gained a lot of purpose."[216] The joint committee was able to move Ernest McMillan from state to federal prison, where he filed several writs on his case and was eventually freed in 1974.[217] Upon being freed, McMillan went to work for a time in the office of Eddie Bernice Johnson on her prison reform committee.[218]

Black Panther Party Redux

By 1974, the Black Intercommunal Party, which had been in existence for three years, withered away. In Haynes's words, "by that time battle fatigue had set in [and] people were getting older and trying to figure out what they were going to do with their lives."[219] Meanwhile, another version of the Dallas chapter of the Black Panther Party was coming into existence. At the helm was another former SNCC activist, Fahim Minkah, who maintains that "the Texas state chapter of the Black Panther Party began in 1973."[220] The new leadership core was small, consisting of Minkah as coordinator and Marvin Crenshaw as assistant coordinator. Charles Hillman was director of the People's Free Pest Control Program. Hillman had gotten involved with the party after graduating from Thomas Jefferson High School. He remembers, "I was ready to join the Panther Party.... I had been reading Jimmy Baldwin. I was angry.... The whites at my high school were racist... [and] hearing white students use the word 'nigger' was commonplace, plus the school's fight song was 'Dixie'.... I had gotten to the point where I wasn't going to continue singing that racist song so I helped organize a boycott to ban it."[221]

Both Hillman and Crenshaw were worker bees. Akintunde Funso says, "Crenshaw was a very good person, someone who could get things done... he was a veteran... he was a logistics genius."[222] Although Crenshaw was an Austin native, as a kid he had lived in Wichita and St. Louis. After graduating from Austin's L. C. Anderson High School in 1965, Crenshaw joined the army and served until 1968, with two of those years spent in Germany. After being discharged from the army, Crenshaw, by now a married man, decided to enroll in Augsburg College in Minneapolis in 1969 at the age of twenty-two. It was there that he met another nontraditional student, Kenny "Mo" Burton, who headed the NCCF there in Minneapolis. "Burton introduced me to the party... [and] when I read the ten-point program it blew my mind," says Crenshaw.[223] Burton was ten years Crenshaw's senior. Crenshaw aspired to play football at Augsburg, but after making the team his attention turned elsewhere, and he worked with the NCCF. In 1971 Crenshaw returned to Texas and landed in Dallas, where for a time he did custodial work. Given his experiences working with the NCCF in Minneapolis, it was only a matter of time before he joined the Black Panther Party in Dallas. Says Crenshaw:

When I returned to Texas I had hoped to reconnect with the Black Panther Party. I was in Dallas for two years before I met Fahim in the summer of 1973. My daughter was in a day-care center where Fahim's wife happened to work, so I had heard of Fahim. Then a white guy by the name of Charlie Young, who headed a local group of white radicals that followed the principles of the Black Panther Party, told Fahim about me ... [and] the next thing I know, Fahim shows up at my apartment. His entire conversation was about him going to Oakland and getting permission to start a Dallas chapter of the Black Panther Party.... If he got permission to start a chapter, he wanted me to be a member. After he gets back from Oakland he informs me and others that he got the charter.[224]

Upon getting permission to start a chapter, one of the first orders of business was finding an office. The revived Dallas party's first headquarters was an old house located on Hamilton Street in South Dallas and in serious need of repair. Crenshaw was assigned the unenviable responsibility of staying overnight there and keeping an eye on the place. Fortunately the newly sanctioned Panthers found more suitable accommodations a week or two later.[225]

The size of the Dallas chapter of the BPP is difficult to even approximate. Minkah says, "I didn't talk about numbers then and I don't intend to do it now.... As Malcolm used to say, 'those who know don't tell and those who tell don't know.'"[226] Hillman remembers that the chapter consisted of "approximately fifteen members; people joined and left ... it was like a revolving door." [227] Other members of the chapter included Antoinette and Chester Mitchell, Deborrah Molo and her brother McClellan Molo, and William Morehead. That Panther officials at the national level tapped Minkah as the chapter's leader caught some by surprise. Several Panthers in the Dallas area remember him as Fred Bell and as having been for years opposed to joining the Black Panther Party. Says Funso, "I remember vividly Fred saying to me one time that he had no interest in becoming a Panther, so when he was chosen to lead the chapter I was surprised."[228] What accounted for Minkah's change of heart is not entirely clear. Hillman, who considers Minkah to be one of the smartest people he has ever met, reasons that Minkah's change of heart about the party was directly related to the Newton-Cleaver ideological rift that turned many people off, Panthers included. When it became apparent that Newton's position of serving the people was going to win out over armed revolution, Minkah became receptive to joining the party, says Hillman.[229] Whatever the reason, Minkah wasted little time in getting the chapter off the ground.

In no time at all, members of the newly revived Dallas chapter of the BPP were selling the Panther newspaper. Deborrah Molo, a Louisiana transplant, remembers hawking the newspaper in various locations in South Dallas, West Dallas, and downtown Dallas.[230] For the most part under Minkah's leadership, the community programs resembled those in other parts of the country where

Panther chapters and branches existed. Says Crenshaw, "Paul Laurence Dunbar Elementary School was just four or five blocks away from our headquarters so we would go to the kids' homes and walk them to school."[231] Unlike the earlier incarnation of the chapter there was no free breakfast program, but, says Minkah, "we had a People's Free Legal Clinic that was held one night a week.... We also had a program called Prisoners, Families and Friends for Action.... This program was also held weekly... the objective was to press for better treatment for inmates."[232] Hillman is most proud of the pest control program over which he presided. "This program was hugely popular," Minkah says. "A lot of the places where we did pest control badly needed it... for example there was one project that was built on top of a landfill, so you know the problems that came with that.... Roaches and rats were not uncommon sights."[233] A private company trained members of the party and others in pest control.[234] Hillman remembers the time and energy that went into making the community aware of this program: "We put out hundreds of leaflets and handbills... we went door to door and handed them out."[235] For Crenshaw it was the program for families and friends of prisoners that was most significant. "Although I was not involved in this program the idea of helping inmates and those close to them deal with some of the issues that come with incarceration was one that really appealed to me," says Crenshaw.[236] From Minkah's standpoint, the programs were "organizing devices;... not only were we serving the people... we were educating the people."[237]

The chapter also conducted political education and was conscientious about educating residents about their rights as tenants. "Tenants' rights information was a big thing with us," says Hillman. "A lot of tenants didn't know their rights... landlords knew this and would take advantage of them."[238] They did a lot of work with those who lived in the West Dallas Housing Projects, a thirty-five-hundred-unit housing complex that by the early to mid-1970s had seen better days. Over the next few years the Dallas chapter of the BPP also made its presence known by engaging in a number of high-profile events. For example, when branch members got word that employees at a store on Hamilton Boulevard were selling glue and paint to kids who used them to get high by inhaling them, they approached store personnel and requested that they refrain from selling these products to youth. After store managers scoffed at the request, the Panthers, with the support of the community, threw up a boycott that lasted three months. "We not only impacted their sales, because residents honored the boycott, but we also educated the community on the dangers of kids having access to those kinds of chemicals," says Hillman.[239] Crenshaw remembers the boycott but recalls a different reason for it: "Yes, we did boycott the store in February 1974, but I remember boycotting the store because its owner had shot and killed a young brother by the name of Jody Brown. Naturally, he accused Brown of stealing. I organized community residents to boycott. Every evening around six o'clock we would start boycotting the store until it closed around 10:00 to 11:00 p.m. In fact I was arrested for my participation in that boycott, along with James Curtis Wilson, Michael Tubbs, and Willis Stafford."[240] A March 15, 1974, memorandum sent from the FBI's Intelligence Division in Dallas to the director of the FBI in Washington described the boycott and arrests: "Average of four to eight persons, with picketing usually from 12:00 noon until approximately 9:00 pm. Picketers have not violated law except for an arrest of three Negro males on March 13, 1974 at 9:00 pm on a charge of obstructing a highway. Picketers were blocking street adjacent to Miller's Drive-In grocery when DPD asked them to clear street. Persons cleared street except for Marvin Eugene Crenshaw, James Curtis Walton and Willis Stafford. Walton and Stafford are not known militants."[241]

The boycott was just one of the Panthers' public expressions of dissidence. In the spring of 1974 the Panthers publicly called for the firing and arrest of two white police officers who they charged with the death of an off-duty black police officer in February of that year.[242] Fearing that the police officers in question would escape punishment, the Dallas chapter of the BPP filed a suit against the city, charging it with violating chapter 16, section 15, of the Dallas City Charter. This part of the Dallas charter stipulated that if three or more citizens brought written charges of misconduct against any civil service employee on the city's Classified Service list, the Dallas Civil Service Board was required to conduct "an open and public trial." If not for the extensive research done by Fahim Minkah, who possessed keen legal insight and knowledge of the Dallas City Charter, the public would have remained unaware of its power to hold civil servants accountable in this way.[243] Among the citizens who brought said charges against the city were Black Panther Party members: Deborrah Molo, Marvin Crenshaw, Margie Graves, and Charles Hillman.

Despite the fact that chapter 16, section 15, had been city law since 1931, the city attorney arbitrarily and illegally decided that this section of the charter did not apply to police officers. It was after this that the Panthers' attorney filed suit. The city's response was predictable: it refused to process the complaint. Attorney Mike Daniels remembers Fahim Minkah coming to the Legal Services office where he worked: "I was a lawyer by then.... I took the case... I was glad to take it.... It was the kind of case that interested us, that we should have been taking, so I took it." The suit was filed, but a district court judge ruled against the complainants. Daniels appealed the decision, at which point an appeals judge overturned the district court's ruling, ordering the city to process the complaint.[244] Although the complaint was then processed, the officers were neither indicted nor did they lose their jobs. Supporters of the police in turn embarked on an effort to ruin Panther leader Minkah, while insulating civil service employees, by placing the matter on the ballot. Minkah, who was seen as the driving force behind the lawsuit, drew the ire of establishment leaders not only for that but also because of his insistence on a citizens' district police board.[245] "They tried to get Fahim fired from his job at Dallas Legal Services... I know this because I worked there," Daniels recalls. Dallas residents overwhelmingly supported the Dallas Police Department and the city. "I remember the vote being something like 70–30 in favor of protecting Dallas's civil servants from that kind of legal redress," says Daniels.[246] City attorney Alex Bickley maintained that any grievance against the police force or its individual officers "should be left in the hands of the chief of police.... He has the exclusive right to suspend his men."[247]

In 1974 the Dallas chapter of the BPP lost one of its key members, Marvin Crenshaw, who departed that spring, leaving Hillman to take over the assistant coordinator responsibilities. Hillman would leave the following year. Upon leaving the party, Crenshaw enrolled at El Centro College for the school's second summer session in 1974.[248] Crenshaw remembers stopping by the Panther office one day after Deborrah Molo, with whom he was in a relationship, had informed him that Hillman and another friend, William Morehead, had stopped by looking for him.

"I remember it like it was yesterday," says Crenshaw. After enrolling at El Centro he had immediately begun reviving the Black Student Union. Black Students for Pride and Identification, the school's dormant BSU, had once been a vibrant organization under Kathy Davis, who served two terms as president, 1973–74 and 1974–75.[249] However, after Davis left El Centro for North Texas State, the organization appears to have been inactive for a period. "When I found Charles at the headquarters," Crenshaw says, "I told him what I was doing and that he needed to come with me.... I didn't encourage him to quit the party... I just told him he needed to join me at El Centro."[250] Not long after that, Hillman left the party and joined Crenshaw at El Centro where Crenshaw had already begun the arduous task of reactivating the BSU. Now Crenshaw had Hillman to share the load. Crenshaw and Hillman assumed control of the BSU and renamed it Black Students for Community Survival. Although neither Hillman nor Crenshaw was a member of the party any longer, they continued working together in the spirit of the BPP. In fact, says Hillman, "we based the organization on BPP ideology."[251]

During Hillman's tenure as BSU president, Crenshaw was responsible for much of the organizing that took place. Like many who hold the position of vice president within service-oriented organizations, Crenshaw did the tedious and laborious work. It was Crenshaw who gathered and filled out all the necessary paperwork required to get the BSU up and running after a period of inactivity.[252] Crenshaw's work as the BSU's vice president was just an extension of the responsibilities that he carried out as a member of the party. The same can be said for Hillman. So why did he leave the party? Hillman says, "There were some internal struggles going on.... There were people coming into the party that I didn't know or trust.... Paranoia set in ... people were generally hesitant to trust one another."[253] Crenshaw expressed a similar sentiment recalling an incident that has stayed with him over the years: "One day I ran into someone who held a leadership position within the party, and he urged me to go by the party's headquarters.... I was out of the party by then, no longer a member.... So I go to the office the following day, and seconds later the police was kicking the door in.... To this day I can't help but wonder whether or not this was a coincidence."[254] The police were supposedly looking for stolen library books.[255] After that experience Crenshaw never went back to the party's office.

Crenshaw admits that he was actually purged from the party by local leaders.[256] Although being ousted stung, he did not let that setback prevent him from serving the people. "Marvin has always been a consistent and tireless worker ... a warrior, a dragon on behalf of the people," Hillman says. "He loves his community and has shown it time and time again, that's why as soon as I became president of the BSU I knew I wanted Marvin as my VP."[257] Actually, it was Crenshaw who urged Hillman to take on the presidency. "I wanted Charles to be president because he was closer in age to many of the students who were attending.... I knew they would be able to relate to him better than they would me, because I was older," says Crenshaw.[258] The activities in which Hillman and Crenshaw engaged while serving as officers in the BSU were in the spirit of the BPP. The BSU pushed for the creation of black studies courses and established a very popular Black History Month program that included speakers and performers such as James Baldwin, the Dance Theatre of Harlem, and Freddie Hubbard. Donna Miller, a student at El Centro at the time and a member of the BSU, remembers bringing James Earl Jones to campus, a move that seemingly ruffled the feathers of administrators as the BSU violated certain protocols in extending the invitation directly.[259] The BSU also initiated a campaign of disinvestment in South Africa and worked on behalf of Vietnam veterans and mothers who were recipients of public assistance.

While Hillman and Crenshaw were furthering the Panthers' legacy through their work with the North Texas State BSU, the Texas state chapter of the BPP under Minkah continued to fight the good fight.

On April 26, 1975, the Panthers, along with the Brown Berets and Bois d'Arc Patriots, a white activist group, led one thousand Dallas residents in a protest march. Chanting "We want jobs!," the marchers paraded through downtown and rallied on the steps of City Hall, where community leaders urged the demonstrators to present their grievances before the Dallas city council. Besides jobs, the marchers wanted an end to police brutality against minorities and poor people. Weeks earlier a young man had reportedly been choked to death by a police officer in the Dallas jail. "We had an ongoing campaign against police brutality," says Minkah.[260] Police officials claimed that twenty-three-year-old David Carroll Walker had committed suicide by hanging himself "in a telephone booth."²⁶¹ Walker's death had set off an April 4 demonstration of two hundred people who packed the chambers of the city council and prompted an independent investigation of Walker's death. According to the *Black Panther*, more than twenty-three hundred signatures had been presented to members of the city council. Minkah warned the council that they should be thankful "that black and poor people are still coming before you in an orderly manner."²⁶²

Police brutality was a fact of life against which the Panthers were constantly fighting. Surprisingly, in December 1975, Dallas Civil Appeals Court judge Claude Williams ruled in favor of the Panthers' suit. Determined to thwart the Panthers' efforts, the Dallas city council unanimously voted to appeal Judge Williams's decision to the Supreme Court of Texas. In the meantime, the council decided to revise chapter 16, section 15, to be voted on at a special election the following April. Minkah maintained that this was "merely a stall tactic to delay the upcoming hearings against certain cops."²⁶³ Win or lose, Minkah could be counted on to fight the good fight. In the following years, Minkah, with a cadre of recruits different from the original members of the party in Dallas, continued to organize and serve the community in various ways. The Panthers' opposition to police misconduct was ongoing. In 1978, Minkah resigned from the party. "By the late 1970s the party was again ordering all Panthers to move to Oakland.... I thought central headquarters should have been dispatching comrades to the South and Southwest.... I wasn't going to Oakland so I sat down and wrote a well-crafted letter that was addressed to the chief of staff, central committee, informing them that I was resigning with honor," says Minkah.²⁶⁴

Conclusion

The Black Panther Party in Dallas took on different iterations at different times, but the goals and objectives remained the same. Haynes maintains that "while Dallas was the key... we made the biggest impact in Denton by spreading the Panther ideology and philosophy."²⁶⁵ The Dreamland projects, out of which the BIP organized, at Russell and Denton Street, were fertile ground for its message. The residents rallied around the BIP and welcomed what the group's members were trying to accomplish.²⁶⁶ Although neither the Dallas Panthers nor its offshoots such as the BIP have received the historical attention they deserve, their imprint on Dallas and Denton is undeniable. The Panthers inherited a rich legacy of activism that dates as far back as the nineteenth century, when those blacks who were held as slaves sought to win their freedom by any means necessary.

In the sterile, gray shadows of Dallas's Central Expressway—the highway that connects the city's southern sector to outlying, northern suburbs, bisecting the once-thriving African American community known as Freedman's Town—there is a wrought iron gate. This gate would go unnoticed by motorists or customers hastily rushing into the Walmart next door if not for the two proud African statues, in brilliant onyx, situated to its left and right. Perhaps this gate, with its African protectors on either side—one male and one female—still goes unnoticed by the average Dallasite. Regardless, it was there that the expressway's burgeoning expansion was made to halt some thirty years ago.[267] Construction workers discovered bones, chipped bits of shell and glass, and other human remains. In the midst of forklifts and cement trucks were the unmarked resting places of tens of thousands of African Americans whose remains had been paved over by a manifest destiny–obsessed oligarchy that sought to replace Freedman's Town with Walmarts, condominiums, expressways, and contemporary markers of gentrified colonialism.

This space, now a consecrated historic landmark, was the place of rest for both enslaved and free blacks. After having been condemned by the City of Dallas almost a century ago, it lives again as a testament to those early people who chose to move or were forced to settle in Texas. Freedman's Cemetery now serves as an example of Dallas's modus operandi with black inhabitants of the city.[268] The history of the civil rights and Black Power movements in Dallas, not coincidentally, fell victim to a similar fate.

Keeping the movement and its history alive in Dallas today is of utmost importance. So is including the entire history of Dallas in public curricula. Teaching Dallas's black citizens their history could be a point of departure for reinvigorating larger movements within the city. While movements in the struggle for dignity and rights entail failures as well as successes, these movements and their organizing tactics could be studied in civics, history, and social studies classes. After all, they developed organically and centered around genuine care and concern for community and people.

As a principal organizer in the movement, Ernest McMillan shares his final thoughts on this. "I wish [this study] could help discover, [teach, and revitalize] what were some of the methods that may have been used and that might be applicable to today [for youth interested in championing human rights], so [that there can be a] kind of like passing the baton on this historical piece. It can [serve] the future as well as by clarifying [past] acts and deeds and providing a sense of what we can and could do."[269] McMillan stresses the need for youth to play an active, central role in the movement. He feels that the people in Dallas's movements of the sixties and seventies, who also did not have the full support of elders to guide their endeavors, now ostracize the youth of today. The veterans of the movement, McMillan says, have to "resist being a 'sage on the stage' and [instead] listen to youth [because] the youth have their own roles as co-creators in this [new] leg of the movement. There has to be a dynamic of side-by-side struggle and giving and taking. Vets have to learn that we don't know the dimensions of their struggle."[270]

It is our hope that this essay will be a catalyst for reenergizing the struggle in Dallas, giving key organizers their rightful place in history, and inspiring the research of similar movements elsewhere.

NOTES

1. Stefanie Decker, "Women in the Civil Rights Movement: Juanita Craft versus the Dallas Elite," in *Blacks in East Texas History*, ed. Bruce A. Glasrud and Archie P. McDonald (College Station: Texas A&M University Press, 2008), 133. A similar sentiment is detailed in W. Marvin Dulaney, "Whatever Happened to the Civil Rights Movement in Dallas, Texas?" in *Essays on the American Civil Rights Movement*, ed. John Dittmer, W. Marvin Dulaney, and George C. Wright (College Station, Texas A&M University Press, 1993), 79.

2. Randolph B. Campbell, *An Empire for Slavery: The Peculiar Institution in Texas, 1821–1865* (Baton Rouge: Louisiana State University Press, 1989).

3. Michael Phillips, *White Metropolis: Race, Ethnicity, and Religion in Dallas, 1841–2001* (Austin: University of Texas Press, 2006), 3.

4. Ibid.

5. There is a local myth that Dallas was named after the grand wizard of the Ku Klux Klan at the time of its founding. However, many believe the city was actually named after the eleventh vice president of the United States, George Mifflin Dallas, although he was not yet in office at the founding. See Sam Acheson, *Dallas Yesterday* (Dallas: Southern Methodist University Press, 1977), 3–4.

6. Ibid., xv.

7. Harvey J. Graff, *The Dallas Myth: The Making and Unmaking of an American City* (Minneapolis: University of Minnesota Press, 2008), 49.

8. Ibid., quoting Gervase Rosser, "Myth, Image and Social Process in the English Medieval Town," *Urban History* 23 (1996): 25.

9. Jim Schutze, *The Accommodation: The Politics of Race in an American City* (Secaucus, N.J.: Citadel Press, 1986), 51, 52.

10. Decker, "Women in the Civil Rights Movement," 134.

11. Robert B. Fairbanks, *For the City as a Whole: Planning, Politics, and the Public Interest in Dallas, Texas, 1900–1965* (Columbus: Ohio State University, 1998), 238.

12. Mark Herbener, conversation with Ava Wilson, March 16, 2010.

13. Schutze, *The Accommodation*, 8. Schutze refers to the Dallas Citizens Council, a still-extant iteration of the southern anti-desgregation white Citizens' Councils.

14. "Bloom, Sam R.," in *The Handbook of Texas*, Texas State Historical Association, https://www.tshaonline.org/handbook/online/articles/fblvh.

15. Sam Bloom, *Dallas at the Crossroads* (Dallas, 1961).

16. Fairbanks, *For the City as a Whole*, 238.

17. Ibid. The African American committee members would change. Two texts provide the names of some of the members of this committee but provide no dates. Dulaney, "Whatever Happened to the Civil Rights Movement," 67–69, names A. Maceo

Smith, NAACP chapter president and a founding member of the Dallas Negro Chamber of Commerce; W. J. Durham, NAACP attorney; C. Jack Clark, of the prominent African American funeral home Black and Clark; local businessmen Ed Reed, Henry Lenoir, and George Allen; and the Reverend B. E. Joshua. Schutze, *The Accommodation*, 7–8, also names these members of the biracial committee: the Reverend Robert L. Parish and the Reverend Bezaleel R. Riley.

18. Quoted in Gary Cartwright, "The Bad Brother," *Texas Monthly* 11, no. 5 (1983): 202.

19. Quoted in ibid.

20. Dulaney, "Whatever Happened to the Civil Rights Movement?," 79.

21. Dulaney, "Whatever Happened to the Civil Rights Movement?," 79.

22. Ibid. This would explain why an initial review of materials published by the *Dallas Express*—namely the years of 1960–63—did not have any information about city or state civil rights movement activity. All that was publicized that could remotely be juxtaposed with civil rights were editorials from the NAACP's *Crisis Magazine*. It must also be noted that Decker's text explains that white newspapers were not censored.

23. John Geddie, "Activities of Dallas FBI Outlined," *Dallas Morning News*, December 14, 1977.

24. Decker, "Women in the Civil Rights Movement," 134; Graff, *The Dallas Myth*, 134–35; Phillips, *White Metropolis*, 5. None of these incidents that led to negative press entailed African American Dallasites.

25. Randolph B. Campbell, *Gone to Texas: A History of the Lone Star State* (New York: Oxford University Press, 2003).

26. John Hope Franklin and Loren Schweninger, *Runaway Slaves: Rebels on the Plantation* (New York: Oxford University Press, 1999), 115.

27. China Galland, *Love Cemetery: Unburying the Secret History of Slaves* (New York: HarperCollins, 2007).

28. Anna Irene Sandbo, "The First Session of the Secession Convention of Texas," *Southwestern Historical Quarterly Journal* 18 (1915): 162.

29. Ibid., 163; Julia Kathryn Garrett, *Fort Worth: A Frontier Triumph* (Austin, Tex.: El Chino Press, 1972), 176.

30. John William Rogers, *The Lusty Texans of Dallas* (Dallas: Dutton, 1960), 93.

31. Kevin Shay and Roy H. Williams, *And Justice for All! The Untold History of Dallas* (Dallas: CGS Communications, 2000).

32. Garrett, *Fort Worth*, 176.

33. James M. Smallwood, "Black Texans during Reconstruction," in *Blacks in East Texas History*, ed. Bruce A. Gladrud and Archie McDonald (College Station: Texas A&M University Press, 2008), 52.

34. Dulaney, "Whatever Happened to the Civil Rights Movement?," 67.

35. Patricia E. Gower, "The Price of Exclusion: Dallas Municipal Policy and Its Impact on African Americans," *East Texas Historical Journal* 39, no. 1 (January 2001): 51.

36. Merline Pitre, "The Evolution of Black Political Participation in Reconstruction Texas," in Glasrud and McDonald, *Blacks in East Texas History*, 69, 79.

37. Dulaney, "Whatever Happened to the Civil Rights Movement?," 68.

38. Ibid., 69.

39. Karen Kossie-Chernyshev, "Constructing Good Success: The Church of God in Christ and Social Uplift in East Texas, 1910–1935," in Glasrud and McDonald, *Blacks in East Texas History*, 113.

40. Ibid.

41. "Protesters of COGIC [Church of God in Christ] presence allegedly doused the tent where the early church met with kerosene and 'set it afire' in a futile effort to destroy 'the very symbol' of the COGIC. Petitions were circulated to have the church declared a public nuisance." Ibid., 111.

42. "White Primary," in *The Handbook of Texas*, Texas State Historical Association, https://tshaonline.org/handbook/online/articles/wdw01.

43. Dulaney, "Whatever Happened to the Civil Rights Movement?," 71.

44. Eva McMillan, interview with Ava Wilson, December 16, 2009.

45. Dulaney, "Whatever Happened to the Civil Rights Movement?," 77.

46. Decker, "Women in the Civil Rights Movement," 134.

47. Michelle L. Gillette, "The Rise of the NAACP in Texas," in *The African American Experience in Texas: An Anthology*, ed. Bruce Glasrud and James Smallwood (Lubbock: Texas Tech University Press, 2008), 371.

48. Dulaney, "Whatever Happened to the Civil Rights Movement?," 76.

49. Brian D. Behnken, "The 'Dallas Way': Protest, Response, and the Civil Rights Experience in the Big D and Beyond," *Southwestern Historical Quarterly* 109, no. 1 (2007): 4.

50. Dulaney, "Whatever Happened to the Civil Rights Movement?," 77.

51. Schutze, *The Accommodation*, 6.

52. Ibid., 18, 23.

53. William H. Wilson, *Hamilton Park: A Planned Black Community in Dallas* (Baltimore: Johns Hopkins University Press, 1998).

54. Dulaney, "Whatever Happened to the Civil Rights Movement?," 77.

55. Ibid.

56. Behnken, "Dallas Way," 15.

57. Dulaney, "Whatever Happened to the Civil Rights Movement?," 32n. The United Political Organization was a Texas organization "almost wholly composed of Negroes committed to the policy of providing support to candidates who would promise to provide jobs for Negroes." Joseph Parker Witherspoon, *Administrative Implementation of Civil Rights* (Austin: University of Texas Press, 1968), 54.

58. Herbener conversation.

59. Ibid.

60. "Pickets March at Building of School Administration," *Dallas Morning News*, April 28, 1964.

61. Allen had been sued by the Piccadilly Cafeteria for inciting pickets that caused the franchise to lose a substantial amount of money. See "Dallas Cafeteria Picketing Halts," *Victoria Advocate*, June 28, 1964.

62. Many refer to McMillan as one of the progenitors of the Dallas student movement. See Ava Wilson's transcribed conversations with Marilyn Clark, Edward Harris, Mark Herbener, Jacqueline Hill, and Eva McMillan.

63. "25 Arlington Students Protest 'Rebel' Theme," *Dallas Morning News*, October 28, 1965. It must be noted that the electronic archives of the University of Texas, Arlington, only have information on related protests and rallies from 1968 to 1971.

64. Ernest McMillan, "SNCC 1964–1969: Georgia, Alabama, and Mississippi," Civil Rights Movement Veterans, http://www.crmvet.org/vet/mcmille. Second set of brackets appears in original.

65. Ibid.

66. Cartwright, "Bad Brother," 200.
67. Eva McMillan interview.
68. Carolyn Barta, "Dallas–Fort Worth Panelists See Hope in Racial Situation," *Dallas Morning News*, February 1968.
69. Eva McMillan interview.
70. Edward Harris, conversation by Ava Wilson, March 16, 2010.
71. SNCC Field Notes, November 1968; "Harassment, Dallasite Says," *Dallas Morning News*, June 28, 1968.
72. John Geddie and Tom Johnson, "Orders Served Welfare Sit-In," *Dallas Morning News*, November 27, 1968.
73. Eva McMillan interview.
74. The Kerner Report was released by Lyndon Johnson's National Advisory Committee in 1968 in response to riots after Dr. Martin Luther King Jr.'s death.
75. *Call to Action: The SNCC Experience in Dallas* (Dallas, Sixth Floor Museum, 2006), DVD.
76. SNCC Field Notes, November 1968.
77. McMillan, "SNCC 1964–1969."
78. Herbener conversation.
79. Eva McMillan interview.
80. SNCC Field Notes, November 1968.
81. Eva McMillan interview.
82. Marc Powe, "SNCC Leaders Charged in Raid on Store," *Dallas Morning News*, July 12, 1968. This article mentions that the damage was estimated at $211.
83. Eva McMillan, interview.
84. McMillan, "SNCC 1964–1969."
85. "Trial Set Aug. 19 for SNCC Pair," *Dallas Morning News*, August 6, 1968.
86. "Youth Says He Saw Two Destroy Goods," *Dallas Morning News*, August 22, 1968.
87. James Ewell, "Store Chain to Sell," *Dallas Morning News*, July 26, 1968.
88. Carolyn Barta, "Store Threats under Study," *Dallas Morning News* July 27, 1968.
89. "U.S. to Aid SNCC in Store Buy," *Dallas Morning News*, August 8, 1968.
90. "McMillan Delinquent, Board Says," *Dallas Morning News*, July 30, 1968.
91. Bill Hunter, "Judge Reduces Bail, if Passport Yielded," *Dallas Morning News*, November 14, 1968.
92. United States of America, Plantiff—Appellee Versus Fred Louis Bell and Charles Lavern Beasley, Defendants—Appellants, United States Court of Appeals, Fifth Circuit, March 23, 1972.
93. "Dallas Man Arraigned in Airliner Hijacking," *Dallas Morning News*, September 13, 1968.
94. William Tucker, "Passengers Freed in Canadian Drama," *Dallas Morning News*, September 10, 1968; Dallas SNCC FBI Files, November 4, 1969.
95. "Dallas Man Arraigned in Airliner Hijacking."
96. Bob Hayes, "Air Canada Plane Hijacked," *Montreal Gazette*, September 12, 1968.
97. "Dallas Man Arraigned in Airliner Hijacking."
98. Robert Finklea, "2 SNCC Leaders Arrested in Dallas," *Dallas Morning News*, April 29, 1969.
99. "SNCC Official to Be Arraigned on Draft Charge," *Dallas Morning News*, May 28, 1969; "Arraignment for McMillan Is Postponed," *Dallas Morning News*, May 29, 1969.

100. Ernest McMillan, unaddressed letter to judge, July 1969.
101. Ibid.
102. Dallas SNCC FBI Files, November 4, 1969.
103. Akintunde Funso, telephone conversation with Judson L. Jeffries, July 30, 2015.
104. Huston-Tillotson was founded in Dallas at the St. Paul United Methodist Church, one of the oldest black churches in the city, the same church where Ernest McMillan's father acted as associate minister. (One McMillan ancestors was a church founder.)
105. Leroy Haynes, telephone conversation with Judson L. Jeffries, May 17, 2015.
106. Joyce Halton, telephone conversation with Judson L. Jeffries, July 29, 2015.
107. Glenn Currier, telephone conversation with Judson L. Jeffries, November 6, 2016.
108. James "Skip" Shockley, telephone conversation with Judson L. Jeffries, July 20, 2015.
109. Leroy Haynes, telephone conversation with Judson L. Jeffries, July 21, 2015.
110. James "Skip" Shockley, telephone conversation with Judson L. Jeffries, July 21, 2015.
111. Halton conversation.
112. Leroy Haynes, telephone conversation with Judson L. Jeffries, May 18, 2015.
113. Donald Lister, conversation with Ava Wilson, February 20, 2010.
114. "Conversation with Dr. Leroy Haynes—2003: A History of the Development of the BPP in Texas," http://www.itsabouttimebpp.com/, accessed August 2009.
115. Floyd W. Hayes III and Francis A. Kiene III, "'All Power to the People': The Political Thought of Huey P. Newton and the Black Panther Party," in *The Black Panther Party Reconsidered*, ed. Charles E. Jones (Baltimore: Black Classic Press, 1998), 167.
116. "Black Panthers Forming under Two New Fronts" *Rome (Ga.) News-Tribune*, June 1, 1970.
117. Shockley conversation.
118. Odinga Kambui, telephone conversation with Judson L. Jeffries, August 2, 2015.
119. It was widely reported that before his death Bunchy Carter had supposedly tape-recorded a message that in the event of his death Pratt was to succeed him as deputy minister of defense of the Southern California chapter of the BPP. Whether or not this is true is anybody's guess, as we have no way of verifying it.
120. Curtis J. Austin, *Up against the Wall: Violence in the Making and Unmaking of the Black Panther Party* (Fayettteville: University of Arkansas Press, 2006), 241.
121. Jack Olsen, *The Tragedy and Triumph of Geronimo Pratt* (New York: Doubleday, 2000), 35.
122. Leroy Haynes, telephone conversation with Judson L. Jeffries, May 21, 2015.
123. Leroy Haynes, telephone conversation with Judson L. Jeffries, June 23, 2015.
124. Leroy Haynes, telephone conversation with Judson L. Jeffries, July 15, 2015.
125. Ibid.
126. James "Skip" Shockley, telephone conversation with Judson L. Jeffries, June 16, 2015.
127. Kambui conversation.
128. Haynes conversation May 21, 2015.
129. Kambui conversation.
130. Leroy Haynes, telephone conversation with Judson L. Jeffries, June 3, 2015.

131. James "Skip" Shockley, telephone conversation with Judson L. Jeffries, 12 June 2015.

132. Leroy Haynes, telephone conversation with Judson L. Jeffries, June 3, 2015.

133. Shockley conversations.

134. Dallas SNCC FBI Files, October 22, 1969.

135. Ibid.

136. Haynes conversation, June 3, 2015. When the Dallas city council condemned low-income housing in South Dallas as part of an expansion of Fair Park, residents were offered as little as $600 to leave their homes. As founder of the Fair Park Homeowner Association, J. B. Jackson fought to get reasonable prices for South Dallas homeowners. See Camille Davis, *Dallas Morning News*, July 1, 1998.

137. James "Skip" Shockley, telephone conversation with Judson L. Jeffries, July 9, 2015.

138. Haynes conversation, July 21, 2015.

139. Leroy Haynes et al., Plaintiffs, v. Dallas County Junior College District, et al., Defendants, United States District Court, N.D. Texas, Dallas Division, December 2, 1974.

140. "Dallas NCCF Disbanded," *Black Panther*, February 20, 1971.

141. Lister conversation.

142. Haynes conversations.

143. Huey Newton regarded the idea of building an underground movement as stupid and counterproductive. See David Hilliard and Lewis Cole, *This Side of Glory: The Autobiography of David Hilliard and the Black Panther Party* (Boston: Little Brown, 1993), 310.

144. Ibid.

145. Shockley conversation, June 16, 2015.

146. Jack Olsen, *Last Man Standing: The Tragedy and Triumph of Geronimo Pratt* (New York: Doubleday, 2000), 71–72.

147. Flores Forbes, *Will You Die with Me? My Life and the Black Panther Party* (New York: Atria Books, 2006), 55.

148. Aaron Dixon, *My People Are Rising: Memoir of a Black Panther Party Captain* (Chicago, Illinois: Haymarket Press, 2012), 185.

149. Ibid., 173.

150. Wayne Pharr, *Nine Lives of a Black Panther: A Story of Survival* (Chicago: Lawrence Hill Books, 2014), 294.

151. Khalif Hasan, telephone conversation with Judson L. Jeffries, July 8, 2015.

152. See Olsen, *Last Man Standing*, 53–73, for suspicions within the party that Pratt was an informant and for tensions between Newton and Pratt.

153. Hilliard and Cole, *This Side of Glory*, 310.

154. Forbes, *Will You Die with Me?*, 57.

155. Huey Newton, "On the Expulsion of Geronimo from the Black Panther Party," *Black Panther*, January 23, 1971.

156. Olsen, *Last Man Standing*, 72.

157. Stuart Hanlon, telephone conversation with Judson L. Jeffries, June 24, 2015.

158. James "Skip" Shockley, telephone conversation with Judson L. Jeffries, July 1, 2015.

159. Shockley conversation, July 20, 2015.

160. Ibid.
161. Ibid.
162. Bob Parvin, "Students Protest 'Mess,'" *Beaumont Enterprise*, March 24, 1972.
163. U. S. Williams, "My Memories: Memories of a Soldier," unpublished diary in possession of authors, 2.
164. Bonnie Oglethorpe, "Officials' Door 'Is Open,'" *Beaumont Enterprise*, March 24, 1972.
165. U. S. Williams, letter to Judson L. Jeffries, September 17, 2015.
166. U. S. Williams, email to Judson L. Jeffries, December 26, 2016.
167. Haynes conversations.
168. James "Skip" Shockley, telephone conversation with Judson L. Jeffries, July 15, 2015.
169. Paula Ransom, telephone conversation with Judson L. Jeffries, August 7, 2015.
170. Haynes conversation, July 15, 2015.
171. Ransom conversation.
172. Shockley conversation, July 15, 2015. Founded in 1946, The Links, Incorporated, today "consists of nearly 14,000 professional women of color in 283 chapters located in 41 states ... committed to enriching, sustaining and ensuring the culture and economic survival of African Americans and other persons of African ancestry." "About The Links, Incorporated," http://www.linksinc.org/about.shtml.
173. Diane Ragsdale, telephone conversation with Judson L. Jeffries, November 7, 2016. Ragsdale had been a student at Texas Women's University when she decided to get involved with the Panthers. Although Ragsdale was a community worker she also maintained membership in the Southern Christian Leadership Conference.
174. U. S. Williams letter.
175. Ransom conversation.
176. B. L. Smith, telephone conversation with Judson L. Jeffries, July 3, 2015.
177. Shockley conversation, July 15, 2015.
178. B. L. Smith, telephone conversation with Judson L. Jeffries, July 3, 2015.
179. Ransom conversation.
180. Shockley conversations.
181. Haynes conversations.
182. Ibid.
183. B. L. Smith conversation.
184. Haynes conversations.
185. Khalif Hasan, telephone conversation with Judson L. Jeffries, July 15, 2015.
186. Haynes conversations.
187. James "Skip" Shockley, telephone conversation with Judson L. Jeffries, July 31, 2015.
188. Richard Yahr, telephone conversation with Judson L. Jeffries, August 1, 2015.
189. Ibid.
190. U. S. Williams letter.
191. Yahr conversation.
192. Elected to the city council with Miller were George Schneider and Morris Kibler with 1,668 votes.
193. Haynes conversation, November 18, 2016.
194. Lister conversation.

195. Kambui conversation.
196. Lister conversation.
197. Lister conversation. Lister would serve only eleven years in federal and state prisons due to a reversible error in his case, which he researched and successfully appealed.
198. "Curtis Gaines, Red Dog, Grassroots Org, Busted! The Contradictions," *Ghetto Eye* (Dallas), May 1973.
199. Ibid.
200. Kambui conversation. Lister is referred to as "Red Dog" by Kambui, but he does not answer to that moniker any longer since it was given to him by Gaines.
201. Lister conversation.
202. See United States of America, Plantiff—Appellee Versus Fred Louis Bell and Charles Lavern Beasley, Defendants—Appellants.
203. Kambui conversation.
204. Hasan conversation, July 8, 2015.
205. Akintunde Funso, telephone conversation with Judson L. Jeffries, June 26, 2015.
206. Akintunde Funso, telephone conversation with Judson L. Jeffries, July 17, 2015.
207. Ibid.
208. B. L. Smith, telephone conversation with Judson L. Jeffries, July 3, 2015.
209. Rev. Peter Johnson, interview by Ava Wilson, March 15, 2010.
210. Ernest McMillan conversation.
211. John Geddie, "Man Believed to be Ernie McMillan Captured in Ohio," *Dallas Morning News*, February 9, 1971; Henry Tatum, "Suspect Held in Ohio Reported Not McMillan," *Dallas Morning News*, February 11, 1971.
212. "Ex-Leader of SNCC Ordered to Prison," *Dallas Morning News*, August 18, 1971.
213. John Geddie, "Fugitive Militant Captured," *Dallas Morning News*, December 9, 1971.
214. "Polk Asks Trial Transfer," *Dallas Morning News*, December 24, 1971.
215. Earl Golz, "McMillan Returned to Dallas, Faces Trial Feb. 22," *Dallas Morning News*, January 29, 1972.
216. Eva McMillan interview.
217. Ernest McMillan interview with Ava Wilson, December 14, 2009.
218. Juila Scott Reed, "Ms. Johnson Looks Back," *Dallas Morning News*, January 5, 1975.
219. Haynes conversation, June 3, 2015.
220. Fahim Minkah, telephone conversation with Judson L. Jeffries, July 7, 2015. Minkah refers to the Black Panther Party initiative as a chapter, not a branch and says that branches were supervised by chapters, while chapters reported to the national office.
221. Charles Hillman, telephone conversation with Judson L. Jeffries, October 23, 2016.
222. Akintunde Funso, telephone conversation with Judson L. Jeffries, June 29, 2015.
223. Marvin Crenshaw, telephone conversation with Judson L. Jeffries, July 16, 2015.
224. Marvin Crenshaw, telephone conversation with Judson L. Jeffries, January 5, 2017.
225. Ibid.
226. Ibid.

227. Charles Hillman, telephone conversation with Judson L. Jeffries, July 1, 2015.
228. Funso conversation.
229. Charles Hillman, telephone conversation with Judson L. Jeffries, June 29, 2015.
230. Deborrah Molo, conversation with Judson L. Jeffries, December 4, 2016.
231. Marvin Crenshaw, telephone conversation with Judson L. Jeffries, August 10, 2015.
232. Minkah conversation.
233. Ibid.
234. Ibid.
235. Hillman conversations.
236. Marvin Crenshaw, telephone conversation with Judson L. Jeffries, July 17, 2015.
237. Minkah conversation.
238. Hillman conversations.
239. Hillman conversation, July 1, 2015.
240. Marvin Crenshaw, telephone conversation with Judson L. Jeffries, August 4, 2015.
241. Federal Bureau of Investigation Communications Section, regarding Marvin Eugene Crenshaw, file 157-6-12-1096.
242. "Racist Dallas Power Structure Launches Attack on Black Panther Party," *Black Panther*, April 6, 1974.
243. Crenshaw conversation, January 13, 2017.
244. Mike Daniels, telephone conversation with Judson L. Jeffries, January 13, 2017.
245. Minkah proposed to create a citizens' district police board (CDPB) in each of the city's nine police districts. His proposal says in part: "Said board shall have the powers, duties and composition to determine all policies, regulations and procedures of patrolmen within their respective districts or divisions." It continues, "Each district board shall set policy... with respect to all affairs of the police in its district that insure the safety, justice and general welfare of the citizenry of each district. Each board shall have the power, by majority vote, to suspend or fire patrolmen on duty in their respective divisions." The proposal also provides that all "records and files related to police matters... shall be available to CDPB members... as they deem necessary." The document also includes proposed election procedures for board positions and the stipulation that all powers of the various city agencies and branches including the mayor's office, "as related to the Dallas Police Department," be transferred to the citizens of Dallas at large. See "Racist Dallas Power Structure Launches Attack on Black Panther Party."
246. Daniels conversation.
247. Ibid. Quoted by Daniels in Daniels conversation.
248. Marvin Crenshaw, telephone conversation with Judson L. Jeffries, January 3, 2017.
249. According to Kathy Davis, the name "Black Students for Pride and Identification" was a decided by a group. "The name 'Black Student Union' didn't do much to identify us. This was the 1970s, and we were a proud group. There was a need for pride and unity in the air. And we felt that name showed it." Email exchange between Kathy Davis and Judson L. Jeffries, December 13–14, 2016.
250. Crenshaw conversation, January 3, 2017.

251. Charles Hillman, telephone conversation with Judson L. Jeffries, November 19, 2016.
252. Marvin Crenshaw, telephone conversation with Judson L. Jeffries, August 7, 2015.
253. Charles Hillman, telephone conversation with Judson L. Jeffries, July 15, 2015.
254. Marvin Crenshaw, telephone conversation with Judson L. Jeffries, July 22, 2015.
255. Charles Hillman, telephone conversation with Judson L. Jeffries, July 22, 2015.
256. Crenshaw conversation, July 22, 2015.
257. Hillman conversation, July 22, 2105.
258. Marvin Crenshaw, telephone conversation with Judson L. Jeffries, January 9, 2017.
259. Donna Miller, telephone conversation with Judson L. Jeffries, January 9, 2017.
260. Minkah conversation.
261. "Dallas B.P.P. Leads 1,000 in March for Jobs," *Black Panther*, May 12, 1975.
262. Ibid.
263. "Dallas B.P.P. Wins Suit on Citizens' Review of Police," *Black Panther*, February 1976.
264. Minkah conversation.
265. Ibid.
266. Ibid.
267. *Facing the Rising Sun*, ongoing exhibition, African American Museum, Dallas.
268. "Freedman's Cemetery reportedly grew into the 1920s, when the City of Dallas Sanitation Department forced its closure, supposedly because of overcrowding, a claim later proven false." Galland, *Love Cemetery*, 180.
269. Ernest McMillan conversation.
270. *Call to Action*.

Conclusion

The Black Panther Party in Summation

CURTIS AUSTIN

In 2017, fifty-one years after its founding, the Black Panther Party remains one of the most studied groups of the civil rights movement and Black Power eras. Dozens of books and hundreds of articles have been written about it, and increasingly films are being made in an attempt to capture the true essence of the organization and its contributions to the fight for human rights in general and to the black freedom struggle specifically. Courses on the BPP flourish on college campuses, and grade school students expand their academic horizons by researching and conducting oral histories with former members of the party for National History Day and Black History Month projects. Federal, state, and local government entities celebrate the Panthers with plaques, markers, and statues, most recently by giving it an honored place in the newly constructed National Museum of African American History and Culture that sits on the National Mall in Washington, D.C.[1] Politicians from Congresswoman Barbara Lee in California to former mayor Moon Landrieu in New Orleans have extolled the virtues of the Black Panther Party. Other elected officials, including such former Black Panthers as Illinois congressman Bobby Rush, have attributed their visions and goals as public servants to the hard work and dedication the BPP exhibited as a grassroots organization seeking to bring about revolutionary change. Political leaders as far afield as New Zealand, England, and Cuba have held the Panthers up as the quintessential example of how to engage "the people" in community-centered efforts to engender change from the bottom up. Members of recent movements like Occupy Wall Street and Black Lives Matter see the BPP as a template for their own mass-based efforts. From the vantage point of time, it seems that the BPP outperformed all its organizational contemporaries in the black freedom struggle. Surely, the recognition conferred upon organizations such as US, the Republic of New Africa, the Congress of African People, and the Revolutionary Action Movement pale in comparison to the BPP's impact in distressed communities across America. No other Black Power movement organization fed as many children, provided health care to as many residents, educated as many adults, and clothed as many people as did the Panthers over a period of nearly two decades.

One cannot help but wonder how it is that the BPP has become such a popular and prominent example of sixties and seventies activism given the successful efforts on the part of the U.S. mass media and the state to vilify the group. The police as well as state and federal government agencies viewed and treated the Panthers as if they were a threat, and some of today's retiring politicians made their bones on denigrating the BPP. The answer should be apparent to anyone who has read this book, along with its predecessors *On the Ground: The Black Panther Party in Communities across America* (2010) and *Comrades: A Local History of the Black Panther Party* (2007).[2] In a nutshell, the Black Panther Party both talked the talk and walked the not so easy walk.

The BPP accomplished these feats because from the start its members were endowed with a healthy dose of the strongest force on earth: the power of love. BPP members loved their people so much that they were willing to die to secure their freedom. Oral histories of the Panthers demonstrate that without this quality, the Panthers might not have even come into existence.

This book is part of a larger project presenting a more complete portrait of the Black Panther Party by looking away from its headquarters in Oakland to Panther history in outlier cities. Had Huey Newton and Bobby Seale not stood up to the brutal and murderous street-level bureaucrats in the Bay Area, the group would have never caught the attention of those who eventually joined the organization. Only deep feelings of love for something and someone, plus an element of craziness mixed with daring and courage, could have sustained them in the face of such overwhelming odds. Publicly telling marauding police officers that their days of running roughshod over the Bay Area's black communities were over, the founding Panthers displayed acts of love on par with the sacrifices of Toussaint L'Ouverture and Jean-Jacques Dessalines, Harriet Tubman, David Walker, Frederick Douglass, and John Brown.[3] The Panthers accepted early on that their public stand against the imperialist nation they referred to as Babylon, which Dr. Martin Luther King Jr. termed "the greatest purveyor of violence on earth," would likely lead them to an early grave. Still, they soldiered on. As this book has demonstrated, it was not the Black Panthers' guns that most struck fear in the hearts of those who were determined to maintain the status quo. It was their insistence on the freedom of oppressed people everywhere but particularly black people, whose very humanity was being threatened by capitalism, sexism, and militarism.

Very early on, the BPP's leaders abandoned Panther police patrols after California's passage of the 1967 Mulford Act, which prevented people from carrying loaded weapons in public.[4] By then the Panthers had made their presence felt. They said, through their actions, speeches, and in their newspaper, that they were not going to stand idly by while black women, children, and men were cut down in the streets by those who had ostensibly vowed to serve them. While the Panthers continued to use militant rhetoric, it is safe to say that 99 percent of all Panther activity after 1967 was based in nonviolent community activism. Because the press chose not to explain that the Panthers had all but abandoned their early insistence on armed struggle, most people today, as at the time, have the erroneous understanding that the Panthers existed solely to kill white people in general and white police officers in particular. Again, as this book has shown, nothing could be further from the truth.

What one discovers when one peels back the many layers of history associated with Panther chapters and branches across the country in the years following the upheaval of 1967 (i.e., the murder of Denzil Dowell, the march on Sacramento, and the imprisonment of Huey P. Newton) is that many people who joined the party did so because the original Panthers made it clear that black people, with a strong interracial network of allies, needed to fight on all fronts to secure their liberation. So, for example, the Panthers' efforts fostering political education contributed to the creation and development of black studies on campuses across the nation, thanks partly to working with like-minded Asian Americans, Latinos, and Native Americans. Demanding education that "exposes the true nature of this decadent American society" and that "teaches us our true history and our role in the present-day society," the early Panthers organized study groups that evolved into political education classes serving thousands of people across the nation. Panthers in Boston, Dallas, Washington, D.C., and Atlanta followed these examples and helped change the mindsets of students and administrators in such a fashion that education has not been the same since. It is doubtful that black, Latino, Asian American, and Native American faculty would be as represented on college campuses as they are today if not for the Panthers' efforts. While some of these gains have been rolled back by conservative and racist policies of federal and state lawmakers, it is no less true that the Panthers literally changed the face of higher education in the United States.

To be sure, we must be careful to qualify assessments and not attribute to the BPP things that are not its due. Regarding higher education, it is not the case that only one group pushed community members, students, and even administrators to think about the fact that tax dollars were being used to fund the education of white males, for the most part, while the rest of the nation suffered. The NAACP, SNCC, CORE, and the Urban League certainly played a role in fighting for equality in higher education, but they did not energize a mass of young people across the nation the way the Panthers did.

Indeed, the BPP's ability to energize, galvanize, and inspire people from all walks of life, at home and abroad, is what caused FBI director J. Edgar Hoover to dub the group "the greatest threat to the internal security of the United

States."⁵ Hoover wasn't afraid of the Panthers' puny arsenal of AR-15s and AR-180s. The Panthers were able to convince people that capitalist hegemony was not only inherently unjust but also threatened to usher in full-fledged fascism. This politics is what prompted America's power elite to conduct meetings at the highest levels of government, where they considered the importance of destroying the Black Panther Party. Once the Panthers convinced people that they could actually do something to stop repression, they became Public Enemy Number 1. So, despite the fact that the Panthers never launched an all-out assault on the nation's power brokers or infrastructure, as it was often depicted in its own newspaper, they were treated as if they had. Panthers across the country were arrested on trumped-up charges, often convicted, and in some cases given lengthy sentences. Those who were released from jail or prison after relatively short terms typically came back to communities that had already "moved on" for the most part. While there are exceptions, most chapters and branches that lost their leadership for any significant amount of time limped on briefly and then eventually petered out.

Then there are those who put lie to today's laudatory words about the Panthers being great influences and who more than counter the fact that a former Panther now serves in Congress. On December 31, 2016, decades after the party's heyday, it was reported that sixteen Panthers were still behind bars, while eight had died in prison, two of whom had served over forty years.⁶

By keeping Panthers in prison on false charges of murder, the state continues to control and perpetuate the "armed to the teeth" mythology that surrounds the Black Panther Party. It also tampers with the nation's memory and understanding of the past by helping to create the impression that illegal acts committed by members of the Black Panther Party are no different than murders committed by the Klan and racist police during the era of the civil rights movement. By spending money to keep Panthers in prison, the federal government is sending a message to Americans in general and activists in particular: there is no statute of limitations where you are concerned. If you challenge the power of the state, you will be met with a punishment most severe.

Despite such maneuverings of the state, the BPP continues to elicit a positive response on the part of young people, many of whom are female. No organization composed of men and women is completely free of patriarchy or sexism, but at least the Black Panther Party sought to engage the question of gender equality and struggled to end sexist practices. It has taken nearly two hundred years for entrenched institutions such as the Democratic and Republican Parties to acknowledge the importance of women and their contributions. The BPP, on the other hand, had existed for only a few years when women members rose to positions of power throughout the party. While we have read earlier of Panther personalities such as Elaine Brown, Kathleen Cleaver, and Ericka Huggins, this book has allowed us to understand how women like Audrea Jones and Paula Ransom helped propel the party. Uncovering and publishing their stories helps to debunk negative media portrayals of the BPP as a hyper-masculine organization whose male members were insensitive to the importance of making space for women to flourish. Whether it was leading political education courses, serving children breakfast, providing health care to community members, or writing articles in the party's newspaper, Panther women enjoyed more opportunities to demonstrate their agency than women did in any other organization of the Vietnam War era. Undoubtedly the Panthers picked up some of these ideas about gender equality from their reading of Frantz Fanon, who spoke directly to the role of women in revolution.[7] Equally important were the BPP's close ties with the Student Nonviolent Coordinating Committee, which served as something of an incubator for feminists.[8]

The Panther-SNCC nexus in places like Atlanta, Dallas, Washington, D.C., and Boston helps us to understand the deep soil from which the party grew. The Panthers were not an upstart organization that came from nowhere in the wake of mid-sixties rebellions that set fire to Watts, Cleveland, and Detroit. Many who founded Panther chapters had prior experience in the black freedom struggle. From Chico Neblett in Boston to Tim Hayes in Atlanta to Leroy Haynes in Dallas, it is evident that much serious Panther organizing was done by those who had already attended the school of hard knocks. Because SNCC activists had been nurtured by older NAACP activists, who themselves had been schooled in organizing by leftists whose activist genealogy stretched back to the late nineteenth century, it is no wonder that the Panthers had organizing prowess beyond their years. They used organizing techniques that had been used since blacks began to organize politically after the armistice was signed at Appomattox Courthouse in Virginia. As this deep history is one reason for the Panthers' success, it can also be seen as one of the reasons why some chapters did not fare as well as others.

Atlanta is a case in point. Because the city enjoyed a rapidly expanding middle class and an emerging black majority electorate, the Panthers found it more difficult to operate there than Panthers found in Boston or Dallas. In Atlanta, many blacks could envision that one day they too would enjoy the middle-class accoutrements of nice homes, good schools, and well-paying jobs. The overwhelming majority of poor blacks who counted on this bright future have experienced dashed hopes and remained poor. But it is nevertheless true that their hopes prevented them from giving too much sway to the Panthers, an organization that the press showed as violent, murderous, and undemocratic. This is likely the reason the Panthers in Washington, D.C., fared about as well as their counterparts in Atlanta. A burgeoning black middle class there seemed to operate as a strong magnet for those who found themselves on the margins of society yet so close to the seat of power. To be sure, the Panthers in both Atlanta and D.C. had their own shortcomings that made it hard to attract a critical mass of supporters. However, the years of marches, legal victories, and the opening up of educational and employment opportunities had heightened blacks' hopes of securing the power of the almighty dollar in their own hands.

Books like this one must be given the widest possible exposure. Unless the truth of the past is told and historical lessons are learned, there will be little hope for future progress. The sexist and racist assault against minorities and women epitomized by the election of Donald Trump to the presidency of the United States will not be stanched unless old and young alike come to grips with what has actually happened in the nation's capital. When a critical mass of people come to understand that the Black Panther Party was not a roving band of hoodlums and thugs who sought revenge on white people in Nat Turner fashion, the people may simultaneously discover that the government, and many of its policies to which they pay allegiance, is at the root of their suffering.

If this volume does nothing else, it should convey that the Black Panther Party, rhetoric notwithstanding, was one of the most nonviolent groups of the Black Power era. It implemented its many community service programs with a level of compassion, dedication, and tenderness seldom seen before or since. For most people, this isn't the image that first comes to mind when the subject of the Black Panthers is brought up. However, the Panthers did not brandish guns when they escorted elders to medical appointments. They did not threaten to shoot anyone when they treated the indigent at their free health clinics. Guns were not involved in the voter registration campaigns in Dallas, and they certainly had no place in the free breakfast programs that operated in many of the cities with a Panther chapter or branch. Besides dismantling the myths, this book has helped us extract a major lesson the Panthers taught. Their attempt to fight racism by forming coalitions with whites, Latinos, Asians, and Native Americans was wise: this is the only way to effectively deal with the problems presented by today's neoliberal world order. Not only are we doomed to repeat the mistakes of the past if we do not know our history, we may also find ourselves in a situation where "the 1 percent"—a powerful minority of the superrich—controls not only the economy but even the air we breathe and the water we drink. We have seen that this tiny ruling cabal has little respect for our lives and aspirations. Indeed, it has no respect for the lives and aspirations of the majority of the world's citizens.

Just as the Panthers realized that their literal call to arms was a tactic that could only be useful for a while, today's activists must find and employ tactics that work—and then keep moving, keep growing. The Panthers found a way to do this, but they were met with laws and policies that have resulted in today's mass incarceration. If we do not learn from their example of trying to secure power for all people, it may not be long before a new set of laws makes it easy to incarcerate anyone who challenges the very notion of state power. In other words, we must all do our homework and due diligence to find out what we can about what works to effect substantive social change. If we fail in this task we may find that the Panthers were correct when they intoned, "No investigation, no right to speak."

NOTES

1. Fifty percent of the costs of the planning, design, and construction of the museum were to have been federally funded. "H.R. 3491, National Museum of African American History and Culture Act," https://www.congress.gov/bill/108th-congress/house-bill/3491.

2. Judson L. Jeffries, ed., *On the Ground: The Black Panther Party in Communities across America* (Jackson: University of Mississippi Press, 2010); Judson L. Jeffries, ed., *Comrades: A Local History of the Black Panther Party* (Bloomington: Indiana University Press, 2007).

3. Lerone Bennett Jr., *Before the Mayflower* (Chicago: Johnson Publishing, 2007).

4. Curtis Austin, *Up against the Wall: Violence in the Making and Unmaking of the Black Panther Party* (Fayetteville: University of Arkansas Press, 2006).

5. John Ehrlichman to J. Edgar Hoover, December 22, Black Panther Party, WHSF-John Ehrlichman, box 15, Nixon papers, in author's possession; Director to SACs Albany et al., September 3, 1968, no. illegible, FBI-Hampton Files, in author's possession.

6. Bakari Kitwana, "The 16 Black Panthers Still behind Bars," *Colorlines*, December 31, 2016, https://www.colorlines.com/articles/16-black-panthers-still-behind-bars.

7. Frantz Fanon, *Toward the African Revolution* (New York: Grove Press, 1967).

8. See Jack White, "The Women of SNCC," *The Root*, April 17, 2010, http://www.theroot.com/the-women-of-sncc-1790879231.

CONTRIBUTORS

JUDSON L. JEFFRIES is professor of African American and African studies at the Ohio State University. He earned his PhD in political science at the University of Southern California in 1997. He is the author of seven books. His most recent book is *The Portland Black Panthers: Empowering Albina and Remaking a City* (Seattle: University of Washington Press, 2016).

CURTIS AUSTIN is an associate professor of African American and African studies at the Ohio State University. He earned his PhD in history from Mississippi State University in 1998 and began his teaching career at the University of Central Florida in Orlando. He is the author of *Up against the Wall: Violence in the Making and Unmaking of the Black Panther Party (2007)*, which *Choice* designated an Outstanding Academic Title of the year. His current research projects include a textbook on African American history and a book covering the history of the Black Power movement.

CHARLES E. JONES is professor and head of the Department of Africana Studies at the University of Cincinnati. He is past president of the National Council for Black Studies and the editor of *The Black Panther Party Reconsidered* (1998). Prior to going to the University of Cincinnati, Jones was the chair of the Department of African American Studies at Georgia State University. He has published widely in the area of black politics, including journal articles and book chapters on the Black Panther Party.

AVA TIYE KINSEY is a native of Dallas, Texas. Steeped in a long tradition of activism, Kinsey is a descendent of the revolutionary McMillan family who sparked social change in Dallas. She received a bachelor and master's degrees in Africana studies from Howard University and Temple University, respectively, and seeks to make it her life's work to magnify indigenous cultures as a means to liberate and commune with herself and others. Ava currently serves as the codirector of the DreamYard Center in the Bronx, New York, which is an arts and social justice organization that serves youth and families.

DUNCAN MACLAURY is a high school history teacher in Massachusetts. He received a bachelor's degree in history and Master of Arts of Teaching from Tufts University, the latter focusing on middle school and high school history education.

SARAH NICKLAS currently works in the medical field at Harvard Vanguard Medical Associates. She has earned two master's degrees, one in world history from Northeastern University and one in political science from Fordham University. Earlier she attended Emmanuel College, earning a bachelor's degree in history and political science in 2010.

JOHN PREUSSER is the chairman of the History and Art History Department at James Sprunt Community College in North Carolina. A native of Fairfax County, Virginia, Preusser earned his bachelor's degree in history from George Mason University in 1996 and then worked for five years at the *Washington Post* until 2001. He earned a master's degree in American history from the University of North Carolina, Wilmington, in 2006. Since 2007 Preusser has been employed at James Sprunt Community College.

INDEX

Abernathy, Ralph, 30
airport protest, in San Francisco, 1
Alcohol, Tobacco, and Firearms, Bureau of, 64
Algiers, 5, 21
Alkebulan, Paul, 22, 26
All-African People's Revolutionary Party, 59, 72, 75
All African Youth Party, 20
Allen, Frederick, 14, 15
Allen, Ivan, 17
Allen, Phoebe, 157
Allen, Waverly Patrick, 73
Allen Temple Christian Methodist Episcopal Church, 154
Alston, Marion, 102
American Civil Liberties Union, 72
American Indian Movement, 80, 82
Anderson, Malik, 167
Angela Davis Liberation Committee, 173
Angela Davis People's Free Food Program, 77
Atkins, Michael, 98
Atlanta Civic Center, 20
Atlanta Constitution, 36, 40, 41
Atlanta Daily World, 30
Atlanta Fund Appeals Review Board, 40
Atlanta Journal, 36
Atlanta Life Insurance Company, 30
Atlanta Police Department, 38–39
Atlanta University, 19, 25, 31, 32, 33
Austin, Carl, 165
Austin, Curtis, 53
Australia, 6

Bailey, Greg, 32, 33, 40
Baldwin, James, 176, 181
Baraka, Amiri, 2
Barbados, 6
Barry, Marion, 57, 62–63, 68, 83
Bay State Banner, 96, 110, 120, 124
Beasley, Charles Lavern, 153
Bethea, Jacob, 73–74
Bey, Colonel Hassan Juru-Ahmed, 61
Bible, Sen. Alan (D-N.V.), 59

Bickley, Alex, 180
Big Apple (supermarket), 36
Birth of a Nation, 142
Black Citizens for Justice, Law, and Order, 175
Black Defenders, 55, 83
Black Federated Alliance, 35
Black History Month, 31, 181, 194
Black Intercommunal Party, 164–71, 176, 182
Black Liberation Army, 32, 37
Black Lives Matter, 194
Blackman Development Center, 61
Blackman's Volunteer Army of Liberation, 58, 61, 66
Black Panther (newspaper), 40, 42, 53, 56, 70, 72, 74, 99, 100, 103, 104, 107, 108, 116, 120, 123, 173
Black Shirts, 15
Black Student Federation, 106, 119
Black Students for Pride and Identification, 180
Black Student Unity, Organization of (OBSU), 22
Black United Front, 56, 57, 58, 61, 66, 69, 72, 75, 117, 119, 121, 151. *See also* Boston Black United Front
Black Workers Congress, 20, 35
Bloom, Joshua, 4–5, 12
Bond, Julian, 20, 30
Boone, Joe, 35
Boston Black United Front, 98, 104, 108, 117, 119, 120, 121. *See also* Black United Front
Boston Globe, 93, 94, 95, 96, 98, 102, 113, 114, 120, 123
Boston Housing Authority, 113, 119, 123
Boston Police Department, 92, 94, 98, 106, 107, 108, 112, 117, 120, 122, 124
Boston Redevelopment Authority, 106
Bourne, Wendell, 96, 98
Bowden, Nicole "Nicky", 33
Boyce, Ernest, 36
Bradley, Williams, 122
Brewer, Philomena, 119
Bronzeville (Columbus, Ohio), 3
Brooke, Sen. Edward W. (R-Mass.), 95

203

Brown, Elaine, 6, 8, 78, 82, 123, 170, 197
Brown, H. Rap, 60, 62
Brown, John, 195
Brown, Sherry, 65, 72, 73
Brown, William Wells, 89
Brown Berets, 22, 181
Brown v. Board of Education (1954), 138
Brunson, Charles, 57, 63, 69, 73–74, 79, 81
Bryan, John Neely, 137
Bryan, Robert, 7
Bullard, Robert, 19, 20
Burston, Stacey, 119
Burton, Kenny "Mo," 176
Bussey, Jerome, 44
Butler, Emily, 35
Butler Street Christian Methodist Episcopal Church, 35
Buttermilk Bottom (Atlanta, Ga.), 19, 20

Calhoun, Donald, 45
Carmichael, Stokley, 56, 58–60, 62–63, 72, 76, 100; resigns from BPP, 21
Carter, Ron, 13, 30–31, 37–40, 42, 43
Cass, Melnea, 90
Cawthon, O. B., 15
Central Intelligence Agency, 64
Chambers, Winfield, 108
Cheatham, John, 106, 122
Chicago, Ill., 2, 21, 56, 57, 68, 108, 110
Church of God in Christ, 143
Civil Rights Act of 1964, 53, 147
Citizens' Board of the Pilot District Project, 68
Citizens Council, 139, 145, 149
Clansman, The, 142
Clark, John, 69
Clark, Mark, 21, 38, 57
Clark, Ron, 79, 83
Cleage, Pearl, 43
Cleaver, Eldridge, 1, 2, 6, 21, 23, 54, 62, 64, 80, 97, 101, 156, 160, 161, 163
Cleaver, Kathleen, 6, 29, 62, 101, 164, 196
Clement, Rufus, 17
Cleveland, Ohio, 54, 198
Coalition against Racism and Fascism, 63
Cochran, Johnny, 163
COINTELPRO (FBI Counter Intelligence Program), 28, 39, 64, 72, 98
Collins, John, 94
Colonial Stores, 30

Columbus, Ohio, 3, 4
Commerce Club, 18
Committee on Internal Security of the U.S. House of Representatives, 24
Community Relations Commission, 30
Congress of African People, 194
Congress of Racial Equality, 27, 32, 58, 196
Conrad, Emmett, 139
Cook, Rodney, 14
Cox, Donald "DC," 100
Craft, Juanita Jewel, 144
Creamer, Donald, 160
Crear, Bunchy, 173
Crenshaw, Marvin, 177, 178, 179, 180, 181
Cronkite, Walter, 139
Cuba, 28, 194
cultural nationalists, 55, 56, 58, 60, 61, 72, 73, 83, 100

Dallas Bethlehem Center, 165
Dallas Chamber of Commerce, 138, 139
Dallas City Charter, 179
Dallas Community Committee, 140, 145–46
Dallas Coordinating Committee on Civil Rights, 147
Dallas Express, 140, 142
Dallas Morning News, 140, 150, 151, 152, 175
Dallas origin myth, 138
Daniels, Mike, 179–80
Davis, Angela, 35, 156
Davis, Kathy, 180
Dawkins, Willie Lee, 57, 62, 68–69, 72, 74, 79
Deep Elm (Dallas, Tex.), 145
Deep South, 15, 148
Delaney, Henry, 35
Democratic Radical Union of Maryland, 71
Dessalines, Jean-Jacques, 195
Detroit, Mich., 3, 16, 22, 24, 34, 54, 56, 99, 117, 125, 198
Deville, Alton, 25, 38, 39, 41–42
District of Columbia Home Rule Act, 54
Dixie Hills (Atlanta, Ga.), 16, 19, 32
Dobbs, John Wesley, 14
Dodd, Mike, 149
Donner, Frank, 20
Douglass, Frederick, 195
Dowell, Denzil, 196
Dreamland (Denton, Tex.), 166, 167–68, 182
Drinan, Robert F., 94–95

Dunwoody (Atlanta) office, 28; armed robbery of, 43

Eaves, Reginald, 44, 117, 122
Edwards, Reginald "Malik," 7, 57, 64, 77–78, 79
El Centro College, 154, 155–56, 159, 160, 164, 174, 180–81
Emancipation Proclamation, 65, 141
England, Kenneth, 31
Essex, Mark, 43
Estell, E. C., 140
Evers, Medgar, 60

Fair Housing Act of 1968, 59
Fair Park (Dallas, Tex.), 146, 157, 159
Fair Park Homeowners' Organization, 145
Fanon, Frantz, 96, 115, 198
Farmers and Merchants State Bank, 153
Farrar, Delano, 96, 98, 99
Farris, Milton, 14
Federal Bureau of Investigation, 20, 21, 26, 28, 37, 38–41, 61, 64, 65, 70, 72, 73, 82, 98, 104, 106, 113, 123, 124, 140, 150, 153, 158, 159, 161, 163, 174, 179, 196
Ferguson, Gene, 13
Flanagan, Minnie, 144
Flippen, Karen, 99
Fonda, Jane, 26, 172
Ford Hall, takeover of, 98
Forrest Gump, 52
Franklin Lynch People's Free Health Center [Medical Center], 92, 111, 114, 116, 118–21, 123, 124, 125, 126
Franklin Park, 90, 106
Free All Baptist Church, 35
Freedman's Town, 145, 183
freedom school, 33–34, 35
Freedom Summer, 59
Freedom Trail, 106
Free Huey campaign, 1, 29, 96, 97, 124
Freeman, Charles, 174
Freeman, Thomas, 25
Fulton County Commission, 14
Funso, Akintunde, 173–74, 176, 177

Gaines, Curtis, 157, 158, 160–61, 162, 163, 171, 172
Garvey, Marcus, 34
Gayle, Addison, Jr., 2
Georgia Black Liberation Front, 20, 23, 25

Georgia State University, 31
Georgia Tech, 23
Ghetto Eye (newspaper), 172
Gilliam, Sam, 32, 40
Glaspy, Kay, 99
Grassroots Incorporated, 171–73
Graves, Margie, 179
Gray, L. Patrick, 37, 41
Gray v. Sanders (1963), 17
Great Migration, 89
Great Society programs, 63
Great Speckled Bird (newspaper), 28
Green, Steve, 25
Guevara, Ernesto "Che," 97, 115–16

Halton, Joyce, 155
Halton, Nathaniel, 160
Hamilton Park (Dallas, Tex.), 145
Hampton, Carl, 22, 35
Hampton, Fred, 6, 21, 38, 57, 62
Hanlon, Stuart, 164
Harding, Kitty, 105
Hardwick, Floyd, 100, 104–5, 108–9
Harriet Tubman Mother's Club, 90
Harris, Eddie, 149, 153
Harris, Edward, 149, 153
Harrison, Bobbi, 44
Hartsfield, William (Atlanta mayor), 15–18
Hasan, Khalif, 157, 163, 169, 173–74
Hayden, Tom, 59
Hayes, Tim, 25, 27, 32, 198
Haynes, Leroy, 8, 160, 161, 164, 165–66, 167, 169, 170–71, 176, 182, 198; and founding of Dallas National Committee to Combat Fascism (NCCF), 154–57, 158, 159
Heard, Robert "Big Bob," 107–8, 111
Heller, James, 68
Herbener, Mark, 139, 146, 150
Hewitt, Raymond "Masai," 7, 156, 163
Hill, Jesse, 30
Hilliard, David, 1, 21, 25, 29, 55, 64–66, 69, 118, 156, 163, 164, 169, 173
Hilliard, June, 30, 42, 173
Hillman, Charles, 176, 181
Hilltop (Columbus, Ohio), 4
Hobbs, Leon Valentine, 4
Holley, W. W., 38
Holloway, Sidney, 133
Hoover, J. Edgar, 39–40, 64, 104, 196–97

Horn, Al, 36, 38
Hornsby, Alton, 16, 17
Howard, Elbert "Big Man," 70–71, 74, 79, 83
Howard University, 54, 55, 57, 63, 74, 76, 78
Howard University Mississippi Project, 78
Howell, Donna, 114, 115, 117, 124
Hubert, Dennis, 15
Huey Newton Defense Committee, 1
Huggins, Ericka, 108, 197
Hughes, Frank, 96, 99
Hutton, Bobby, 1, 97

Inman, John, 37, 39, 40–41
Institute of the Black World, 35, 44
Interdenominational Ministerial Alliance (IMA), 140, 145–46
Israel, 6

Jackson, Bob, 102
Jackson, Gregory, 108
Jackson, Larry, 155
Jackson, Maynard, Jr., 14, 43, 44
Jackson, Maynard, Sr., 143–44
James, Rhett, 145–46
Jefferson, Ruth, 153
Jefferson, Thomas, 7
Jenkins, John, 36
Jeru (ex-Panther informant), 64
Johnson, Clark, 160
Johnson, Deborah, 38
Johnson, Eddie Bernice, 166, 175–76
Johnson, Flozell, 112
Johnson, Leroy, 17, 18
Johnson, Lyndon B., 54, 57, 62–63, 140
Johnson, Matthew, 149, 152–53, 175
Johnson, Peter, 174
Jones, Audrea, 8, 91, 100, 109–10, 111, 113, 118, 124, 197–98
Jones, Frank, 44
Jones, Gene, 100, 104, 106, 107, 108, 111, 112, 120, 123
Jones, Gregory, 100, 102, 104
Jones, Mack, 19, 43
Jonsson, Erik (Dallas mayor), 139, 149
Juneteenth Independence Day, 141

Kambui, Odinga, 156, 158, 164, 167, 171, 172, 173
Karenga, Maulana, 56
Keating, Larry, 16, 19

Kennedy, Edward M., 95
Kennedy, John F., 32, 140
Kennedy, Robert F., 60
Kent State University, 57–58, 65, 84n21, 113–14
Kilson, Martin, 124
King, Ester, 22
King, Lonnie, 20, 30
King, Martin Luther, Jr., 2, 8, 54, 56, 60, 65, 97, 99, 146, 195
King v. Chapman (1945), 17
Kirkwood (Atlanta) headquarters, 26, 28, 29, 32, 33, 34, 35, 38, 42
Kroger, 33, 36
Ku Klux Klan, 15, 29, 60, 142, 184n5, 197

Lafitte, Jean, 141
Landrieu, Moon, 194
Laurence, Maurice, 67, 68, 79
Lee, Rep. Barbara (D-Calif.), 194
Leland, Mickey, 175
Lemons, Jennifer, 44
Leone, Sergio, 2
Lester, Phillip, 44
Lewis, Janice, 165
Lincoln Memorial, 54, 65
Linzau, Jean, 78–82
Lipscomb, Albert, 139, 166
Lister, Donald, 155–56, 161, 171–72
literacy tests, 18
Lorton Reformatory, 61, 77
Los Angeles, Calif., 2, 3, 7, 16, 21, 23, 54, 99, 156, 157, 161, 162
L'Ouverture, Toussaint, 195
Love Field Airport, 158
Lundy, Charles, 39, 41–42, 44
Lundy, Sam, 39, 40, 41

Maddox, Lester, 29
Malcolm X, 55, 60, 96, 155, 177
Malcolm X Community Information Center, 111
Malcolm X Memorial Park, 106
Malcolm X Park, 62, 66, 74, 76
Maltise, Rebecca, 43
Mao Zedong, 55, 64, 97, 100, 115, 116
Marable, Manning, 8, 27
March on Washington, 18, 54, 147
Martin, Emma Jean, 25, 32–34, 42
Martin, Waldo, 4–5, 12
Massell, Sam, 14, 29

Massen, Ona, 66, 72
Mays, Benjamin E., 17
Mays, Irene, 167
McCutchen, Steve, 9, 69, 81
McMillan, Eva "Mama Mack," 143, 149, 150, 151, 175
McMillan, Marion Ernest, 147–51, 174–76, 183–84
McNamara, Edmund, 95
Means, Russell, 80
Medical Student Association, 78
Meridian Hill Park, 62, 66, 74
Mexican Revolution, 141
Mills, Tommy, 7
Minkah, Fahim, 153, 173, 174, 176, 177–82
Miranda, Doug, 30, 91, 95, 99–107, 109, 111, 113–14, 118
Miranda v. Arizona (1966), 1
Mission Hill (Boston, Mass.), 111, 113, 123
Mitchell, Chester, 177
Molo, Deborrah, 177, 179–80
Moore, Albert, 73
Moore, Andra, 26
Moore, Douglas E., 57, 61, 75
Moore, Howard C., 73
Morehead, William, 177, 180
Morehouse College, 15, 16, 17, 25, 32, 147, 148
Morricone, Ennio, 2
Morris, Aldon, 18
Mothers for Adequate Welfare (MAW), 93, 95
Mount Olive Lutheran Church, 139, 158
Muhammad, Elijah, 39
Muhammed, Ali, 112
Mulford Act (1967), 195
Murchison, Russell, 108

Nasson College, 98
National Association for the Advancement of Colored People (NAACP), 27, 30, 58, 61, 95, 117, 138, 142–45, 167, 196, 198
National Committee to Combat Fascism (NCCF), 4, 23–24, 57, 63, 64–66, 69, 70, 78, 81, 105, 117–18, 154, 156, 159, 169, 173, 176
National History Day, 194
National Museum of African American History and Culture, 194
National Park Service, 74
Nation of Islam, 27, 39, 58
Native Americans, 6, 196, 199

Neblett, Chico, 96, 99, 100, 198
Neblett, Rene, 99
Negro Achievement Day, 144
Newark, N.J., 16, 54, 56
New Hope Baptist Church, 145
Newton, Huey, 1, 6, 8, 13, 20–21, 26, 28–32, 43, 44, 54, 56, 64–65, 75, 79, 80, 91–92, 99, 101, 108, 111, 112, 116, 160–64, 171, 177, 195, 196
Nixon, Richard, 54, 58, 62, 64, 65–66, 80
Nommo X, 4
North Shore Community College, 101
November Action Committee, 109
Nzinga, Yazid, 99

Oakland, Calif., 1–7, 12–13, 22, 25–31, 33, 41–44, 53, 55, 57–58, 61, 63, 70, 77, 79, 82, 91, 96, 97, 104, 105, 108, 114, 118, 123–24, 169, 173–74, 177, 182, 195
O'Bryant, Tilmon, 68
Occupy Wall Street, 194
Old South, 15
Oliver, Kouson, 39, 41–42
Oliver, William B., 155
Operation Exodus, 117, 122
Order of the Black Shirts, 15
Ordinance 13–28, used in harassment efforts, 41
Organization of Black Student Unity (OBSU), 22

Page, E. M., 143
Pan-African Cultural Festival, 21
pan-Africanism, 56, 61
Parents for Justice in Welfare Rights, 106
Partee, Clifton, 143
Pauley, T. D., 98–99
People's Free Busing Program, 34
People's Free Clothing Program, 34
People's Free Day Care Center, 34
People's Free Health Center, 92, 111, 114, 115, 117–18, 119–20, 121
People's Free Health Clinic, 78
People's Free Health Service, 78, 81
People's Free Legal Clinic, 178
People's Free Medical Center, 118, 124, 125–26
People's Free Pest Control Program, 34, 176
People's Liberation Party, 42
People's Party II, 22, 137, 173
Peoplestown (Atlanta, Ga.), 19

People United for Justice for Prisoners, 175
Pharr, Wayne, 163
Pinderhughes, Cappy, 90
Pointer, Gwen, 167
political prisoners, 23, 74, 108, 175
Polk, Ed, 175
poll taxes, 18, 143
Porter, George, 142
Porter, Ron, 44–45
Portland, Ore., 7, 8, 9, 154
Powell, Clayton, 37
Powell, Maurice "Mojo," 7
Pratt, Geronimo (Geronimo ji Jaga), 7, 23, 157–58, 161–64
Pride, Inc., 57, 62–63, 66
Prince George's County, Md., 56
Progressive Citizens League, 143
Progressive Labor Party, 20
Progressive Voters League, 143–44, 148
Pugh, Devon, 121

Rackley, Alex, 106, 109
Ragsdale, Diane, 167
Rahim, Malik, 7
Ramparts (magazine), office of, 1
Ransom, Paula, 165, 167–68, 198
Ransom, Ruby, 103
Rayburn, Patricia, 167
Reconstruction era, 141–42
Red Guards, 22
Republic of New Africa, 22, 194
Revolutionary Action Movement, 194
Revolutionary Conference for a United Front Against Fascism, 22. *See also* United Front Against Fascism conference
Revolutionary People's Constitutional Convention, 26, 58, 65, 70, 74, 76
Ricks, Willie, 20, 148
Rippy, Robert, 55–56, 61, 83
Robinson, Gwendolyn, 20
Robinson, John, 67
Rogers, Robert, 108
Rudd, Mark, 59
Rush, Bobby, 194
Rush Memorial Congregational Church, 35

Sacramento, Calif., 1967 protests in, 1, 196
San Francisco, airport protest in, 1
Schoop, Maxine, 57, 62, 78

Schoop, Robert, 72, 74
Scott, Charles, 31
Scruggs, Frank, 44
Scruggs, Patricia, 44
Seale, Bobby, 5, 6, 9, 21, 23, 31, 54, 64, 65, 82, 108, 113, 123, 169, 195
Seale, John, 42
Seattle, Wash., 4
Shabazz, Betty, 1
Shakur, Zayd, 69
Shockley, James "Skip," 155, 156, 158–62, 164–65, 167–69, 170
Showell, Catherine, 78
Simeon, Antionette, 167, 168, 173
Simeon, Charles, 167
Simms, John, 121
Slaton, Lewis, 41
Smethurst, James, 20
Smith, A. Maceo, 143
Smith, B. L., 161, 164, 165, 167, 168, 169, 174
Smith, Melvin "Cotton," 162, 163
Smith, William Armstrong, 23
Smith v. Allwright (1944), 144
Socialist Workers Party, 20, 35, 74
Southern Christian Leadership Conference, 20, 27, 31, 35, 58
Spence, J. R., 39
Stafford, Willis, 179
Stafford, W. J., 35, 42
Stevenson, Adlai, 140
St. John Missionary Baptist Church, 140
Stone, Clarence, 16, 20
St. Philip Catholic Church, 96
Stroud, Anita, 78, 81
St. Stephen's Episcopal Church, 75, 76
Student Non Violent Coordinating Committee (SNCC), 198; in Atlanta, 13, 20, 24, 26, 27, 28; in Boston, 95, 97; in Dallas, 143, 148–58, 174–75; in Washington, D.C., 55, 58, 59–61, 62, 63
Student Organization for United Liberation (SOUL), 154
Students for a Democratic Society (SDS), 55, 56, 72, 96, 109, 110
Styron, William, 2
Summerhill (Atlanta, Ga.), 16, 19, 26, 29, 33, 34
Sydeman Hall, takeover of, 98

Taart, Marilyn, 108
Talmadge, Herman, 14

Talmudic Jews, 6
Tate, Horace, 14
Texas Southern University, 22
Thompson, Fletcher, 29
Trump, Donald, 199
Tubbs, Michael, 179
Tubman, Harriet, 34, 195
Turner, Nat, 2, 199
Tysinger, Jim, 23

Unitarian All Souls Church, 63
United Black Brotherhood, 55–56, 58
United Farm Workers, 96
United Front Against Fascism conference, 55, 156
United Planning Organization, 55
University of New Mexico, 65
Upper Cardozo (Washington, D.C.), 83
Urban League, 58, 119, 196
US Organization, 194

Verone, Jerry, 96
veterans, 7, 20, 53, 57, 60, 101, 150, 152, 171, 176, 181
Vietnam War, 7, 53, 57, 60; protests against, 96, 106, 109, 113; veterans of, 7, 57, 150, 181
Vine City (Atlanta, Ga.), 19, 26, 33, 35
Voting Rights Act of 1965, 17, 53

Waddell, Joseph, 35
Walker, David, 195
Walker, David Carroll, 181–82
Wallace, George, 59
Walston, Ida, 106–7
Walton, James Curtis, 179
Ward, Columbus, 44
Ware, Bill, 20
Washington, Walter, 54, 62, 70

Washington Afro-American, 67, 77
Washington Daily News, 67, 68, 74, 77
Washington Evening Star, 67, 68, 77, 81
Washington Post, 67, 76, 77, 78
Watts, Ernest, 33, 39
Watts revolt in Los Angeles (1965), 16
Waxie Maxie (record store), 72
Webb, Robert, 100
Wells, Ammon S., 142, 143
West Baton Rouge Parish Jail, 32
West Dallas Housing Projects, 158, 178
White, Ellis, 7
White, LuLu B., 144
Williams, Hosea, 155
Williams, Jim, 58, 63, 65, 69, 71, 79, 80, 82, 83
Williams, Kwesi, 153, 174
Williams, U. S., 166–67, 168, 170
Williamson, Q. V., 17, 26
Wilson, Linda, 78
Winston-Salem office, 3, 12, 23, 24, 26, 30, 34, 35, 40
World War I, 90
World War II, 90, 101, 145
Wright, Richard, 2
Wright, S. M., 140, 146

Yahr, Richard, 170
Young, Andrew, 30
Young, Carl, 171
Young, Charlie, 177
Young, James, 111
Young Lords, 22, 66, 74
Young Patriot Party, 110
Youth International Party (Yippies), 71, 74

Zinn, Howard, 113
Zulu, Chaka, 81

www.ingramcontent.com/pod-product-compliance
Lightning Source LLC
Chambersburg PA
CBHW011756220426
43672CB00018B/2978